SMB3000720

114

£18.99

MVR U (Hon)

Women, Gender a   **.J, 1700–1870**

British Studies Series

General Editor JEREMY BLACK

Published

John Charmley   **A History of Conservative Politics, 1900–1996**
David Childs   **Britain since 1939**
John Davis   **A History of Britain, 1885–1939**
David Eastwood   **Government and Community in the English Provinces, 1700–1870**
W. H. Fraser   **A History of British Trade Unionism, 1700–1998**
Brian Hill   **The Early Parties and Politics in Britain, 1688–1832**
Katrina Honeyman   **Women, Gender and Industrialisation in England, 1700–1870**
Kevin Jefferys   **Retreat from New Jerusalem: British Politics, 1951–1964**
T. A. Jenkins   **The Liberal Ascendancy, 1830–1886**
David Loades   **Power in Tudor England**
Alexander Murdoch   **British History, 1660–1832: National Identity and Local Culture**
Anthony Musson and W. M. Ormrod   **The Evolution of English Justice: Law, Politics and Society in the Fourteenth Century**
Murray G. H. Pittock   **Inventing and Resisting Britain: Cultural Identities in Britain and Ireland, 1685–1789**
Nick Smart   **The National Government, 1931–40**
Andrew Thorpe   **A History of the British Labour Party**

British Studies Series
Series Standing Order
ISBN 0–333–71691–4 hardcover
ISBN 0–333–69332–9 paperback
(*outside North America only*)

You can receive future titles in this series as they are published by placing a standing order. Please contact your bookseller or, in case of difficulty, write to us at the address below with your name and address, the title of the series and the ISBN quoted above.

Customer Services Department, Macmillan Distribution Ltd
Houndmills, Basingstoke, Hampshire RG21 6XS, England

WOMEN, GENDER AND INDUSTRIALISATION IN ENGLAND, 1700–1870

Katrina Honeyman

First published in Great Britain 2000 by
MACMILLAN PRESS LTD
Houndmills, Basingstoke, Hampshire RG 21 6XS and London
Companies and representatives throughout the world

A catalogue record for this book is available for the British Library

ISBN 0–333–69077–X hardcover
ISBN 0–333–69078–8 paperback

First published in the United States of America 2000 by
ST. MARTIN'S PRESS, INC.,
Scholarly and Reference Division,
175 Fifth Avenue, New York, N.Y. 10010

ISBN 0–312–23178–4 (cloth)

Library of Congress Cataloging-in-Publication Data
Honeyman, Katrina.
Women, gender, and industrialization in England, 1700–1870/Katrina Honeyman.
p. cm. — (British studies series)
Includes bibliographical references and index.
ISBN 0-312-23178-4 (cloth)
1. Women–England–History. 2. Women–Employment–England–History. 3. Sexual
division of labor–England–History. 4. Industrialization–England–History. I. Title. II.
Series.

HQ1599.E5 K37 2000
306.3'615'0942–dc21   99-055824

This book is printed on paper suitable for recycling and made from fully managed and
sustained forest sources

10   9   8   7   6   5   4   3   2   1
09 08 07 06 05 04 03 02 01 00

Printed in Hong Kong

Contents

Acknowledgements

This book stems from my interest in the making of industrial society and the impact of feminist history on our understanding of that process. It is the outcome of a number of years of teaching and researching questions related to the process of industrialisation and the history of gender and work. It is founded on the notion that recent developments in economic and social history and in gender history have converged to allow a gendered history of industrialisation to emerge. It argues that gender was made in a special way during industrialisation and that men and women continue to live with its consequences. The shape of the book is informed by the preoccupations of modern feminism. It should be recognised that the struggles of women in today's labour market are connected to equivalent struggles of 200 years ago. The association of women with domestic activities and with a subordinate working position was constructed or confirmed in the process of industrial change.

My work has been influenced by students and colleagues at the University of Leeds. I have taught various courses in social history, the history of industrialisation and women's and gender history during the past ten years and I am grateful to the students on those courses for their enthusiasm and commitment. I should like to thank my friends from the challenging yet supportive gender and work research group, especially Jean Gardiner, Sarah Irwin and Sylvia Walby, not only for their intelligent and perceptive comments on an earlier version of this book, but also for the stimulating and wide-ranging discussions that we regularly enjoy. Jill Liddington, with whom I have shared the pleasures of teaching gender history at the University of Leeds, has also read parts of the text and offered insightful suggestions. I am grateful to her. I am indebted to an anonymous reader from the publisher who offered constructive criticism of an earlier draft that I valued greatly. This book attempts to reflect the work of a large number of creative and talented historians. It shows that there is still much to be done to remedy the neglect of women and gender in the understanding of industrialisation and its outcome, as in many other fields of historical enquiry, but if the huge progress made by historians of gender in recent years is sustained, the wider historical project will be greatly enriched.

Leeds, June 1999

1   Feminist History and the Historiography of the Industrial Revolution

The objective of this chapter is to identify strands in women's and gender history and in the history of industrialisation, in order to provide a framework for the following chapters which together comprise a case study in feminist history. Until quite recently, women were shamefully ignored in historical investigations. Even now the neglect is still apparent, and much history remains gender blind. In the last 20 years, however, enormous strides have been made in uncovering the lost history of women. Progress in feminist and gender history has been particularly impressive in the study of gender, work and employment. At the same time, the historiography of industrialisation has continued to reflect to some extent 'the preoccupations of the present'[1] and in so doing has become more sensitive to issues of gender as well as those of race and ethnicity. It is argued here that there has been a convergence or interaction in the two important areas of historical thinking, and that gender history is beginning to challenge the theoretical underpinnings of conventional history. There is some evidence to indicate that the 'mainstreaming' of gender history has been most successful within the context of analyses of industrialisation. This book is mainly concerned to test whether this is so and how useful it has been.

Although women's history, gender history and feminist history differ from one another, some of their distinguishing characteristics are subtle, and not all their distinctions are uniformly understood by historians. In the following paragraphs I shall outline what I consider to be the most important developments in the broad field of feminist history, while recognising that not all feminist history is concerned with women and that not all histories of women are feminist. I shall also attempt to identify the evolving relationship between feminist history and what is unsatisfactorily described as 'mainstream' history. During the last 20 years, the approaches to historical investigation adopted by women and/or feminist historians have varied. Not only have they changed over time, but a range of possible methods has existed at any one moment. Like any evolving discipline, feminist historiography can be explored through the debates that it engenders and the issues that it investigates. In the mid 1970s, the first volume of the *History Workshop Journal* was prefaced by a statement from the feminist history position. This emphasised both the influence of contemporary feminism and the neglect of women in historical investigation to that point.

It is well known that women received little or no attention in traditional history writing, but even among radical and socialist historians they are all too often mentioned as an afterthought, if at all, tagged on rather than present in their own right. . . . Sexual divisions are being questioned now because of the women's liberation movement, and it is through investigating the problems which feminism has raised that we can expect the most useful women's history to emerge. One priority of feminism is necessarily the history of women, but the purpose is not simply to slot women in wherever they have been left out. . . . For women are *workers* too, both waged and unwaged; and capitalism is as dependent on its 'unskilled' sweated labour force as on its skilled engineers.[2]

Such a statement now appears unexceptionable, yet in the 1970s profound disagreements influenced the direction of feminist thought. Feminist history of the 1970s, influenced as it was by the political movement of second-wave feminism, was driven by attempts to understand and explain women's historical oppression. The published research of the period was also marked by the conviction that it was possible to generalise and to rethink historical epochs. It was the early efforts to develop a theory of gender oppression that gave rise to one of the longest running debates within feminist history which focused on the utility of patriarchy as an explanatory tool. The concept of patriarchy was central to embryonic efforts to provide feminist history with a theoretical foundation, but its controversial impact can be illustrated by the late 1970s interchange between Sally Alexander and Barbara Taylor on one side and Sheila Rowbotham on the other.

Recognising the theoretical paucity of gender history, Alexander and Taylor proposed the use of patriarchy as a framework for analysing women's oppression which empirical research alone could not provide. In response, Rowbotham argued that a concept such as patriarchy was incapable of capturing the dynamic processes involved in exploring the differences between the subordination of women and class. Rowbotham was also anxious that the sometimes positive relationship between men and women might be engulfed by a term that assumed the oppression of women by men. 'There are times when class or race solidarity are much stronger than sex-gender conflict', she argued.[3] While disagreement over the use of the concept of patriarchy continues to fester unproductively,[4] the early debate signalled the contest between historians on the political left over the relative merits of class and gender as tools of analysing oppression within industrial capitalist society. Alexander and Taylor felt strongly that 'without a theory of gender relations, any attempt to "marry" the concepts of sex and class will simply do for the theories of sex what marriage usually does for women: dissolve them into the stronger side of the partnership. It was precisely because a Marxist theory of class conflict, however elaborated, could not answer all our questions about sexual conflict that we tried to develop an alternative.'[5] In the initial phase of feminist history, therefore, the focus was on identifying women's oppression through history and on ways of analysing and explaining this oppression.

Within a decade these dominant characteristics of early 'feminist history' had been replaced by a more conciliatory approach employing a more neutral terminology. As Judith Bennett observed, while the 'founding mothers of women's history wrote freely and often about patriarchy and women's oppression', by the later 1980s women's agency had replaced notions of victim, and 'subordination' had taken the place of oppression.[6] In the mean time 'gender' as an analytical tool was increasingly used to replace the more descriptive 'woman' as the discipline began to move on from 'women's history', which filled some of the gaps in 'official' history, to 'gender history', which recognised gender systems as primary categories of historical analysis. Because women's exclusion from history had been so total, it was believed, in the early days of the discipline, that 'every rectification must be welcome'.[7] It was considered important, however, to make the distinction between adding women to history and adding women's history to history. In this second phase of the development of feminist history, therefore, steps were taken to understand the gender system as a 'critical feature of all social relations'. In practice this allowed women to be restored to the historical process and enabled feminist history to move 'beyond the deadend of attempting to establish sexual difference as an agent of historical causation'.[8] This was a significant step in the process by which women came to be analysed as active historical participants, rather than victims of both historical events and historical analysis.

By the early 1980s, therefore, several strands of feminist history could be discerned. One of these was 'women's history' which Joan Scott termed 'her-story'. Most of the research which can be placed in this category focused on women as historical subjects and provided a narrative of women's experience. Information retrieval was and remains central to what is known as women's history. Such an approach,[9] while demonstrating the need for sex and gender to be conceptualised in historical terms and filling in many of the missing gaps, did not mount a direct challenge to conventional history. Feminist historians have criticised this branch for its separatist position and for its failure to stimulate a rewriting of history. A second contemporary approach – in which women were incorporated into social and working-class history – might be attacked for its overzealous integration by subsuming women 'within received categories of analysis'.[10] Neither category of feminist history in the early 1980s undermined the foundations of traditional history, nor was that the aim. Both women's history and social and working-class history broke new ground and engaged in empirical and theoretical areas of enquiry that were vital to subsequent approaches. Thus the rewriting of history, to which many feminist historians ultimately strive, was able to make more substantial progress. The third approach of the 1980s, therefore, can be described more explicitly as 'feminist history' in which social definitions of gender were re-examined, most fruitfully through 'specific studies of discrete periods, movements or events'.[11] Feminist history shows how conflicts about women or sexual difference 'fit the distribution of social, economic or political power'.[12] Evidence that all strands coexisted during the 1980s is confirmed by the work of Marilyn Boxer and Jean Quataert, whose introduction to an edited volume entitled 'Restoring women to history' suggests that 'old interpretations take on new meanings when a new category of analysis – gender – is added to the historical perspective'.[13]

By the later 1980s, feminist history moved to a more central and self-confident position within the discipline of history, and signs of 'accommodation' were apparent. The tendency to 'mainstream' women's history, however, was viewed as precipitous by some historians.[14] Judith Bennett, for example, who has done more than most to keep the idea of patriarchy alive, and a great deal besides, believed that the two-way negotiation necessary for successful incorporation within 'conventional' history had not yet been achieved. While acknowledging the value of Joan Kelly's exhortation to write women's history with a view to transforming the very practice of history, Bennett insisted that to have a productive dialogue with other historians, 'we must not only critically assess questions of general interest but also command a general interest in our own questions'.[15] Like Joan Scott, who emphasised the importance of politics, Bennett believed in the need to 'regain political nerve'. She criticised feminist historians for examining women's agency in preference to issues of oppression and patriarchy. It is true that in moving forward, feminist historians may have left behind much that was important. Bennett warned of the danger that feminist historians might not only fail to confront real oppression, for example, but also that they might inadvertently collude in their own oppression. She reaffirmed her own position that by exploring the operation of patriarchy through history, women may be seen as both victims and agents. She believed that by making patriarchy the central problem of women's history 'we will produce not only good feminist history but also better history'. Thus 'in making the central issue of feminism the central subject of women's history, we will be working not only within the very best traditions of history . . . but also within the very best traditions of feminism'.[16]

The concept of patriarchy was less evident in the writing of feminist history by the late 1980s, when the analysis of gender and specifically gender relations had gained broad acceptance. It remained implicit, however. In 1989, the issue of women's subordination, if not their oppression, was still considered to be important. The editorial of the first issue of *Gender and History* which appeared in that year emphasised men's monopoly of superior positions which they could afford to take for granted. Such male privilege is relevant both to historical processes themselves and to the way in which history has been produced. As Catherine Hall has written elsewhere, 'the dominant rarely reflect on their dominance in the ways that the subjected reflect on their subjection'.[17] Since it is 'men who have been responsible for the doing and writing of history', Hall believes, 'it is their definition of the legitimate historical project which has prevailed'. In order to understand both history and the project, therefore, gender has to be made central. According to Hall, 'gender is not only a set of lived relations, but is also a symbolic system. Gender operates at every level: the creation and reproduction of gender is a process changing over time.'[18] This position has been supported by other historians, including Gisela Bock, who has argued that 'gender should not be seen as more important than anything else but rather that gender relations should be seen as equally important as all other human relations'.[19]

The placing of gender more centrally in the analysis of historical processes has gained strength, and is particularly evident in recent investigations of industrialisation. Before turning to explore the way in which feminist history has informed or interacted with the historiography of industrialisation, it is necessary to make reference to a further approach and a further controversy which has appeared in the past decade. Post-modernism, or post-structuralism, has offered a new theoretical approach to a range of disciplines in recent years. Joan Scott was instrumental in applying the idea of post-structural analysis to feminist history, but her most important contribution has been to confirm the central place of gender in historical approaches. She suggested that history should be less concerned with things that have happened to women and men and their reaction to such things but rather how 'categories of identity have been constructed'.[20] In this way the concept of gender would be revitalised, 'to generate new knowledge about women and sexual difference'. Because gender 'illuminates all history whatever its specific topic, by historicising gender it is possible to identify the contradictory meanings attributed to sexual difference'.[21] Adherents of a post-structuralist approach believe that it has provided more depth and complexity to women's history, by avoiding generalisation – especially that of women's oppression – and by developing greater sensitivity to context, diversity and contradiction.[22]

It is not altogether clear how far post-structuralism has influenced the development of gender history as distinct from women's history, or whether changes in the subject were taking place anyway. There seems little doubt that during the 1980s, possibly in response to post-structuralism, attention shifted from attempts to find overall explanations for women's subordination towards exploring gender relations in clearly defined groups.[23] The post-structuralist recognition that neither men nor women constituted uniformly homogeneous categories was clearly of value to all historical investigation, not solely to gender history. The injection of intellectual rigour into women's history can also be seen as a contribution of the new methodology, but it by no means certain that women's history would have languished in the absence of post-structuralism.

There is some debate about the position of post-structuralism in gender history. Some historians have assumed that gender history is post-structuralist by definition, which has caused Joan Hoff, among others, to rail against it.[24] Hoff's opinion is that gender 'as a category of analysis' did not need to be reinvented using a special linguistic jargon unless it was to eliminate women in the new field of gender history. Post-structuralism apparently asserts the intellectual and apolitical superiority of gender history over women's history, and instead of promoting women's history into the mainstream, it has removed the possibility of generalisations about the 'shared experiences' of women.[25] June Purvis broadly supports Hoff's position and she and others have argued that to study women as women neither ignores heterogeneity nor inevitably results in generalisation. Neither women's history nor feminist history claims, as post-structuralists seem to assume that they do, that 'all women's shared experiences have been experienced equally'.[26]

Others see gender history as political and feminist and thus intrinsically alien to the apolitical post-structuralism. Catherine Hall, for example, believes that post-structuralism is at best superfluous to the needs of gender historians, at worst it has borrowed their ideas. Some of the insights that are attributed to post-structuralist theorists, she argues, have been thought of in other ways by feminists. 'We do not need post-structuralism to develop gender as a category of analysis . . . feminists do not need Foucault to understand that power operates on many sites or post-structuralism to understand that historical writing was a male-centred form of knowledge.'[27] Yet other historians, among whom many of the above group would be included, see gender as a 'less overtly political' synonym for women, and gender history as an academic field that recognises the importance of the construction of masculinity and femininity and the relationship between women and men.

It is not always easy to distinguish feminist history, women's history and gender history, nor is there agreement about the meaning of them. The differences between them, however, should not be exaggerated. As Hannah Barker and Elaine Chalus have recently argued, any lens that historians use to look at the ways in which men and women interacted with each other and with society increase our understanding of the past.[28] Nevertheless, it is necessary to accept that feminist historians can be motivated by different interests and political positions and be influenced by different methodologies. It is also important to acknowledge that the distinction between the various strands may not always be very great. In any case, whatever the theoretical and methodological advances made by practitioners of feminist, women's and gender history, such progress means little unless it leads to acceptance by or dialogue with the broad body of historical scholars. This is important not just for gender history but for the entire project of history. According to Pam Sharpe, 'women's history needs to be inserted into the mainstream, not simply in the interests of completeness but to challenge the mainstream historical view, to open fresh debates and to provide new perspectives in the pursuit of history'.[29]

Until recently it was believed that women's history had not advanced sufficiently to allow mainstreaming to occur.[30] The information retrieval stage of historical research on women has flourished especially with respect to the period of industrialisation,[31] but in order to maximise its value, women's history or gender history has to become more visible in the core of academic history. It is still sometimes characterised as a subdisciplinary specialism 'like business history or transport history'.[32] The mainstreaming project is impeded by data deficiencies and other methodological problems, but it seems most promising within the context of industrialisation. Historians of women and work have produced some of the most stimulating reinterpretations of the Industrial Revolution period.[33] Maxine Berg and Pat Hudson, for example, both separately and together, have argued that the employment of women and children in the Industrial Revolution constituted a significant break with the past.[34] There is growing evidence of the contribution made by women and children to the family budget,[35] and the concept of the industrious revolution[36] takes full account of the role of women and children. Such research effort has revised ideas about the nature of industrialisation as well as perceptions of women's role within it. In other words, the feminist project has challenged traditional wisdom on the Industrial Revolution and thus achieved its objective to engage in a dialogue with the mainstream.

Until recently, interpretations of the Industrial Revolution tended to marginalise both the contribution of female labour and the relevance of a gendered workforce to the process of industrial change. This reflected the gender-blind approach typical of historical analyses but was compounded by the insensitivity of economic historians to gender issues. By the mid 1990s the gender agenda had progressed further in social history and 'mainstream' history than was the case in economic history.[37] Traditional approaches to the study of economic history were not inherently hostile to the inclusion of women, as the work of Ivy Pinchbeck, Alice Clark and others in the early twentieth century prove. Yet there was a reluctance to continue the trend established by these pioneer economic historians, for cultural reasons or because of the contemporary preoccupations of economists. Some recent strands of economic history, especially that of quantification, have been distinctly inhospitable to women.[38] The neo-classical frame of reference that informs the method of the so-called cliometricians has effectively submerged a gendered perspective.

The historiography of the Industrial Revolution provides an example of economic history's tendency to marginalise women. Up to and including the 1960s, the Industrial Revolution was generally accepted as a fundamental transformation, associated with great inventions and negative social outcomes. The analysis of change within this perspective drew on the measurements of growth rates from which a periodisation emerged. A more gradualist vision of industrial development, nevertheless founded on the same kinds of changes, characterised the thinking of the 1970s. Since the 1980s, analyses which tend to underplay the idea of a sudden break have become popular. They fall broadly into one of two categories. The first – championed by Nicholas Crafts and still dominated by his influential work – can be described as 'new' quantitative analysis. The findings generated by the sophisticated measurement techniques of its exponents reveal slower growth in manufacturing industry than was previously assumed. This conclusion questions the existence of a period of industrialisation before the mid nineteenth century. The quantitative version of events is ill equipped to contemplate the subtleties of gender and work issues, and fails to accommodate the regional and structural variations within the national economy. In brief, it is a narrow approach which views industrialisation as a purely economic process and which fails to acknowledge its social and cultural dimensions. The second main strand in recent work is more amenable to a gendering of the historical process and also offers a more complete understanding of the complexities of industrialisation. Although it cannot be easily categorised, its methodology is qualitative and is informed by elements of social and cultural theory. Interpretations within this strand are more subtle and nuanced and although their conclusions vary – ranging from support for the notion of continuity or absence of major transformation to an emphasis on the 'rehabilitation' of the Industrial Revolution – they accommodate the heterogeneity of experience. Because the extensive work in this category has been particularly influential in developing an understanding of industrialisation and because it contains at least an implicit gender component, its main contributions will be considered below. The debate about whether or not an industrial revolution took place is not to be discussed here. The objective of the following sections is to identify the main themes from recent writings on industrialisation and to explore their significance for gender history. Consideration will also be given to the intervention of feminist enquiry in the rewriting of industrialisation.

It was previously assumed that the process of industrialisation was reflected in the growth of large-scale manufacturing and the introduction of capital-intensive technology. It was also assumed that the factory replaced smaller, less efficient and more labour-intensive forms of production and that all or most industries followed the same course of organisational and technical development. Much recent work has reassessed the traditional view of such a linear transformation. By adopting a more imaginative approach to definitions of technique and organisation forms and by paying greater attention to labour, employment and the nature of work, it has found transformations less in centralised production units and expensive technology and more in the varied experience of work.[39] A departure from simplistic notions of linear change that recent ideas indicate, does not necessarily mean that concepts of change are replaced by ones of continuity, but rather that 'circular and cyclical ideas must be at least as germane to our understanding of industrialisation'.[40]

As new research has challenged the previously dominant belief in a linear progression of organisational systems from rural domestic and urban putting out to the centralised factory, it has provided evidence that the expansion of industrial output between 1700 and 1914 was achieved by a continuous interaction of industrial forms that gave rise to an intricate industrial structure. Centralised factory manufacture was only one of the many possible choices in industrial organisation and was by no means the most popular, having failed to supersede other forms by the late nineteenth century. Smaller-scale, less capitalised forms of industrial production were not only not inferior to those of mass production but under certain circumstances they could be economically preferable and entirely consistent with the demands of industrial capitalism.[41]

This revisionism should be understood in the light of the more complex understanding of technical change that has emerged in the past decade. There are two main strands to this recent historiography. The first underplays the ubiquitous use of novel machines during industrialisation. It has been found that conventional techniques often persisted alongside new methods and were adapted to changing economic circumstances. The second strand develops a wider definition of technical change which incorporates not only mechanical inventions but also the novel use of hand tools and the development of new skills. Research has shown that manufacturing output and productivity increased within a relatively unchanging technical context, typically through changes in the division of labour and a flexible supply of cheap female and child labour.[42] In this way it was found possible to adapt customary practices to the requirements of dynamic and market-oriented production.[43] This is consistent with the thesis of Raphael Samuel who, 20 years ago, argued that hand labour and small-scale production, rather than mechanisation, was central to British industrial change, which created a new range of labour-intensive jobs.[44] His investigation suggests that labour power and its 'strength, skill, quickness and sureness of touch' formed the basis of growth.[45] More recently, Kristine Bruland has taken this a step further by arguing that not only was alteration in the division of labour the basis of technical change, 'it was technical change. Even without changes in tools and equipment, changes in methods ought to be considered as technical change.'[46] In order to understand industrialisation more thoroughly, therefore, it is necessary to adopt a broader concept of innovation and a greater awareness of the role of working women and children.[47]

Such challenges to received wisdom place labour more centrally in the process of industrialisation. The nature of the organisation of work, the use of technology and the division of labour should be considered in terms of the positions of both men and women and the way in which they interacted. For example, in many sectors of the economy, an expansion of outwork took place alongside mechanisation and the growth of factory employment and this often involved a gender division of work in which men were employed in factories and women in the home or in domestic workshops.[48] The changing understanding of the nature of industrial transformation influences or is influenced by the positioning of women within that transformation.[49]

What appears to be important in much of the rethinking of the nature of industrialisation is not only the central role played by labour in the process but a greater awareness of the significance of the gender of that labour. A hierarchical division of labour based on gender was not new to the period of industrialisation but it assumed a new importance for the experience of work, for the organisation of production, and for the relationship between labour and employers. Evidence suggests that women's position in the labour force had been consistently undermined since the sixteenth century when they were found in the lowest paid, least stable and most unrewarding occupations. Urban trades were male dominated and although women were, exceptionally, employed in skilled occupations, they found it increasingly difficult to enter the more prestigious trades. During the eighteenth century the expansion of industrial production occurred mainly along traditional lines, but the most significant area of growth was in rural manufacturing. Within this context the gender division of labour was similarly hierarchical. High status jobs in textile production such as weaving, combing and carding were dominated by men. Women were concentrated in low status spinning, lace making, stocking making or calico printing. Women's work was more protean and irregular than men's and, though vital, was undervalued.[50]

Manufacturing in the early stage of industrialisation made a special use of women's position in the secondary labour market, in the elasticity of their labour and in the seasonality of their work. Much industrial employment through the eighteenth and nineteenth centuries was irregular and it was the adaptability of women workers that permitted the survival of many enterprises, and it was their cheapness and flexibility that allowed the persistence of hand and intermediate techniques.[51] Inexpensive female workers provided employers with a range of profitable organisational options, but it could be argued that women's subordination then became a necessary element in the continued operation of capitalism.[52] It is possible that the emphasis on low cost, easily exploitable female labour discouraged investment in skills.

Changes in technique and organisation of production heightened the complexity of the relationships between the classes and the sexes. Just as women and men had performed specific functions in manufacturing before the factory, so this continued to be the case subsequently but in a more complicated way.[53] As female labour became more clearly categorised as cheap and expendable, so men were able to define their own position as more skilled. This did not happen without a struggle, however, and recent research has confirmed that industrial change was associated with crises in gender and class relations.[54]

The above discussion indicates that recent work on the history of industrialisation has paid greater attention to the social and cultural context of what has traditionally been seen as an economic process.[55] Industrialisation can be seen 'as a process of cultural change, [generating] the production of new meaning and practices as much as of commodities', so markets, especially labour markets, were culturally constructed. Gender was very much at the centre of such constructions.

In the last 10 or 20 years, therefore, analyses of the nature of industrialisation and the main strands of thought on women's history and gender and history have converged. Certainly, many of the important features of the historiography of industrialisation both inform and are informed by issues of gender. The current state of the two historiographies is reflected in the structure of this book. The organisation of the text is influenced by two assumptions that derive from a meeting of these historiographies. The first is that industrialisation cannot be understood without reference to female labour. Although the contribution of men is not to be disregarded, women's specific activities are seen to have played a crucial role in the progress of industrialisation. The second assumption is that industrialisation, and the social, cultural and political changes associated with it, should be understood as a gendered process. This does not mean that issues relating to class should be marginalised, but rather that such issues be gendered. The gendered response to industrialisation can be analysed most effectively in the context of labour movements, political protest and factory reform which reveal the interaction of male labour and employers as well as the relationship between men and women of the working class. The outcome of such contests and negotiations – often confused and conflictual – can be described as a gendered working class.

The process of industrialisation, whatever doubts remain about its nature, was one in which women engaged fully. They may have been marginalised and undervalued, both by contemporaries and possibly more so by historians, but this very marginalisation was nevertheless crucial to the short-term evolution of industrial society.[56]

The rest of the book examines the mechanisms by which industrial society in the nineteenth century emerged as one centrally defined by gender. Chapter 2 questions the extent to which the early industrial period before 1800 was marked by a transition in gender relations. The eighteenth century is sometimes identified as a 'Golden Age' for women. It was, however, a time when shifts in ideology disadvantaged women, and when clear gender differences in the experience of work, poverty and the standard of living were visible. Particular characteristics were attributed to women workers in the context of domestic industry and protoindustry and these provided the basis of the new industrial labour force. Chapter 3 explores the way in which women's cheapness, flexibility and alleged docility were used profitably by early industrialists, and identifies other means by which women contributed to industrialisation. While recognising the value of the detailed investigations of early historians of women,[57] the chapter attempts to reflect the more recent approaches, which consider the proactive role of women in the process of industrialisation. There now seems little doubt that the labour of women influenced the development of particular industries and the course of industrialisation as a whole.

Chapter 4 will investigate the view that industrialisation developed as a gendered set of practices through the actions of male and female labour, the employers, the state and the labour movement. Particular attention will be given to the emergence of the gender division of labour and gender divisions between industries, the gendered experience of work and pay, and the gendering of skill and machinery. In Chapter 5 the main features of women's employment in the new industrial economy will be identified. The heterogeneity of work, regional distinctions, structural changes and the difference between the formal and the informal economy will be emphasised. The chapter shows that not only did women's labour offer a viable labour-intensive alternative to mechanised and centralised production, but women's outwork, casual and sweated labour provided a much-needed flexibility and sometimes a lifeline to the often inefficient factory forms of production.

Chapter 6 explores the interface of home and work in the construction of differential gender identities. It examines the nature of the family during industrialisation as it moved from a co-operative production unit where all members contributed to the survival of the whole, to a structure in which hierarchy played a more obvious function by placing men at the apex as breadwinners and women in a supportive domestic role. The significance of the diffusion of the complementary ideologies of domesticity (for women) and the breadwinner wage (for men) in the construction of the working-class family are identified. Chapter 7 places gender in a central position in analyses of the outcome of industrialisation. It explores the responses of working men and women to the economic and social changes introduced by industrialisation with particular reference to the objectives and activities of working-class associations.

By the late nineteenth century, English society was defined by both industry and gender. The remainder of this book explores the processes by which England became a gendered industrial society. Gender distinctions at work and in the home were not new to the period of industrialisation, but gender took on a new significance during that time. Gender was made in a particular way during the period of social and cultural change associated with industrialisation. Each component of the new industrial society was constructed through a process of negotiation. That industrial society took the gendered form that it did was by no means inevitable. That women became confined to the least skilled and lowest paid sectors of employment and to a subservient position within the domestic division of labour was the result of prolonged intervention by their husbands and fathers, by paternalist employers and the state. Such an outcome was not merely unfortunate for women but was disastrous for the English economy. Long-term social and economic progress was clearly hampered by the rigid gendering of work that was established and sustained during the period of industrialisation. The legacy of the creation of a gendered industrial society for the status of women and for the quality of available human resources is clearly felt in the present day.

2 Gender and Work before Industrialisation

Much recent research by feminist historians has been located in the century or so before the onset of industrialisation. There are several reasons for this emphasis. The first is that among the group of highly influential female economic historians writing in the inter-war years, the position of women in the pre-industrial period was of particular interest. These pioneers influenced the direction of women's history and enhanced its status within contemporary historical scholarship.[1] Their research generated abundant information on women's work before industrialisation on which subsequent generations of feminist historians have built.[2] The second reason for the focus on the pre-industrial period is that the findings of some, but not all of these pioneer researchers, indicated – or have been interpreted as suggesting – that before industrialisation women had access to greater equality of opportunity than was to be the case subsequently. For second-wave feminists there was political significance in the conclusion that the history of women was not simply one of persistent oppression. Finally, because the period from the late seventeenth century has been viewed as one of transition in economic and industrial terms,[3] the possibility existed that a transformation in gender relations might be located there. The operation of a pre-industrial family production unit, where all members contributed to the family's survival, is believed to have permitted a flexibility in gender roles which was to disappear thereafter.

The idea of an eighteenth-century 'golden age' in women's economic and social experience, pervades interpretations of the transition to industrial capitalism. The notion has appealed to feminist historians, especially those investigating women's position in the labour force. Historians of gender, above all those wishing to identify a time in the past when women occupied a position of relative economic equality with men both in the domestic sphere and in the labour market, have assumed that industrialisation disadvantaged

17

women to a greater extent than men. Evidence for a *bon vieux temps*, when women enjoyed a harmonious if hardworking existence before they were downgraded into 'social parasites or factory fodder under the corrupting hand of capitalism', however, has proved to be elusive.[4] This chapter will investigate the possibility that the period between the late seventeenth and the late eighteenth centuries was one in which gender relationships were relatively fluid, and where women enjoyed better opportunities at work than they did during industrialisation. It will also consider the significance of the debate between those historians who have tended to see women's work as moving from a 'golden age', in which there was overlap between the activities of men and women, to one where gender roles were distinct, and those who argue that women's opportunities were as limited in the pre-industrial period as at any other time.[5]

Despite this disagreement, aspects of women's working position before industrialisation are undisputed. There seems little doubt, for example, that the work of women in the pre-industrial period was flexible and did not always fall into formal or clearly recognised occupations. Women's engagement in manufacturing altered according to the requirements of the family enterprise, their marital status or domestic and family commitments.[6] The work of women was different and more varied than that of men. Women's and men's work identities were quite distinct. It was not unusual for women to change occupations several times during their lives or to perform several jobs simultaneously. As a result, women's identification with any one occupation was typically weak.[7] Women's work also took different forms in the countryside and in the towns, in different regions and localities, at different stages of economic cycles or according to individual family circumstances.

Although much recent work in this period has explored the particular dynamics of rural industry and the interaction of town and countryside, earlier research focused on the identification of women's work in the urban context. Alice Clark, an influential member of the first wave of feminist historians, produced a research monograph in 1919 that suggested high female participation in the pre-industrial urban labour market.[8] Clark's exploration of seventeenth-century women's work, while analytically slim, nevertheless indicates that in the period before industrialisation, women had access to a reasonably wide range of employment opportunities. Women commonly worked within a structure that Clark terms

'Family Industry' where parents and children toiled together. Within such home-based employment, any income earned was regarded as family, rather than individual, property. From her research, Clark concluded that in the seventeenth century, it was comparatively rare for a man to support his wife, and that the family existed as a co-operative unit of production and consumption.[9]

With respect to occupational structure, Clark found, as others have subsequently confirmed, that women dominated the spinning of most kinds of textiles until the late eighteenth century and engaged extensively in linen and silk making. She discovered that women were employed in various skilled occupations, mostly in upholstery, millinery and silk production. In non-textile activities women were to be found in large numbers in printing, bookbinding and retailing, but they tended to be located in the relatively low status sectors of the trades. Occupations which could be carried out in domestic settings were most likely to be female dominated. Those trades that required a separation from the home were typically monopolised by men. Such a distribution of work by gender appeared to be determined more by location than by skill, so women were more likely to be pewterers and smiths, occupations that could be home-based, and less likely to be carpenters and masons where activity away from the home was more typical.[10]

Alice Clark successfully identified many occupations in which women participated before industrialisation. Apparently satisfied to find that women were economically active, she engaged in little qualitative analysis to illuminate the status and value of women's work. A clear gender division of work in the pre-industrial era was indicated by Clark's work, and although she recognised such distinctions she failed to scrutinise their implications. The conclusions she reached about women's pre-industrial position were unduly optimistic. The undoubted quality of Clark's scholarship notwithstanding, her identification of a substantial group of economically active women is unsurprising. Although her work has inspired recent feminist historians, doubt has been cast upon her case for a seventeenth-century golden age. Her favourable interpretation of the organisation of production, for example, has been challenged. Clark presented an idealistic picture of self-sufficient family life in the seventeenth century. She believed that the family-based economy made more productive use of women's mental and practical skills than was to be the case within industrialisation.[11]

Several of Clark's near contemporaries, including Dorothy George, Lillian Knowles and Ivy Pinchbeck, however, rejected the idea of equality within the family system of manufacture. George believed that the domestic system of manufacture depended on the excessive and low-paid labour of women and children. From her work on eighteenth-century London she concluded that 'there is no work too heavy or disagreeable to be done by women, provided it is also ill-paid'.[12] Pinchbeck argued that the family production unit in the pre-industrial period established a tradition of low wages that affected women's pay when they subsequently entered the factory.[13] Lillian Knowles, however, whose influence on Pinchbeck's work is evident, formed her particularly negative view of domestic industry from a reading of parliamentary papers produced in the nineteenth century when home-based manufacture was in a debased state.[14] She, like Pinchbeck, broadly welcomed the changes introduced by the Industrial Revolution.

More recent research has also cast doubt upon Clark's positive interpretation of women's employment status in the pre-industrial town. Peter Earle's analysis of seventeenth-century London court records, which, he believes, offer a reasonably representative sample of women workers in the capital, suggests that the range of occupations to which women had access was both narrow and of low status. His evidence indicates that women worked flexibly and seasonally in such casual occupations as domestic service, the making and mending of clothes, in charring, laundry work and in nursing,[15] and that much commercial activity and business ownership was, by law and custom, normally confined to men. Women and men were rarely found co-operating in business, and although widows occasionally continued the trade of dead husbands as was statutorily permitted, only a small number succeeded for more than a short period. Such analysis of occupational distribution in the light of contemporary custom and social structure is entirely inconsistent with the idea of a golden age. It indicates a very clear inequality of opportunity. Urban women may have worked for a living before industrialisation, but their choice of employment was severely circumscribed and largely confined to work that resembled domestic chores. Women were barred from sharing in men's work, and there was a rigid gendering of skill.[16]

It is suggested, therefore, that Clark presented partial evidence, which she interpreted over-optimistically. Her failure to appreciate the complex and uneven transition to industrial capitalism and thus the real implications of her work for women's status has been criticised.[17] Apparently, 'a meticulous reading' of Clark's argument shows her to be of the opinion that the majority of female producers were 'little affected by the rise of capitalism before the spread of factory industry in the eighteenth and nineteenth centuries'.[18] In other words, her framework makes no allowance for the capitalist organisation of industry in various forms of the putting-out system. By moving straight from family industry to capitalist factory industry, Clark's model fails to accommodate an interim 'proto' industrial stage of capitalism that was so vital to both the process of capital accumulation and to the restructuring of the sexual division of labour.[19] The idea of a transitional phase of industrial manufacture between the early modern and the industrial age, however, was less discussed among Clark's generation than it has been since, so its absence from her work is hardly surprising.

The concept of protoindustry post-dates the publication of Clark's book yet it provides a useful framework within which to examine the possibility of a pre-industrial golden age. In the eighteenth-century economy, protoindustry was one of several interacting forms of production that comprised a complex industrial system. Protoindustry was a distinctly rural and regional phenomenon in which agriculture and manufacturing operated in symbiosis.[20] Rural manufacture was organised in a variety of ways, but the putting-out system was typical. Much of the labour force consisted of family groups, working at home and organising industrial work around agricultural commitments. The distribution of both farming and manufacturing employment – commonly in textile production – had a clear yet variable gendered nature. Male family members were more likely to be fully employed in agricultural occupations than women and girls who performed the bulk of the industrial work – specialising in textile spinning – and who helped with the harvest. Because the preparatory and finishing stages of textile production were generally completed in the towns under the supervision of the merchants, rural workers concentrated on spinning and weaving, usually working simple machines that they owned. The merchant putter-out was frequently, but not necessarily, urban-based and had access to substantial markets both locally and overseas.[21] In most regions of protoindustry, manufacturing provided a solution to structural problems in the economies of both town and countryside.

The ability of protoindustry to fit into existing systems of production and to permit the widespread growth of manufacturing output was a reflection of its dynamism and strength. Its expansion was based on the employment of inexpensive and mainly female rural labour.

The concept of protoindustry has been used by a number of historians as a means of analysing traditions in women's work before industrialisation as well as providing a wider framework for understanding the early phases of industrial development.[22] Some historians believe that the protoindustrial family economy provided a golden opportunity for the establishment of sexual equality in work. The model of the protoindustrial family economy presented by Hans Medick, for example, was one where its survival required a 'maximum of familial co-operation' and which was characterised by a minimal gender division of labour and 'flexibility in the role responsibilities of the family members'.[23] Generally the 'protoindustrial situation was characterised by a strong degree of assimilation between the production functions of men and women. Women as cutlers, nailmakers and organisers of the marketing of industrial products, were as common as men in the roles of spinners and lacemakers. . . . Occasionally . . . it could lead to men's assuming traditional women's roles.' The distribution of family labour was therefore distributed 'without regard for sex and age'.[24] Both the extent and the novelty of gender role flexibility, however, have been questioned by historians. Rab Houston and Keith Snell, for example, are not convinced that a blurring of gender divisions within the protoindustrial family economy was unprecedented. They argue that such role flexibility resembled the pattern in earlier artisan family economies.[25] Other historians, among them Pat Hudson, doubt the very existence of gender role fluidity in the protoindustrial family economic unit. Hudson has challenged the assertion that protoindustrial employment had a liberating effect on women, and argues that there was a hierarchy of labour in most protoindustrial trades, processes and households which may have 'endorsed female subordination' at the expense of women's emancipation.[26]

It is probable that manufacturing activity spread into the countryside from the late seventeenth century because of the prevalence of cheap and unregulated female labour, which contrasted with the highly regulated and relatively expensive male labour that dominated the urban manufacturing labour force. The expansion of the protoindustrial system relied on a family economy in which cheap and adaptable female labour was central. Protoindustrial activities increased the intensity of labour, and the productive effort of women and children made a significant contribution to the family subsistence wage, but 'their work effort was underpaid'.[27] The highest paid female workers of the eighteenth century were apparently girls and young women who worked away from home in workshops in the hand weaving, calico printing and pottery trades, in metal and hardware workshops and in small jenny factories.[28] Even where there was great pressure on labour supply, as in cotton and wool spinning, protoindustrial women's work was low paid because it was regarded as low status and was supplemental to household income. That excess demand for female labour did not become translated into higher female wages is evidence of a segmented labour market.[29]

As far as the distribution of household tasks in the eighteenth century was concerned, there is little indication that men seriously engaged with domestic chores. Women's involvement in manufacturing in the home does not seem to have liberated them from traditional domestic pursuits, as Medick suggests it did, even when the demand for female labour in manufacturing exceeded that for men. Women's relatively poor earning capacity served to confirm unequal gender roles. Manufacturing activities for women in the protoindustrial family economy were additional to, rather than substitutes for, women's 'normal' work in the home or in agriculture. 'Protoindustry added to the drudgery of female existence' just as homeworking and sweatshop working were later to do.[30]

Although interchangeability of tasks did sometimes take place, the extent of co-operation between men and women within the rural industrial family economy has probably been exaggerated by Medick and others. A gender division of labour was a crucial element in the rural industrial system throughout the eighteenth century. Men's work and women's work remained distinct. The expansion of protoindustry took place mainly on the basis of cheap and flexible female and child labour, which retained many of the characteristics of women's work in the urban economy. Despite the importance of female labour to the protoindustrial system, it was grossly undervalued. Women had few job options and none of them paid well. Men's jobs were more specific and were consistently better paid than women's.[31] There is, therefore, evidence to suggest that the association of women's industrial work with low wages was cemented during the so-called 'golden age' of the eighteenth century as Ivy Pinchbeck and others argued several decades ago.

Many historians have associated the alleged decline of the family economy in the context of industrialisation from the late eighteenth century with a more specific gendering of work and a more marginal position for women workers. Yet there is no doubt that the 'rough and ready equality' assumed to exist within family enterprise of the pre-industrial period was by no means common.[32] The patriarchal nature of the family economy probably outweighed its egalitarian characteristics. Not only was the division of labour gendered, but women were also subordinated to men in the family's productive functions.[33] Men's work was central and women's less specialised. Women performed a variety of tasks which consigned them to the position of 'eternal amateurs'.[34] The eighteenth-century economy was a flexible one, where family production could be balanced against consumption by intensifying or extending work effort. In this context women's flexibility was crucial. When additional labour was required at harvest time or because of the illness of an apprentice, 'it was the woman who rallied to supply the need'.[35] Women's ability to fill in the gaps and their willingness to turn their hand to any necessary task were indispensable within the context of the family economy and in the wider productive system.

The greater flexibility and generality of women's work do not necessarily provide evidence for their relative subordination in the eighteenth-century economy. The particular and vital role played by women in the pre-industrial struggle for subsistence and the association of women with low wages and general work, can be connected with family co-operation. Dorothy Thompson has asserted that 'men and women shared a vocabulary of work as well as family, understood and respected each other's contribution, recognised the interdependence of their various jobs and shared in the training and rearing of children'.[36] Popular politics and plebeian culture acknowledged the productive role of women more explicitly than was to be the case subsequently.[37] The food riot, for example, in which women were fully engaged, was a major point of intersection between the household economy and the community political body. John Bohstedt's analysis of newspaper reports of all recorded riots between 1790 and 1810, indicates that when women did participate in food riots, which they did in just under half of all cases, they were equal to men in the communal polity and economy.[38] The same research found that it was those areas with the highest ratio of non-agricultural occupations in which women were most often found co-operating with men in food riots and were particularly prominent in the Black Country. These findings tentatively suggest that some forms of protoindustrial employment in some areas gave women an economic role in the family that was less differentiated from men's than was to be the case later, and that this gave women some political status within the local community.

Women's position in food riots, therefore, was not symbolic of a special female role of family shopper. Riots were 'complex assertions of shared memberships and beliefs and obligations'.[39] The household economy was defended by all members of that household. The material contribution of women to the family, the community and the wider economy during the eighteenth century was acknowledged. Deborah Valenze's analysis of later eighteenth-century writing in political economy indicates that women were praised for their industriousness, and their productive effort was recognised to have contributed to the wealth of the nation, as well as to individual families.[40] 'When our woollen manufactory flourishes', wrote Francis Moore in 1773, 'the wives and children of small Farmers, Cottagers and Labouring men, can earn nearly as much money from spinning at the wheel, as the men can get by his industry in the field.'[41] Deborah Valenze argues that 'no eighteenth century commentator would have denied that women labourers were important producers of wealth. The fact of widespread expectation of women's labour was unremarkable from the vantage point of eighteenth century society', but after mid century, the positive image of the labouring woman characterised by her 'industriousness and economic potential was challenged by a more critical view'.[42]

Women's flexibility, however, denied them access to the skilled, specialised and higher productivity work which was to be particularly valued from the turn of the century. Not only was pre-industrial women's work ill-defined and narrowly based but there is evidence that it became even more so through the course of the eighteenth century. Women's choice of occupation, already constrained by the actions of male-dominated guilds in the seventeenth century, was further restricted by the operation of the apprenticeship system and by the gendered distribution of rational and scientific knowledge.[43] Changes within the apprenticeship system during the eighteenth century reduced the number of private arrangements, cut the proportion of female apprentices and narrowed the range of tasks for which girls received a formal or semi-formal training. Eighteenth-century apprenticeships were increasingly designed to prepare girls for a life of domesticity either in their own homes or in the homes of others. The work of Keith Snell shows that some boys but few girls enjoyed access to training that would lead to work in a skilled trade. Snell's analysis of parish apprenticeship records in the southern counties indicates that most female apprenticeships in the eighteenth century were in 'housewifery'. Parishes apprenticed girls in housewifery in the belief that such skills would train them in the habits of industry while ensuring their future ability to contribute to their families' self-sufficiency.[44]

Economic opinion of the later eighteenth century objected to apprenticeship on the grounds that it served to restrain competition, yet the system remained the typical contemporary means of providing formal vocational training.[45] Even so, apprenticeships after 1750 had other equally important objectives. They were at least as concerned with the transmission of behaviour patterns as with the passing on of skills, and, in the case of parish apprenticeship, the priority was to alleviate poverty and its associated costs.[46] It is therefore possible to identify clear distinctions in the use of apprenticeship between parish and private indentures. Parish children were apprenticed younger, for shorter periods and for smaller premiums than their privately apprenticed counterparts, and were most prominent in agriculture, services and the primary stages of manufacture. Employers increasingly exploited parish apprentices in an attempt to reduce labour costs and maximise profits, so that towards the end of the century they were often confused with cheap labour.[47]

The allocation of pauper apprentices to the less skilled occupations has implications for their gender distribution. More girls were apprenticed by the parish than privately and the reverse was true for boys. According to research by Deborah Simonton into the operation of apprenticeship in the counties of Essex and Staffordshire, 60 per cent of all female apprentices were put out by the parish compared with only 12 per cent of boys.[48] Her finding, that slightly less than one-third of parish indentures in those counties were girls, is broadly consistent with Keith Snell's conclusions, but less compatible with those of Peter Rushton who suggests a figure of nearer 10 per cent.[49] In private apprenticeship deals, girls were less likely than boys to receive a formal training in skilled work, a tendency that was reflected in the lower premiums that were paid for them. Apprenticeship in domestic service, which was the largest single category in the eighteenth century, required a minimal premium and was almost entirely female.[50]

As the female experience of apprenticeship differed markedly from the male during the eighteenth century, so the gender distribution of training schemes by trade suggests a downgrading of female work and status and a narrowing of occupational opportunities for girls and young women. Formal apprenticeship, however, was only one of several possible routes to the acquisition of skill. Informal training for example, was more common and probably less gendered. Both girls and boys were trained less formally through various mechanisms of which the annual hiring of servants was the most prevalent. Girls and boys also received informal training from family members. It is sometimes assumed that girls learned traditional 'female' skills from their mothers and boys received appropriate instruction from their fathers, but there is evidence that girls who worked for their fathers received an equivalent training to boys.[51]

Whether apprenticeship were formal or informal, the majority of training schemes embodied gender divisions.[52] The smaller proportion of female apprentices was a less important cause of the lower level of perceived skill that women came to possess than was the socially constructed view of women's work as marginal. Women might work entirely competently alongside male relatives without acquiring or possessing a recognised skill.[53] Girls had limited opportunities and were directed to low status occupations with modest future prospects. Apprenticeship served to confirm the status of female work as inferior to that of men.[54] It ensured that women were confined to low productivity work, which further marginalised their position from the late eighteenth century. Above all apprenticeship helped to construct domestic work as appropriate for women.

Employment in domestic service was one of the few growth areas for women during the eighteenth century when traditional occupations were contracting. Domestic service was already a feminised activity before 1700 and thereafter became increasingly female dominated, as men servants became less attractive financially to their employers.[55] After 1750, women monopolised the work in the proliferating single-servant households. The growing femaleness of domestic service also reflected the evolution of 'housework' and its unique association with women during the eighteenth century.[56]

The connection of women with the domestic sphere, which the expansion and feminisation of service helped to confirm, was important in their subordination thereafter. Domestic service offered women employment, but little in the way of status. Women opted for a job in service only in the absence of a satisfactory alternative. It has been suggested that domestic servants could achieve economic independence,[57] but this was unlikely. Evidence indicates rather that the increasing feminisation of service through the eighteenth century was associated with its greater exploitation. This was particularly true where family members were employed as servants or housekeepers, and in the case of pauper children, who both comprised an important component of the supply of servants in the eighteenth century and lowered the threshold at which households could afford a servant.[58] The ubiquity of service appeared to disadvantage those employed in the sector. Employment conditions of eighteenth-century domestic servants were harsh and intensive. Hours of work were longer even than those in other contemporary occupations. Discipline was strict, rigidly enforced and often unjustly meted out. Female servants were exploited sexually by other servants as well as by masters. Remuneration was so inadequate and sporadic that domestic servants were known to engage in prostitution in order to tide themselves over until they were paid or could find a better job.[59] The contemporary condition of the female job market, however, ensured that the latter option was unlikely to be available.

During the eighteenth century, women's employment in a number of traditional activities was curtailed. The decline in farm service was one of the factors contributing to the overall reduction in opportunities for productive work in agriculture, especially for women. The process affected different regions at different times, but began in the middle of the century in the south and east. The growing practice of enclosure after 1750 was not the sole cause of women's unemployment but it hastened a trend that was already in place. Enclosure forced a pattern of seasonal employment that restricted women to poorly paid spring and early summer activities and reduced their opportunities for remunerative customary activities on the common land for much of the rest of the year.[60] The decline in employment opportunities for both men and women led to greater competition in the labour market from which men were most likely to derive advantage. In Deborah Valenze's view, 'the pattern of employment established by enclosure was the key to the fate of women in [late eighteenth and] nineteenth century agriculture'.[61]

Agricultural employment for women contracted further because of increasingly rational methods of farm organisation to which women were deemed unsuited.[62] Women had traditionally dominated the dairying sector of farming, which was seen as an art, but as production became increasingly influenced by commercial as well as scientific principles, the dairy became 'contested territory' and ultimately women lost their position of authority there. Competition developed between long-established female practices and those novel techniques associated with 'rational' man. Changes in commercial dairying, therefore, which displaced women from one of their few remaining positions of strength in agriculture, can be related to a 'general transformation in the nature of work at the end of the eighteenth century . . . [which] paved the way for a denigration of women's work. . . . Under capitalism work was rationalised and tailored to men; traditional women's work was seen as irrational and thus . . . less valuable.'[63]

With the loss of a substantial proportion of traditional occupations and ways of making ends meet, it is not surprising that the eighteenth century witnessed the association of women and poverty. Women, especially widows and spinsters, featured prominently in poverty statistics and records. The assumed characteristics of women's lives, namely the responsibility of caring for others, confinement to menial and irregular jobs in trades that were subject to seasonal and cyclical fluctuations, rendered women highly prone to the threat of poverty.[64] In eighteenth-century society, 80 per cent of those classed as poor were women. Life for all working people at the time was a 'remorseless struggle against poverty', yet it is apparent that women, more than men, failed in the battle to make ends meet.[65] In desperate circumstances, women engaged in begging or encouraged their children to beg. Those on poor relief or on the margins of poverty endured life by scraping together a subsistence income from a variety of sources such as casual labour, charitable donations and petty crime. Women, especially unmarried women and widows or abandoned women with children living in parishes without legal claims to parochial relief, often became the subjects of disputes between parishes under the Settlement Laws. Such poor women were likely to become dependent on the parish for long-term poor relief because the bearing of children, especially outside of marriage or cohabiting partnership, made it more difficult for them to gain employment.[66]

The poverty of women in particular became increasingly severe as traditional commons rights were eroded. In periods of economic crisis, between one-third and a half of the population were forced into poor relief. Often women were employed by the parishes in return for relief, typically in caring activities as nurses, maidservants and caretakers. Not only did this employment benefit the parish, the infirm and the poor, it also reinforced rather than undermined the family economy and did not threaten existing labour pools in other menial trades.[67]

Little of the evidence presented above indicates an eighteenth-century golden age. Before 1800, women were disadvantaged in terms of opportunities for work, yet they made a substantial contribution to the family budget. They ensured family survival by piecing together subsistence from a range of sources. Household strategies of production and consumption were determined and organised by women.[68] Women's industriousness was central to both the family economy and to the wealth of the nation. In the eighteenth century women worked whenever the opportunity arose. They worked hard, for long hours and often at heavy tasks. Much of their work was unwaged and performed within the home. Women were multi-occupied as they moved between jobs that were part-time, irregular and seasonal.[69]

The history of women workers in the eighteenth century highlights the link between poverty and progress. Attitudes towards the labouring poor during the critical period of early industrialisation informed contemporary perceptions about who would work, how well they performed and how they were to be remunerated. For much of the eighteenth century such views were clearly inclusive because women as well as men were seen to be potentially productive.[70] By the late eighteenth century, however, as the level of poverty rose, women became cast as economic burdens rather than assets, and ceased to be regarded as joint supporters of the labouring household. Within the context of the early industrial economy, women became perceived as victims and as objects of pity rather than as equal participants in the project of wealth creation.[71]

This change in attitude towards female labour from the late eighteenth century can be only partly explained by the growing unemployment and underemployment among women. A reformulation of the contemporary meaning of work was also relevant. Women became excluded from jobs as productivity and rationality, with which women were only weakly associated, became increasingly valued. Much of the work that women performed, especially the home-based multi-occupations, lacked the potential for productivity enhancement. The scientific revolution spread the notion that women were less rational than men, but both the importance of productivity and women's tenuous connection with it, were developed in the framework of contemporary political economy. The diffusion of the ideas of later eighteenth-century economists was responsible for the changing perception of women workers. The open view of women workers, in which they were expected to contribute to economic well-being, and indeed were criticised if they did not, can be placed within an early eighteenth-century corporate concept of society.[72] Adam Smith, writing from a later eighteenth-century vantage point, acknowledged the contribution of women workers to the eighteenth-century economy, and while recognising their industriousness also noted their poor remuneration notably within the domestic trades.[73] Female spinners and knitters, for example, 'earn but a very scanty subsistence, who endeavour to get their whole livelihood by either of those trades'.[74] The low wages of women, which had rarely diminished their enthusiastic participation in economic activities, was seen by some contemporaries as a possible deterrent in the future. According to Priscilla Wakefield, a 'discouragement to the industry of women, is the inequality of the reward of their labour, compared with that of men, an injustice which pervades every species of employment performed by both sexes'.[75]

Historians have noted that by the early nineteenth century, when rising national wealth paradoxically coincided with declining public sympathy for the poor, economists associated women with the problems of poverty rather than the habits of industry.[76] Ideologically, therefore, women became excluded from a productive role in society. Such exclusion was compounded by growing criticism of their maternal performance.[77] In Malthusian terms, women were both failures as mothers and inappropriate as workers. Thomas Malthus and some of his colleagues placed the male worker in a central productive role. This lent support to organised male labour's demands for a breadwinner wage and for restricted entry to their trade. Women were implicitly positioned as domestic and dependent beings who operated in a sphere separate from men. It was increasingly assumed that working women were, or should be, caring for young children. Working people, especially working men, and the middle class adopted the ideas of political economists about work and family duty that were considered useful to a new industrial society. The construction of gender roles was an important outcome of such ideas. The identity of labouring women 'vanished behind the collective image of the dependent family'.[78] Positive views of women as workers receded as political economists proposed a more individualist perspective. The idea of the working woman 'as a producer apart from her family seemed to vanish from sight. Her fate was intimately associated with the declining strength of a corporate vision of society as it surrendered before a more individualistic, capitalist orientation towards labour. No longer would plans for an industrious nation include explicit discussion of harnessing the productivity of women.'[79]

During the eighteenth century, new perceptions of the relationship between women and work were generated. There is little doubt, however, that the dominant thinking of the earlier eighteenth century perceived labour in non-gendered terms. All working people, irrespective of age and sex, were expected to contribute to family survival and thus to the well-being of the economy as a whole. Late in the eighteenth century this had changed and the construction of women in terms of dependence and domesticity which had begun by 1800 was to become more central in the making of gender during the following decades.

The pre-industrial years can therefore be seen as a period of 'twists and turns' with respect to women's standing in the economy and society.[80] There was no unequivocal golden age, nor was there an uninterrupted continuity from an earlier epoch. There were moments of fluidity in the relationships between men and women especially within the context of the family economy. For much of the century the sexes were viewed almost as equivalents with respect to their labouring capacity. Women were acknowledged to be hardworking and their contributions were readily recognised. The extent to which women were used as workers, however, was not matched by the value placed on their labour. Women workers were more likely to be low paid and to operate within a secondary labour market of less skilled occupations. Differential access to paid work on the basis of gender was increasingly apparent by the end of the eighteenth century as a prelude to a more robust gendering of labour in the context of nineteenth-century industrialisation. Opportunities for women diminished in the wake of economic and institutional changes and women, more than men, were likely to find themselves unemployed or underemployed.

In attempting to identify a pre-industrial golden age, historians of women's work may well be searching for a non-existent transformation. In so doing, they may fail to discover the subtle changes that were superimposed on the underlying continuities.[81] Neither Judith Bennett nor Bridget Hill, who disagree profoundly on the explanation for women's long-term disadvantage in the labour market, believes the golden age to be a useful concept. Bennett suggests that a simplistic notion of times getting better or worse should be rejected. Having examined a long period of women's working position before industrialisation she advocates an essential continuity in women's low status. Hill justifiably emphasises the heterogeneity of women and of historical periods, but argues that a thesis of an unchanging role for women plays into the hands of male historians who have suggested that women's experience has no part in history precisely because their role has been unchanging.[82] Bennett's view of continuity, however, is not that there has been no change but that there has been less than we would have liked or expected; and this in itself requires explanation.[83]

Many historians believe that the relative economic and social positions of men and women were transformed between the seventeenth and the nineteenth centuries mainly as a result of industrialisation. Women were seen to have been marginalised as the family economy, in which all family members are supposed to have shared the work, was replaced by a wage economy. Historians, including Alice Clark, have regretted the displacement of the relatively equitable gender relationships within the family economy by a more robust gender division of labour. As this chapter has shown, however, the era in which the family economy dominated was by no means one in which the gendering of work was insignificant. Even before the factory, work was neither as household-centred nor as communitarian as has been suggested. Even in the classic protoindustrial family economy there was a division of labour by gender, and elsewhere the concept of separate spheres for men and for women was implicitly accepted.[84] The notion of a golden age has clearly been attractive to feminist historians who seek the origins of women's oppression, but it has so far proved unamenable to empirical research.[85] Industrial developments from the late eighteenth century may have imposed a greater rigidity of women's subordination at home and in employment, but it is clear that a marginal position at work already existed for women. Evidence indicates that women played a critical role in the survival of the family economy especially through their ability to turn their hand to any number of tasks as required. In filling the gaps, women ensured subsistence, yet through such a general and amenable approach to work women set themselves up for exploitation. High productivity was impossible by those multi-occupied, so in an environment where rising productivity was perceived as desirable if not necessary, women found themselves marginalised. For much of the eighteenth century women were expected to contribute to their family's and the nation's wealth, but they were not regarded as eligible for skilled or full-time work. It could be argued that in some contexts gender roles were more flexible than previously or subsequently, but in their willingness to perform any function required of them it could be argued that women colluded in their own oppression.[86]

3   Women and the Making of Industrialisation

During the eighteenth century, manufacturing activity, organised in systems of urban putting-out or rural protoindustry, expanded in response to growing markets. Expansion in output, however, was achieved with increasing difficulty. Typically, production operated on the basis of constant returns to scale.[1] Growth in output by extending the range of putting-out activity was ultimately found by merchant capitalists to be unwieldy and costly. Further geographical dispersal of production generated both greater travelling costs to put the raw material out to individual households and more difficulty in ensuring a standard level of quality and of quantity of product.[2] In order to achieve greater control over the production process and over the producers, a number of merchant manufacturers, especially in the textile industries, centralised their operations. Not only was control over product and process tightened through changes in the social relations of production, but the concentration of capital facilitated further changes in the organisation and nature of work.

From the second half of the eighteenth century, manufacturing began to break out of its traditional confines and to expand relative to agricultural activity. Although agriculture remained an important component of the British economy throughout industrialisation,[3] the process whereby a mainly agrarian economy was replaced by a predominantly industrial one, was clearly under way. Manufacturing output accounted for a growing share of total domestic product. The industrial labour force became absolutely and relatively greater. Work became increasingly specialised as by-employment declined. Such specialisation was associated with changes in the organisation of production, among which the move to the centralised factory structure was one of the most striking.

Industrialisation, which occurred in England between the mid eighteenth and the late nineteenth centuries, was a highly differentiated and regional process. The industrial structure, the nature of work, the organisational forms of manufacturing and the gender and age composition of the labour force all varied across and between regions. Some areas became highly industrial, while in others, manufacturing activity stagnated or declined. During the course of industrialisation, the production of the majority of industrial regions was concentrated in a small number of sectors. Various combinations of textiles, metalwares, coal, engineering and shipbuilding were most common.[4] Lancashire and Yorkshire came to dominate the nation's output of textiles, especially cotton and wool. The Midlands of England, including Birmingham and the Black Country, specialised in metalworking. In the eastern counties, the declining traditional cloth industry was replaced by silk, commercial lace, embroidery, straw plaiting and tailoring.[5]

English industrialisation, therefore, was a process whereby manufacturing became relatively more important, but not in a simple, linear way. Manufacturing expansion occurred flexibly in a combination of new and old settings. Traditional organisational forms proved to be not only compatible with more centralised structures but the two were often used in tandem in order to reduce risk or to combat erratic or unpredictable economic conditions. Within such a dynamic context, labour was deployed in a range of creative ways. The heterogeneity of the workforce,[6] in which the gender of labour was a central feature, formed an essential component of industrial change. Women and men shared in the expansion of industrial manufacturing yet, until recently, women's participation was hardly visible in the historical record. In the past ten years, however, historians have begun to produce detailed descriptions of women's activities during the Industrial Revolution from which it can be concluded that women were not simply passive recipients of industrial change. It is clear that female labour influenced the direction and nature of the industrialisation process itself. Of the small number of early historians who explored women's employment position during the period of industrialisation, the majority focused on the ways in which industrial development affected women, and on the extent to which women's social and economic position was altered as a result of industrial restructuring.

Ivy Pinchbeck, for example, in a remarkable and pioneering investigation of women and the Industrial Revolution, sought to understand the long-term implications of mechanisation and the rise of the factory system. She recognised that women were in some ways disadvantaged during the course of industrialisation, but believed that ultimately they were liberated by it.[7] Such optimism was shared by both Max Hartwell, who identified the Industrial Revolution as marking the onset of female emancipation, and by Rhodes Boyson, who argued that women benefited from the introduction of the breadwinner wage that derived from industrialisation.[8] More pessimistic were: G.D.H. Cole, for whom the decline in the working-class standard of living was compounded by the prevalence of cheap female labour, and Eric Richards, whose early 1970s synthetic work on women's participation in the economy led him to conclude that female labour was not used efficiently within the industrialising economy.[9] Richards believed that it was in the 'full flood of industrialism' that female participation rates fell to a level lower than had been the case in either the preceding or the succeeding periods.[10]

Such early interpretations, whether optimistic or pessimistic,[11] tended to place women in the category of victims. Contemporary commentators also did this.[12] Pinchbeck's conclusions, which rested on substantial, national and especially government data, explicitly presented women as passive recipients of the forces of industrial change, while implicitly recognising that women were themselves important in shaping the character of industrial England if only because of their cheapness.[13] Feminist research of the last 20 years has tended to focus on women's oppression, but increasingly it has acknowledged the importance of women's agency. This has important implications for the understanding of the nature of industrialisation. A coherent analysis of the Industrial Revolution requires a full assessment of the role of women as well as that of men. Women should be seen not as separate, nor as passive, nor as simple victims, but as vital and essential to the making of industrialisation. The remainder of this chapter attempts to provide such an integrated history by drawing on the findings of recent feminist and other research.

Recent developments in the historiography of the Industrial Revolution, outlined in Chapter 1, have included a wider definition of technical change. Industrialisation has often been analysed as a technical process, in which a series of inventions transformed production and raised productivity to unprecedented levels.[14] Recent research has shown, however, that although mechanical developments spread geographically and sectorally through a process of technical complementarity, large sections of British industry were largely unaffected by mechanisation for much of the nineteenth century. Ways of identifying changes in technique other than by the existence of powered machinery have been suggested.[15] A broader definition of technical change and innovation would be consistent with the finding that organisationally, there was no linear progression in structure from small-scale decentralised production to large-scale centralised manufacture, but that a variety of forms interacted to produce a different but no less effective kind of expansionary process. It has been argued that major transformations and even productivity growth took place in the context of apparently traditional sectors, through innovation in the nature of outputs or in the quality of inputs into the production process.

During the late eighteenth and early nineteenth centuries, product innovation was an essential characteristic of both the new trades and many traditional industries.[16] Material inputs altered as innovation influenced the nature of raw materials and intermediate goods as well as final products. Huge changes took place in the metal trades, for example, less through innovation in powered technology than through the introduction of new products and the substitution of cheap alloys for precious metals in the production process. The use of cheaper raw materials generated a price fall and thus a wider market for the finished goods. Industries that achieved high levels of productivity did so not only by the use of new machinery, but also because of innovation in markets, in distribution networks and in the division of labour. Such innovations were often related to changes in the labour force and specifically to a gendering of labour. Female workers were typically introduced into new industries or new settings along with a range of organisational and technical changes. The use of female labour permitted employers to adopt novel ways of organising work, and to introduce those exploitative forms of working that required discipline and intensified effort to generate productivity gains.[17]

According to Maxine Berg, the employment of women can be seen as part of a package of innovation.[18] During industrialisation, labour-intensive techniques were developed along with an advanced division of labour in order to draw on a female labour force. Such techniques in the textile trades included picotage, pencilling and the hand painting of patterns directly on to cloth. This laborious work was, from the start, associated with female labour.[19] In the metal trades of the Midlands, advertisements for button piecers, annealers and japanners specified young female labour. The delicacy of the work in button making and piercing as well as in the hand painting of designs was regarded as the particular province of women and girls who also had a special place in the Birmingham toy trades and in the cheap end of jewellery making.[20]

Innovation in the organisation of manufacturing may also be perceived as an aspect of technical change. The coexistence of a variety of organisational forms was not unique to the early industrialising period. Organisational changes took place during the pre-industrial period as rural manufacturing and some large-scale enterprises complemented the artisanal urban workshop and putting-out systems. In this way a dynamic manufacturing system was generated. During the period of industrialisation, the appearance of the centralised factory may have been remarkable, but it did not herald the demise of pre-existing forms of production. Domestic manufacture remained an essential component of the industrial production system, as did small artisanal craft enterprises. The sweatshop system, based on cheap and flexible female labour and concentrated in urban centres, was new to the later nineteenth century, but in many respects, particularly in its exploitation of women workers, it resembled pre- and early industrial domestic forms of production.

The diversity of production structures was an essential ingredient of development in a range of industries. In the early nineteenth-century Lancashire cotton industry, for example, the spinning and finishing stages of production were completed in large centralised units, while the weaving stage was based on extensive putting-out networks of home-based handloom weavers. Such a system operated for several decades. Female and child labour played an increasingly important role in both centralised and home-based production.[21] The cotton industry developed putting-out and artisanal production, and a dispersed ownership where small and medium-sized factories coexisted with the well-known industrial giants.[22] Even where factories became the dominant form, there were differences in scale and structure. Within the northern textile trades, for example, many of the large factory edifices contained several small enterprises.[23] In the woollen industry of the West Riding of Yorkshire, a company mill structure evolved in which centralised processes of production were shared by artisan clothiers, while in the West Country a combination of highly concentrated ownership, proto-factories and putting-out systems coexisted.[24] In each area, female labour formed the largest component of the work-force.[25] In the equally female-dominated silk industry, the throwing stage of production was the first to become organised in the factory,[26] while weaving remained organised in domestic loom shops or, in the case of ribbon weaving, on the putting-out system. The increase in the demand for silk from the 1850s was met by the expansion of cottage factories.[27] The production of broad silks, the specialism of the nineteenth-century Spitalfields silk weavers, was difficult to adapt to power looms and remained an artisanal trade. In the metal trades, technical change was almost entirely associated with domestic and workshop production and the use of large numbers of women workers.[28] In the Birmingham hardware trades large units were occupied by a number of small artisanal enter-prises, which shared material supplies and distributed to outworkers the production of parts and components.

Early industrialisation was thus characterised by a 'plurality' of manufacturing structures each of which was flexible and responsive to changing market conditions and to institutional and social change.[29] Female labour was crucial to the successful operation of such a flexible system, which was not confined to the early period of industrialisation. Throughout the nineteenth century different forms of subcontracting evolved within manufacturing which served not only to spread or minimise risk but also to enable a sometimes ineffi-cient, or inappropriate, factory system to survive. The garment trade provides an example of this. Until the early nineteenth century, most of the production of clothes, especially tailored garments, was organised on a workshop basis using skilled male labour, with occa-sional support from female relatives. Thereafter expansion in demand for ready-made items[30] rendered such a system untenable and larger numbers of semi-skilled female labour became employed on an outwork basis. In early nineteenth-century Essex, for example, tailoring employed cheap young women working either at home or in workshops, in a system that resembled the slop working of the London clothing industry. Even in the late nineteenth century, Colchester tailoring firms used outworkers in surrounding villages, where women's work supplemented the low agricultural wages of men.[31] From the mid nineteenth century, large-scale production, based on a more detailed division of labour and then using the newly invented sewing machine, appeared in the major urban centres of garment making.[32] Initially the new factories concentrated on the making of trousers, while the more complicated jackets were put out to workshops. Sweatshop working, on the basis of cheap and expendable female labour, performed a vital function for the factories by providing the flexibility for which centralised manufacture was ill equipped. The seasonality of the garment trade meant that the symbiosis of factory, workshop and sweatshop, with the latter recruiting and releasing female labour as required, was the only way in which the factory could survive.[33]

There was, therefore, no single route to industrial change and the outcome for each industry was a distinctive one. In the textile industry, growing competition and technical change in the late eighteenth century intensified existing differences in the structure of production rather than concentrating manufacture in the factory. In engineering and metalworking, centralised production barely influenced the organisation of work. Through the creative use of small-scale and flexible practices, a highly efficient workshop culture developed. This was particularly true among industries around Birmingham and Sheffield, which developed very successful alternative routes to industrialisation.[34] In the Birmingham metal trades the use of flexible labour was key, and the restructuring of manufacturing increased the use of female and child labour and intensified the pace of work. In the Black Country the expansion of women's traditional work was accompanied by the growth of chainmaking, and the making of nails, nuts and bolts which was based largely on low-paid female workers and children.[35] The expansion of industries in the countryside of Essex was likewise based on low-waged female labour.[36] Large-scale production failed to dominate manufacturing in Britain, partly because of its inflexibility, and partly because small-scale production allowed creative and flexible responses to the demands of local and regional markets.

Central to current ideas about technology, innovation and organisational diversity in the process of industrialisation is the role played by labour. Of particular importance it seems is the specific – and flexible – contribution of female and child workers. Industrialisation depended on a cheap and plentiful supply of labour. During the later eighteenth century this was facilitated by demographic change, in particular a rising birth rate. For the first time population growth was sustained and acted as a positive stimulus to industrialisation. In the early stages of industrial development, labour constituted the largest element in production costs. The low price of labour was thus crucial. Its cheapness allowed costs and prices to be contained. This successively encouraged market growth, profitability and investment capital.[37] The supply of, and demand for, female labour in particular was stimulated by eighteenth-century demographic and wage trends and further supported by institutional changes in agriculture. The 'release of labour' facilitated by enclosure and the Poor Law was predominantly female.

The expanding sectors of manufacturing during industrialisation made extensive use of female and child labour. In the textile industries, women and children dominated the labour force, and in leather making and metalworking – especially in the nail making and hardware trades – women were employed in large numbers.[38] Opportunities in the new sectors of industry, however, were insufficient to employ those women displaced by the contraction of agriculture and domestic spinning, yet in terms of the proportionate contribution to the manufacturing labour force, women were more important during the early period of industrialisation than they had been before and were to be subsequently.[39] The majority of working women were found in the areas of manufacturing activity in which change was most pronounced. The dominant parts of the manufacturing sector, and especially the progressive industries to which most of the productivity gains in industry have been attributed, were initially employers of a larger proportion of women than of men. According to the latest quantitative estimates produced by Crafts, only 10 per cent of the adult male labour force in 1831 was employed in the high productivity sector, where women workers were more numerous.[40]

The growth of women's employment in early industrialisation was the product of the ready reserves of cheap and skilled female labour which had characterised traditional domestic and workshop production.[41] The cheapness and easily exploitable nature of female labour, which was highly desirable, even necessary, for the operation of industrial capitalism,[42] had been established within the traditional sector. Protoindustrialisation and the family economic unit established a convention of low wages for women that subsequently affected women's wage levels when they entered the factory.[43]

Female labour did not simply carry the advantage of cheapness, however, and although low wages were important, so too were women's technical dexterity and acceptance of discipline.[44] According to Ivy Pinchbeck, 'women performed generally better than men' in some tasks. Women were also said to 'bear monotonous repetition better than men', and where 'manipulative quickness was required . . . they were more adept. Nor were they inclined to spare themselves in their labours . . . women and children were more easily driven and managed than male labourers.'[45] They were believed to be more 'easily induced to undergo severe bodily fatigue than men'.[46] Women's abilities in textile production were readily acknowledged. According to one early nineteenth-century cotton weaver, 'the woman's talent is equal to the men's when the work is not too heavy; we have some women whose talent is equal to any man's in the middle kind of work'.[47] In silk weaving, where gender equality was common until the mid nineteenth century, a worker asserted that 'my wife is as competent a weaver as I am myself'.[48]

In coal mining 'in spite of their fatigue and exhaustion and the bad conditions under which so many of them worked, women proved to be steady and reliable workers'.[49] Women's alleged lack of ambition, which ensured they remained on the lower rungs of the coal-mining hierarchy, was also recognised and exploited by contemporary employers. According to one collier, women made 'far better drawers than lads . . . when a lad gets to be "half" he is all for getting coal, but a lass never expects to be a coal cutter, and that keeps her steady to her work'.[50] Within the mines as elsewhere, cheap female labour was used as a means of cost containment. Sometimes it was falsely stated that employers could not afford to pay men higher wages if women's labour were withdrawn, nor to make the improvements that male labour would surely demand.[51]

A range of features, therefore, attracted employers to female labour. Cheapness was crucial, and it was also believed that, as a result of their socialisation, women were more docile and less assertive and therefore more adaptable and exploitable than men.[52] The advantages that female labour brought to employers were also inherent in children. Women and children were often grouped together both in the working environment and in the conceptualisation of industrial workers. This was particularly reflected in discussions surrounding the introduction of novel forms of working. Female and child labour influenced the nature of innovation. New technology, work disciplines and organisation forms were tried out first on them.[53] Berg has suggested that women and children were assumed to be the key workforce to be targeted with any novelty in manufacturing methods. Machines and processes were often invented specifically for this workforce, on whom they were initially tested. In calico printing for example, processes were broken down into a series of operations believed to be performed particularly well by teenage girls who combined manual dexterity with high labour intensity. Patent information on machine size suggests that some of the early cotton spinning techniques were invented specifically for children and women. Early developments in metalworking and pottery focused on female labour. This indicates not simply women's ability to perform particular tasks, but also that women were seen to be more amenable to new techniques and work processes. They were less likely to resist new ways of working. In order to assess the optimum operation of a technique or organisational form, employers experimented first on women workers.

Because labour formed the largest component of production costs in all industries through the period of industrialisation, the cheaper it was the better. Women, who were already categorised as cheap labour, became favoured workers. Employers also preferred them for other reasons, mostly related to their capacity to be exploited. That women bore the heaviest burden of the industrialisation process is suggested by their generally declining wage rates. Although data on women's earnings are patchy, it is thought that the disparity of men's and women's wages, while evident in the pre-industrial period, became more marked in the context of industrialisation.[54] Sara Horrell and Jane Humphries have attempted to quantify the income of women and children during industrialisation. They have measured both the participation rates and the earnings of women and children through an analysis of household budgets. Their initial conclusion, that until about 1820 family incomes grew faster than male earnings, suggests either a faster growth of female and child earnings, or an increase in their employment, or a combination of both. After 1820 family income grew more slowly and by the 1840s women and children were less able to supplement the irregular male earnings than had been the case before. Horrell and Humphries argue that women's and children's contribution to family incomes varied according to occupations and the regions within which they lived and worked. Although generalisations can be only tentative, it is suggested that except in the cases of factory and outworker families, the wages of women and children and therefore their contributions to the family income were relatively small in the late eighteenth century and remained so until the mid nineteenth century.[55]

The limited monetary contribution of women and children to family survival was supplemented by non-wage earnings. This can be most clearly illustrated by the example of rural families, though urban women also engaged in a variety of non-monetary transactions through the nineteenth century.[56] In the context of the shift to industrialisation, rural women's contribution to the family budget lay mainly in the mobilisation of common resources. Such operations included gathering and scavenging, food processing – the making of bread and beer and the preservation of meat – the care of livestock and the cultivation of kitchen crops. Ivy Pinchbeck described these activities in the specific case of cottagers who

> either owned or rented houses which carried with them certain common rights, such as the pasturing of specified animals and the right to cut turf from the waste; while in some cases common field rights were also obtained . . . the amount of food raised by the women in their gardens was in many cases quite a substantial contribution to the food of the family, and was often sufficient with the produce from the stock, to change what would have been mere subsistence on wages alone, into an abundant food supply.[57]

Clearly common resourcing could be, and often was, a lucrative activity, central to rather than simply supplemental to family living standards. Pinchbeck's work suggests that 'instances of the wife's management of the livestock together with the earnings of herself and her children in haytime and harvest . . . produce nearly as much money in the course of the year as her husband by all his labour during the same time'.[58] Pinchbeck also cited Cobbett's estimation that the 'profit from a cow was equal every week to two days of the man's wage', and Babington's belief that 'the wives of his cottagers gained a clear profit of from £4–£8 on every cow they kept, most of them keeping two'.[59]

Jane Humphries has established the veracity of these contemporary assessments of activities which, until recently, were dismissed by many historians as economically marginal. Such 'trifling employments', which produced goods for family consumption rather than entering the market, have often been considered to be unamenable to quantitative measurement. Yet they clearly represented the means

by which family members, especially women, could reduce dependence on male wages and make the difference between family survival and destitution.[60] Humphries has attempted to evaluate
women's resourcing. Her work confirms that keeping a cow was economically important and under some conditions could be worth the
equivalent of 50 per cent of a male wage during the course of the
year. Other profitable endeavours were established by Humphries to
include the gathering of logs and twigs for fuel, berry picking and
the collection of heath material to make brooms for sale. Resourcing
from common land, therefore, can be seen to have provided women
with the opportunity of directly contributing to the family maintenance through the provision of food or household necessities.
Pinchbeck's suggestion that 'from the cow she had cream for butter,
milk for cheese and skim milk for porridge, while her stock also provided her with bacon, poultry and eggs' seems entirely feasible and
should not be overlooked. Likewise, those who kept bees, and many
of them did, 'had honey to use for drink and sweetening, and wax
with which to make their rush light for the winter'.[61] It is important,
however, not to exaggerate the extent to which rural labouring families had access to common resourcing. Recent research suggests that
labourers only rarely had access to open field land and that it was
the rural artisan, already enjoying a relatively comfortable standard
of living, who had the most opportunity to exploit such common
rights.[62] While bearing such caution in mind, and recognising the
likelihood of regional differences in the opportunity to exploit
common resources, it nevertheless seems implausible that Poor Law
authorities would have made loans for widows to buy cows if land
did not exist on which they could be kept. 'From enclosure awards,
widows and unmarried women seem fairly frequently to have been
tenants of cottages with common rights and to have rented or
owned small plots of land. In this way they seem to have been able
to earn their own livings and in the case of widows to bring up their
children.'[63]

Less doubt and more consistency surround the value of gleaning
to the family budget. Gleaning – the gathering of post-harvest
residue – remained important to family survival even after enclosure, though its value varied between regions and was far more profitable in areas of specialisation in cereal production and higher
grain yields. According to Pamela Sharpe, where farms engaged in
crop rotation, peas, beans, barley and wheat might all be gleaned in

one village in a season.[64] Ivy Pinchbeck stressed the profitability of gleaning. 'Five or six bushels of wheat is commonly given as the amount a woman herself would glean, and when the price of a bushel of wheat was almost double the weekly wage of a labourer, it will be seen how profitable was this harvest gleaning.'[65] Recent research by Peter King has added support to the notion that gleaning contributed substantially to the household budget. He estimated that in the case of Essex, gleanings could provide a household with flour for the year and might thus account for 10 per cent or more of total family income. For single and widowed women the proportion might be greater, and gleaning was perceived as an effective form of self-help for the poor.[66]

The success of English industrialisation depended on the consumption as well as the production of manufactured goods. Research on early eighteenth-century consumption shows an overall increase in the ownership of household goods across the population. Historians have credited women with stimulating demand, even on a mundane level. Their desire for small consumer goods like metal pins and buttons expanded the domestic market for such products and then created more work for the women who produced them. Consumption became an important part of household management which might then liberate women from some of their more onerous tasks, but also supplemented the definition of women's role.[67]

Increased demand in both the home and overseas markets stimulated changes in the structure of manufacturing activity. By the late eighteenth century, a larger proportion of the working-class population than before were engaged in productive activities. Women and children in particular became wage earners in new manufacturing enterprises, especially in textiles and pottery. This not only increased family income but also raised the level of demand for the products of these industries. The growing importance of women and children as independent wage earners and consumers, together with the possibility that men worked harder in the context of falling or static wage rates, may have influenced domestic demand. The extent of that influence, however, depended not only on the growth of income, but also on existing standards of living and the extent to which the population was already moving beyond subsistence.

An expanding home market for consumption items was an important factor in industrialisation, and women's traditional association with family purchasing decisions was a relevant feature in this growth. The effect of women on home demand, however, needs to be perceived within the context of working families struggling to make ends meet, through a combination of waged and non-waged activities. Women's household role, therefore, enabled consumer demand to rise, albeit slightly, alongside a very small growth in real earnings.[68]

It is probable that as national income was redistributed towards middle-class consumers, spending on a range of consumer items such as stockings, hats and pots increased. The incomes of most families remained below the level at which they participated in this kind of consumption, which generated demand for fashion-oriented domestic manufacture. According to Pat Hudson, it is misguided to infer from descriptions of the dress of working-class people, for example, that they aspired to the garb of their social superiors. Because of the extensive trade in second-hand clothing, such emulation was of only minor importance to the manufacturing sector.[69] Greater influence was exerted by working-class families on demand for such basic household goods as candles, earthenware, food and drink. These items had typically been made by women in the home before they became wage earners in the context of industrial change, and thereafter had to be bought because women had less time to manufacture them.[70] The buoyancy of the home market from the later eighteenth century, therefore, appears to have been created by two types of change in consumption. The first was a growth in demand for fashionable items as a larger middle class adapted to upper-class spending habits, and the second consisted of a growing market for essential goods for the home from that part of the working class which enjoyed increased family income as more members became wage earners. In the context of population growth, income growth and some redistribution of income, the home market expanded and became more differentiated. A mass market existed, however, only for basic household products.

Such a market was important and the influence of women on it, both as contributors to and controllers of the family budget, has been emphasised by a number of historians. Neil McKendrick was one of the earliest to recognise women's particular role in stimulating the home market. He believed that the earnings of women and children generated a surplus over subsistence that would most likely be spent on the consumer industries of the Industrial Revolution.[71] In boosting demand and in contributing cheap labour, women created a Utopian situation for many entrepreneurs.[72] Many manufacturers apparently stated that it was the female market at which they were aiming, and the increasing demand for consumer goods was the direct result of the growing financial independence of women in control of their own earnings.[73] While women clearly did play an important role in stimulating consumption, McKendrick probably exaggerates their influence. Such hyperbolic statements as 'the female consumer should be seen as the most important link between the entrepreneur and the demand side of the economy', and further, it was 'the mill girl who wanted to dress like a duchess' which helped to create the Industrial Revolution, should be interpreted with care.[74] Maxine Berg presents a more nuanced version of McKendrick's position. The growth of a consumer culture, so vital to enduring industrial growth, was influenced, Berg believes, by women's networks. In the early industrial economy, it was consumption that bound community and capitalism together. New industries produced consumer goods and transformed products formerly made by women in the household into commodities to be sold in the world market.[75]

New perspectives on industrial change have allowed the role of female labour to be acknowledged more fully. The need for hand skills, dexterity and work discipline, for example, encouraged the absorption of female and juvenile labour into commercial production. The increase in women's employment in the Industrial Revolution was a product of the reserves of cheap and skilled female labour from domestic and workshop production and as agricultural regions shed female workers. As more of this labour became available, cheaply, it influenced the direction of change.[76] The role of women and children in both capital- and labour-intensive market-oriented manufacturing probably reached a peak during the Industrial Revolution period. Child and female labour were key elements 'in the labour intensity, economic differentiation and low production costs found in late eighteenth century industries. New methods of discipline, subcontracting, putting out, factory production technologies were initially tried out on women and children.'[77]

There is no doubt that industrialisation made a special use of female labour without offering appropriate rewards. Women were valuable but not valued. The early phase of industrialisation witnessed a special interaction of waged work, household subsistence and consumption and community networks. It was women who operated at the interface of these as they had traditionally done, but the mixed nature of women's work that such a position suggested, made women vulnerable to exploitation and their labour lucrative to employers.[78] Women embodied the very attributes that the new capitalist employers desired. Women were more willing than men to work hard, to endure dreadful working conditions and to be paid a pittance. Men were recognised to be more sensitive to the conditions and the status of their work. Women were not obviously averse to performing dull and boring work for many hours. Women were uniquely dextrous but could also perform heavy labour when required. Women were expendable and flexible. They were quick to learn and easy to train. Although they did not earn high wages, they were nevertheless keen and willing to spend what earnings they received on the products of the new industries. This is not to say that men did not possess any of these characteristics. They were less likely, however, to have what it took to be a worker in the early industrial economy. Men had more traditional skills, and were customarily perceived as more highly skilled workers than women. Men had a stronger position to protect, and spent much of the early industrial period trying to defend it from the challenge of the newly created female industrial workers.

Women were vital to the making of the industrial economy. The suggestion that industrialisation was equally important to the making of gender will be explored in the next chapter.

4 Industrialisation and the Making of Gender at Work

Industrialisation created and was sustained by a rigid gender division of labour. The processes involved in allocating occupations, jobs and even machines to labour on the basis of its gender reveal the extent to which contest and negotiation were integral to the gendering of industrial society. Women had been identified as cheap and secondary workers in the centuries preceding industrialisation, but during the early stage of industrial change hierarchical positions within the workforce were fluid and open to potential restructuring. There was, in principle, no reason why status within industrial society should not be achieved on the basis of ability or merit. Some contemporary writers appeared to believe not only that this was indeed the case, but also that it was in the long-term interest of the economy that such a meritocracy should exist.[1] The possibility that women might discard their inferior position in the workplace was perceived during the early decades of industrial development. The challenge that this posed to male workers, especially those of the skilled variety, generated battles between workers over access to employment. The negotiated result of such struggles formed part of the process by which women became confirmed as secondary workers.

Despite the reluctance of historians to view gender as central to economic relations, there is growing evidence that industrialisation developed as a gendered set of practices,[2] through the actions of employers, the state and the labour movement. Because gender became deeply embedded in the structuring of employment, the working situations and experiences of labouring men and women were quite distinct. This chapter, and the ones that follow, will recognise a broader definition of employment for women, whose continued participation in the informal economy – where men rarely intruded – was a significant outcome of the process of industrialisation. Specific characteristics of the gendering of work will be

51

explored especially as it was represented in the gender allocation of jobs, technology and skill, and reinforced by the construction and operation of gender-specific protective legislation. Gender struggle shaped the Industrial Revolution, but the Industrial Revolution itself created the circumstances in which gender conflict, as revealed in male hostility, was aroused. According to Anna Clark, industrialisation exacerbated 'chronic sexual conflict, which was endemic to an economy where women's labour was necessary yet undervalued'.[3]

During the formative stages of industrial change, the relationship between male and female workers was dynamic and negotiable. Women were in a position to gain some advantage, particularly as employers were keen to make use of them, but the clearly structured hierarchy of work that had emerged by the mid nineteenth century was one in which men occupied the higher status occupations with skilled or supervisory components. Women's economic standing thus became marginalised. Once acquired, the superior position and power of men were supported by socially shaped roles for both sexes. Even where women worked alongside men, therefore, they were still considered, by men and by employers, to be primarily domestic beings with a transitory relationship with the world of work. The informal environments in which many women worked, especially after marriage, served only to reinforce the notion that women's connection with employment was weaker than men's. During industrialisation, therefore, differences between men and women as workers were confirmed. The following sections explore the processes by which gender was made.

Although it was not unusual for men and women to perform different functions in the workplace before industrialisation, the allocation of work and occupations according to gender appeared to become more pronounced and rigid as industrialisation progressed. The gendered distribution of work was the outcome neither of the requirements of capitalism[4] nor of economic forces. On the contrary, the sharing of labour and work by gender was probably inefficient. Because the particular form of work segregation was based on the relative superiority of men,[5] substantial benefits may have accrued to male labour. It is possible, though not very likely, that because they operated in a distinct labour market, women were relieved of the competition of men and thus enjoyed some small advantage from the segregation of work. Gender divisions in paid employment that were cemented during industrialisation influenced gender relations in other contexts.[6] During the nineteenth century the very clear definitions of gender roles both at home and in the workplace, which were vital to a particular ordering of society, were sustained by such divisions. Thus job segregation by gender was relevant to the stability both of the industrial capitalist system and of society more generally.

The origins and causes of job segregation may be located in the self-interest of those groups who had most to gain from it. The process by which the labour market became gendered, was neither automatic nor straightforward. Historians have typically viewed the gendering of work as the result of a series of battles and negotiations, which were conducted on an individual industry basis, so that by the later nineteenth century almost every job was associated with a gender.[7] The notions of 'men's work' and 'women's work' became refined and reinforced during the period of industrialisation and were subsequently subject to very little alteration. So firmly embedded were such ideas that nineteenth-century employers were influenced by images of gender when they hired workers, structured the work process and organised their workplaces. Paternalist practices, such as the allocation of punishment and reward, the provision of recreational facilities, and later, the implementation of the marriage bar, were clearly gender specific and reinforced gender relations both at work and at home.[8]

An exploration of the complexity of issues surrounding the gendering of work within industrial society should incorporate ideological forces. Deborah Valenze's recent analysis of contemporary writing reveals that women workers in early nineteenth-century industry were viewed as objects of pity and condemned for their poverty. Such a vision contrasts with that of the mid eighteenth century when women were valued for their contribution to the wealth of the national economy. The ideas of political economists in the late eighteenth and early nineteenth centuries were 'influential in the recasting of women workers in the industrial economy'.[9] That women remained confined to the lower-paid occupations even in the context of substantial changes in the nature and organisation of production, should be understood in relation to contemporary theories about men, women and work. Many of these rated the male relatively highly especially in terms of earning capacity.[10] Male labourers adopted their superior position with alacrity. The notion of the privileged male worker comprised an important component of the restructuring of industrial society, as ideas about appropriate gender roles became crucial to the same enterprise. Opinions about women constantly changed during the period of rapid economic development. According to Valenze, 'the transformation of ways of working also reconstituted understandings of women . . . contemporaneous debates about female labour played a crucial part in determining what paid employment would be assigned to women and men'.[11] The rise of a new set of attitudes promoted through political economy and associated with industrialism marked a turning point in the general view of working-class women. By the early 1800s, the ideas of Thomas Malthus and David Ricardo helped to identify poor women as a problem in need of a solution. Female labourers 'emerged into the new industrial age as "women workers" – part of an industrial working class with separate interests and identities'.[12]

Such ideas seemed to justify the poor conditions of work and level of pay of female labourers compared with their male counterparts. Much of the evidence of women's wages in the early period of industrialisation is partial and piecemeal, yet that which does exist suggests levels of at most 50 per cent of the male wage. Even in the early stages of factory production, women were not offered a 'living wage' because of the assumption that women depended on men for part of their subsistence. Evidence from government enquiries confirms that women were typically placed in lower-level jobs than men, that they were paid less than half the men's rate, that they were more likely to be paid irregularly and by the piece. Although industrialisation and specifically factory employment permitted the emergence of women workers as 'independent' wage earners, the wage that they earned did not allow them to become independent. The level of female earnings was determined on the assumption that a woman's wage was a supplement to some other wage.[13]

Judy Lown's research into the operation of the Courtauld's Essex silk mill during the nineteenth century provides an instance of the dependence of manufacturing on cheap female labour.[14] The wage system at Courtauld's factory reflected the pronounced gender divisions in the workplace. Adult males were paid a weekly rate, while women and girls were paid by the piece and received a fraction of male wages. Piece rates operated not just as a work incentive but also as a means of distinguishing the status of male and female workers. The subordination of female labour was also reflected in conditions of work that imposed greater discipline on women than men. Women were more often than men fined for various misdemeanours and women less frequently received rewards. The employment of women was more likely to be affected by fluctuations and short-time working than that of men.[15]

Other evidence confirms that women's position in the lower levels of the hierarchy of work was reflected in the wages that they were paid and in the conditions of employment that they endured. It is assumed by many historians of women and gender that such disadvantage was socially constructed in order to serve the interests of employers, male workers and society at large. The position of conventional economics, however, is that disparity in wages and participation rates reflects the inequalities in human capital that people bring to the labour market.[16] Neo-classical economics is notoriously insensitive to gender-made issues, yet it is conceivable that women were paid less and remained in subordinate employment positions because of their lower productivity. Such a possibility has been investigated by Joyce Burnette, who challenges the view that women were underpaid because of their assumed dependence on the male household head.[17] Burnette argues that women received a market wage and that part of the gap between male wages and female wages was the result of the lower average number of hours worked by women. The remaining discrepancy is explained as the outcome of women's lower human capital and productivity levels. According to Burnette, men received more training through apprenticeship and possessed more skills than women who then competed less successfully for better-paid jobs. Differences in human capital did not always favour men. Burnette alleges that, although women's productivity was typically lower than men's, women were more productive than men in some occupations – such as lace making, straw plaiting and sewing – because of their greater dexterity.[18] Women, in Burnette's opinion, were generally disadvantaged in the labour market by relative physical weakness and by their role in childbearing which discouraged their investment in human capital. Such a conclusion, which appears to support the conservative view that much of the gap in wages between men and women during the Industrial Revolution was the result of factors other than discrimination, fails to be supported by the necessary evidence.[19]

Although the origin of women's disadvantage in the labour market remains obscure, women became confirmed as low-paid workers in unskilled sectors of manufacturing and service activity during the period of industrialisation. It has been suggested that the gendering of occupations was related to working-class sexuality. Jane Humphries has argued that the gendering of work became institutionalised during the Industrial Revolution partly as a means of controlling the sexual behaviour of young people. The anxiety generated by the potential for heterosexual intimacy and unwanted conception as unrelated men and women toiled together in the same steamy workplace, was dissipated by segregated employment. Humphries supports her hypothesis by identifying a negative correlation between 'regional variation in illegitimacy [and] variation in sex segregation'. In an environment where family survival was precarious, the financial burden of an extra child on a working family could prove disastrous. Before industrialisation the family economy both organised production and supervised sexuality, thus co-ordinating work and social control. During industrialisation, such control mechanisms were replaced by sex-segregated work and the gender division of labour between paid and unpaid work which provided the means to 'manage the explosive potential of heterosexuality in a context of scarcity'.[20] The idea that the gendering of work was a strategy to control working-class sexuality during industrialisation finds further support from the recent research of Anna Clark who highlights the prevalence of illegitimacy and wife desertion during the early nineteenth century as evidence of sexual crisis in plebeian culture. Although working people had traditionally valued chastity less highly than other moral virtues, this began to change from the 1820s as the 'respectable' sexual attitudes of the middle class began to be adopted by those in the working class.[21]

The analyses outlined above hint at the conflicts between men and women that were generated or became more pronounced in the context of industrialisation. The struggle that is implicit in much of the writing on the gendering of industrialisation can be seen most clearly in the constant renegotiations of the gender division of labour. These discussions reveal the oppositional terms in which men and women were constructed from the early nineteenth century.[22] Employers often preferred the cheaper labour of women and children to the relatively expensive skilled men who, as a result, sought to exclude women from the workplace. The outcome of these attempts at exclusion was a divided workforce[23] which ultimately served only the interests of employers.

The struggle over the gender division of labour is typically presented as one that was instigated by male workers, particularly skilled male workers, who perceived an attack on their status and livelihood to emanate from both the deskilling implicit in the technical changes associated with manufacturing production, and the introduction of cheap female and child labour into centralised production units. These two strands of the challenge to male superiority sometimes interacted – when new technology could, in principle, be operated by any worker – but sometimes they were quite distinct – when, for example, cheap female labour was used more intensively as an alternative to mechanisation. In either case the position of skilled male labour was actually or potentially undermined. In a series of contests that spanned more than a century, skilled men sought to limit the damage to their status both at work and at home. Their strategies were designed either to exclude women from the workplace (or marginalise them within it), or to take control of the new technology and redefine the work process. Inasmuch as technology was conceived as a means of raising labour productivity, often in conjunction with reducing the amount of expensive skilled labour, it set in opposition the interests of employers and labour. Because of the particular response of labour, namely male resistance, new technology also cleaved the working class.[24] Men could do little to prevent capitalists engaging women to work in the new industries, so their efforts were directed towards segregating women and maintaining sexual divisions within the factory.[25]

From the late eighteenth century, especially in industries and occupations that were transformed by industrial development, gender segregation became based on and reinforced by the way in which technology was introduced and manipulated. Much evidence suggests that technological change facilitated the gendering or regendering of work, and even that without such change 'regendering seldom occurs'.[26] During the period of industrialisation and beyond, a range of technical developments fundamentally changed the position of women as workers.[27] Manufacturers introduced machinery from the late eighteenth century for a variety of reasons but especially to maximise profit and to extend their control over labour. Innovation challenged the position of male craft workers who, while powerless to prevent the implementation of new technology, could act to limit its impact. The desire of male workers to strengthen their own positions and to undermine those of women, was instrumental in the creation of a gender-segregated workforce and provides an example of the intersection of class and gender.

The actions of male craft workers were co-ordinated by the trade unions that represented them. Initially, skilled men attempted to marginalise women workers by taking industrial action. In the first decades of the nineteenth century groups of hatters, calico printers, tailors and framework knitters each responded to deskilling pressures by striking against female labour in their occupations. Concern over female competition was similarly expressed by warpers, weavers and cotton spinners. Such disputes achieved minimal success and were replaced by alternative strategies which included the division of trades into different branches and the isolation of women into the less skilled, unapprenticed and poorly paid tasks. The latter approach was adopted by bookbinders, who confined women to the sewing and folding of printed pages and refused them admittance to the union, and by tailors, who channelled women into the unpleasant and low-paying production of army and navy uniforms which men were only too pleased to avoid. Other groups, such as shoemakers and London hatters, also used women to perform undesirable functions, which allowed the skilled men simultaneously to avoid the most degraded tasks, and to isolate the competition.[28]

Skilled male cotton spinners also sought to defend themselves from cheap female labour. Gender hostility was more muted among cotton spinners than among the more established skilled artisans, and the division of labour that emerged in cotton and some other textile industries revealed a greater co-operation between the sexes. Such integrated action, however, typically assumed a marginal role for women. As Anna Clark has argued, the traditions of the family labour system meant that within the cotton trade, 'the subordinate labour of women and children was necessary and accepted; buttressing rather than undermining patriarchal authority'.[29] Yet co-operation was not easily achieved, and the way in which men assumed a key role in spinning – a traditional female activity – illustrates the shifts that occurred in the negotiation of the gender division of labour. In the early stages of technical change in the cotton industry, in the 1770s and 1780s, spinning jennies were operated at home by quite highly paid women.[30] The introduction of water-powered mule spinning machines in factories, however, soon undercut their earnings.[31] Women and children were employed on the light mules in the rural factories only until the 1790s when larger steam-driven mules, which apparently required more strength and skill than women possessed, offered employment to male artisanal labour in urban mills. Ivy Pinchbeck argued that because these heavier machines required the strength of men, they became monopolised by a new class of male mule spinners. During this process, mule spinning became skilled work. Pinchbeck, and many writers since, have assumed that because of the need for strength, the work became skilled, and because of biological weakness women could not perform the work.[32] Whatever the justification, it remains the case that within the space of one generation, women lost an occupation that they had dominated for centuries.[33] The new male spinners – nearly all of them drawn from artisanal ranks – were, in contrast to the women spinners they replaced, well rewarded for their work.[34]

For several decades from the 1790s, these mule spinners paid children and young women – members of their family where possible – to assist them as piecers. Such a system of family hiring suggests that the superior strength of men was only one of the reasons why they were preferred as spinners. Their authority and ability to supervise a team of other workers proved equally important.[35] The whole organisation of spinning was oriented around the minder [spinner], and although it was possible for the (mainly female) piecers and ancillary workers to become spinners, this was made difficult by the power of the trade unions, whose major objective was to restrict entry into spinning. The high wages that were paid to the spinners were based more on their quasi-managerial role in production and their ability to contain the supply of labour than on any spinning skills they might possess.[36] Spinners were also in a position to exert considerable control over the labour process. Because of the lack of standardisation of early textile machinery, spinners were responsible for tuning and adjusting their own pairs of mules in their own particular way which made it difficult for men to operate another's machines.[37]

As skilled men usurped the role of women as spinners in the late eighteenth-century cotton industry, so they needed to fight to maintain their acquired position through the early nineteenth century, and to renegotiate the gendering of work in the context of the second generation of spinning technology in the 1830s. Through the early 1800s, frequent industrial disputes reflected the male spinners' hostility to persistent attempts by employers to reduce their high wages and to increase the number of cheap female spinners. Because of the central role played by the spinner in the factory production of cotton yarn, a spinners' strike almost invariably meant a complete stoppage of the plant. Resentment over the power of the spinners that these disruptions represented, motivated factory owners to seek an alternative technology to weaken their influence.[38] In the wake of a major strike of spinners in 1824, several manufacturers approached Richard Roberts to persuade him to construct such a machine. Roberts, a well-known technical engineer and tool maker, subsequently recalled that 'the self-acting mule was made in consequence of a turn out of the spinners at Hyde which had lasted three months, when a deputation of masters waited upon me and requested me to turn my attention to spinning, with a view to making the mule self-acting'.[39] The explicit purpose of the self-acting mule, which was ready for adoption in 1835, was to break the power of the male spinners and to replace them with women and children.

The implementation of the self-actor generated intense struggle. Despite the express wishes of the employers, the self-acting mule remained a male machine. Only in a small number of cases, mainly in Scotland, did women operate the self-actor. At least two explanations have been proposed for the success of the male spinner in maintaining his position within a technical context that was designed precisely to allow a regendering of work. The first appears in the work of William Lazonick who argues that a redefinition of skill based on the ability to supervise was crucial to the reassertion of male control over the technology. Male cotton spinners prevented mule spinning becoming a feminised occupation by transferring the relations of production from the earlier mules to the self-actor. Such a continuity of skill was achieved by the efforts of the Spinners' Union, formed in 1829 as an exclusively male organisation.[40] The spinners' offer – made through the union – to take responsibility for labour recruitment and supervision, was readily accepted by the employers. The spinners were able to restructure the meaning of craft status to include supervisory, machine maintenance and quality control functions, and as they took over some aspects of the work process which would otherwise have been performed by the employer, a position of authority was established.[41] Lazonick argues that men's success in retaining their jobs and skilled status was based on the construction of an artificial monopoly.[42] Mary Freifeld, however, maintains that some real skill was required to operate the new machine and that the overseeing and quality control responsibilities depended upon mechanical training and expertise.[43] Freifeld also suggests that the deskilling implied by the self-actor was only partial, as the adjustment and repair of machinery required knowledge. Although this argument underplays the role of men in creating a monopoly, Freifeld argues that women's exclusion from cotton spinning in the late eighteenth century, rendered straightforward their renewed exclusion in the 1830s. Women's connection with skill in spinning was broken in the 1790s which meant not only that they possessed insufficient practical knowledge to retrieve their position in the 1830s, but also that employers would have been hard pressed to find sufficiently skilled female labourers to replace men on the new machines.[44]

While the male spinners clearly owned an advantage, which stemmed from the 1790s, they did not leave their continued dominance to chance. Until the 1820s, the exclusion of women from spinning tended to be informal and piecemeal. Thereafter the arguments became more robust, and the craft unions came to resemble the pre-industrial guilds in the belief that limitations on entry to their trade were essential to the protection of their industrial position.

Many of the female spinners who became redundant as a consequence of the shift of spinning into factories, became employed in the home-based weaving of cloth with their husbands, who supervised their work and retained control over their earnings.[45] Such a shared engagement in textile weaving continued as the process became mechanised and factory based, to the extent that weaving appears to have been the least segregated occupation within manufacturing industry in the nineteenth century. Throughout, men and women performed similar work, in the same place, for similar rates of pay.[46] Sylvia Walby believes that such unusual gender relations to some extent derived from the unionisation of both men and women at an early stage in the development of power loom weaving in factories.[47] Certainly, once power loom weaving was established as a suitable occupation for women, the situation remained unchanged.[48] Anna Clark explains the tendency of male weavers to recognise the ability of women to perform skilled tasks on a par with themselves, in terms of a distinct and amenable gender culture.[49]

This existed partly because men and women had jointly participated in riots against the introduction of power looms.[50]

For various reasons, male artisans and male textile workers developed different strategies to cope with the threat that cheaper female labour posed to their skill, status and wages. Artisans continued to attempt to exclude women entirely, while male textile workers maintained a tradition in which women and children played an important, if subsidiary, role.[51]

The gendering of technology in cotton spinning implied a reconstruction of the gendering of skill. Feminist economists and historians have emphasised the distinction between skill as a genuine accomplishment acquired through a period of practical training, and skill as a social construct reflecting the position of power of those alleged to possess it. Skill, in both senses, had a gendered quality during industrialisation. Men were more likely than women to have acquired a real ability because of the nature and operation of the formal apprenticeship system. During the nineteenth century and subsequently, men were more likely than women to achieve a socially defined skilled status through strong trade unions and the practice of exclusionary strategies. The attribution of skill to a job on the basis of the sex of the person doing it also tended to advantage men. According to Anne Phillips and Barbara Taylor, 'women workers carry into the workplace their status as subordinate individuals and this status comes to define the value of the work that they do . . . skill is often an ideological category imposed on certain types of work by virtue of the sex and power of the workers that perform it'.[52] Above all skill has been associated with men and absence of skill with women. The identification of men with skill has been central to male dominance in the workplace.[53] The gender bias of skill definitions is indicative of women's relative lack of power.[54]

Part of the process of the making of gender through industrialisation, therefore, was the gendered construction of skill. Increasingly, skill was defined in opposition to women. Skilled work was that which women did not do. Although the gendering of skill can be seen as a process by which men empowered themselves by disempowering women, the identification of women's work with unskilled work ultimately disguised the process through which manufacturing activity in general – including that performed by 'skilled' men – became more routinised.[55]

During industrialisation, men played an instrumental role in the redefinition of notions of skill. By restructuring the meaning of skill and by more clearly defining their own work as skilled, men, especially those who at the outset of industrial change perceived themselves as craftsmen and artisans, were able to drive a wedge between their work and that of women, which in the process became more clearly defined as unskilled.[56] The instances in which men manipulated skill illustrate the interaction of employer and male interest and thus the intersection of gender and class struggle. In such cases, women workers can be seen to have been used in the battle between men and their employers as the former attempted to reduce the immediate challenges posed by the implementation of deskilling technology.

Little resistance met men's attempts to define themselves as more skilled than women. For some time before industrialisation skill had been associated with the construction of masculinity. Skill was synonymous with male qualities. Men's jobs were perceived as skilled, while women were confined to tasks that were defined as unskilled.[57] During the eighteenth century, certain attributes, such as strength and the ability to supervise, became more valued and were uniquely associated with men.[58] Manual dexterity, flexibility and sound powers of concentration, however, all of which were considered vital to new ways of manufacturing production, were associated with women and were defined as natural attributes rather than skills.[59] Before industrialisation, therefore, gender constituted a central determinant of skill. During the process of industrial change the importance of skill as a means of shaping gender definitions became even more pronounced.

From the late eighteenth century a clearer gendering of skill was part of the response by male labour to the process of actual or threatened deskilling. The example of cotton spinning explored above showed how male skilled workers struggled to appropriate components of the work process in the context of technical change in order to maintain their status. Supervisory and organisational functions became central features of the repackaging of male skill during the period of industrialisation. Once accepted, such redefinitions of skill further disadvantaged women because of their alleged incapacity to fulfil those functions. Women's ability to perform a task was understood to be naturally occurring, even when the task was so complex that the natural element was difficult to detect. Women's perceived inability to perform a task was socially constructed and politically motivated.[60] During industrialisation, women were excluded from work that required real skill, because they were denied the appropriate training, as well as from work in which skill was constructed by those whose gender and organisational strength allowed them protect their monopoly. Such was the completeness of the process whereby skill became gendered during industrialisation, that it was unusual for male and female labour to be interchangeable in the workplace.[61] Female abilities were established as different from but complementary to male skills.

During the period of industrialisation, women became barred from work that was recognised as skilled. They nevertheless performed tasks in which the 'real' skill at least matched that of men. Where this was the case, in the nineteenth-century hosiery industry, for example, it was acknowledged neither by employers nor even by the women themselves.[62] In the nineteenth-century woollen industry, there was no overlap between male and female work. The majority of women were involved in the intermediate stages of production, while men were concentrated in the initial and finishing processes. All the jobs performed by male workers in the wool textile industry were described as skilled at some time or other, especially by the men themselves, while few of the women's jobs were perceived as such.[63] The division of labour in the worsted trade, like many others during the period of industrialisation, can be seen as a 'marriage of convenience between the need for manufacturers to cut labor [*sic*] costs to a minimum and the desire of skilled male workers to define and maintain a privileged position'.[64] In the worsted mills, adult men increasingly worked in skilled and supervisory jobs in spinning and weaving and enjoyed higher wages and greater job security. The reorganisation of the worsted industry forced a redefinition of the nature and meaning of skill. Within the mill the skill of labour was based less on machine working than on machine maintenance. In Karl Ittman's opinion, 'the reconstitution of skill was not a neutral process, for it remained the property of adult males and served to set them apart from the rest of the workforce in and outside the mills'.[65] Skilled men justified their positions by reinforcing distinct roles for women. Machine tenders in the worsted industry, for example, 'cited the inability of women to perform mechanical tasks as the reason for the male monopoly among mill mechanics . . . skilled workers also used the rhetoric of domesticity to justify the low status of women in the trade'.[66]

Deirdre Busfield's survey of work in the West Yorkshire textile industry provides further evidence that the term 'skill' has not been used simply as an objective description of the requirement of a job, but rather 'as a means of distinguishing between men's and women's work'. In this case and probably in many others, there was little real difference in the skill content of much of the work done by men and women. Many jobs in the Yorkshire textile industries probably required only a knack that could be learned in a relatively short time.[67]

The gendering of skill, the gendering of technology and the gendering of work were, as the cases above indicate, active and dynamic processes. They were the result of struggles between men and women and employers in a range of industries and occupations. The nature of such struggles varied: sometimes they were overt and violent; sometimes they were barely perceptible. The outcomes of these contests also varied according to the organisational strength of male workers, the extent of competition among employers and prevailing economic forces. The majority of labour disputes in the nineteenth century resulted from competition between men and women for jobs.[68] Even where the two sexes had apparently reached accommodation, gender struggle can be identified. In the case of the cotton weavers of Lancashire, for example, men and women lived and worked as fellow operatives, in the same factories on the same machinery, earning the same piece rates. Yet men could and did differentiate their work from that of women. For example, men monopolised the heavy work on the broad loom, they worked more looms and they alone were able to make adjustments to their machines. Women were not allowed overtime or mealtime working, they were discouraged from seeking overlookers' posts, and were themselves subject to greater supervision. Women were more likely than men to lose their jobs during depression in the trade. Such differences, constructed by trade union leaders, were more substantial than at first appeared.[69]

Within the hosiery industry, there is evidence that the reorganisation of production during industrialisation generated gender antagonisms. The research of Sonya Rose suggests that the traditions surrounding the gendering of work influence the way tasks are assigned to women and men during periods of change in an industry. When hosiery production was organised on the putting-out system, men and women had co-operated on hand-powered

machines. The introduction of factory stocking production, however, resulted in conflict between male and female knitters. As individual wages replaced family payment, struggles over the price of
men's and women's labour generated a gender ideology that portrayed women as different kinds of workers from men. Women were
then allocated low-paid jobs consistent with their gendered position
as supplementary wage earners. Female workers were supervised by
men who alone received training in repair and adjustment of
machines. As men and women shifted from co-participants in
domestic industry to competitors in the factory, so the gendering of
work and skill clarified their distinct roles as workers.[70] In hosiery, as
in other industries, the gendering of work and specifically the gendering of technology was subject to constant renegotiation. During
the early 1860s, and in subsequent periods of economic depression,
factory employers attempted to reduce costs by replacing male
power frame knitters with women. Male trade unionists strongly
resisted this strategy. After prolonged discussion with employers, it
was agreed that women would work only six-headed machines while
the eight-headed ones were restricted to male use. The distinctions
between male and female labour were confirmed by the gendering
of training. Only men were trained to be mechanics, which rendered women unable to operate complicated machinery because
they lacked the technical skills to maintain its operation.[71]

The outcome of contests over the gendering of work occasionally
appeared to favour women. This is well illustrated in the case of the
carpet industry in Kidderminster where a succession of industrial
disputes in the last quarter of the nineteenth century unusually led
to an incremental erosion of the status of male workers. The bargaining position of the male carpet weavers was weakened by
depression and unemployment in the trade and by competition from
other carpet-making districts. Before the 1870s, the weaving of
carpets was a male preserve. In 1874, in order to enhance competitiveness, manufacturers attempted to employ women in the weaving
of tapestries for the working-class market. Immediate and robust
opposition to this by the union on the grounds of lack of alternative
employment for men, successfully prevented the introduction of
female labour.[72] When the issue inevitably resurfaced several years
later it was submitted to arbitration which allowed the male
monopoly to continue but on lower (female) wages. In the early
1880s, to counter further depression in the trade, manufacturers

altered a number of their tapestry looms and hired women for the production of a velvet curtain material. The outcome of the ensuing battle between the union and employers was that men would temporarily be employed on the altered machines, but that when new machines were brought into use men and women would be employed in equal numbers for equal pay. In the depression of the early 1890s, men unsuccessfully attacked the employment of women in the weaving of Axminster carpets. Apparently the Axminster looms were 'so fragile that the men would knock them to pieces'. Systematically, therefore, employers introduced cheaper female labour using 'women's' machines. Equally systematically men resisted this encroachment but ultimately failed to retain the male monopoly of carpet weaving. Depression in the trade and high unemployment clearly influenced both the strategy of employers and the outcome of negotiations with the union.[73]

The gendering of work persisted through the nineteenth century as new technologies and organisational forms of production were introduced in a range of industries.[74] The example of the printing trade reveals the importance of male organisation for the maintenance of gender distinctions in the workplace in the face of technical change and employer preference for cheap female workers. As a traditional male craft, the printing trade had excluded women from most sections for many decades.[75] Successive attempts were made by employers during the nineteenth century to reduce the level of skill required for printing work and to weaken the craftsmen's grip on the work process. Until the 1870s, these efforts were successfully countered by the largest group of printers, the compositors, who restricted entry to the trade society and to the compulsory seven-year apprenticeship. All unskilled workers were excluded by this strategy, yet the arguments used by skilled men against women differed from those used against unskilled male rivals.[76] New opportunities for employers to reassert control of the work process and to reduce labour costs occurred with late nineteenth-century technical developments. The replacement of the flat press by the rotary press in the 1870s and 1880s, however, was not accompanied by the desired introduction of unskilled female labour. Skilled men created a new set of rules in order to sustain their monopoly and the 'very idea of women seriously undertaking to achieve the competence of craftsmen was easily ridiculed'.[77] The skilled men side-stepped the more serious challenge posed by the linotype machine by invoking the requirement for knowledge and experience, and effectively duping the poorly organised employers. The arguments presented by the men were based on women's physical, biological and emotional unsuitability for the work, yet contemporary evidence reveals that the challenge to men's prestige and self-respect lay at the root of their hostility. The definition of masculinity was based on a special relationship to work. Men's status was associated with performing work that only men could do. The male printers 'felt degraded . . . at having to descend to such vile practices as competing with women for work'.[78]

Technical innovation did not always result in a struggle over ownership. Men were not always outright winners when such contests did occur, yet typically they gained an advantage over women. Exclusionary or segregationary strategies based on control of machinery resulted in clear and enduring divisions between men and women in terms of how and where each worked and the level at which each was remunerated for their efforts. Such divisions benefited men at the expense of women as they continue to do. Yet a divided workforce also benefited employers at the expense of workers. Research has not yet produced a satisfactory explanation for men's pursuit of narrow, individually motivated goals rather than a strategy through which a united working class might have successfully resisted the exploitation of capital. Because men could do little to prevent employers using female labour in the new industries, their efforts were directed towards segregating women and maintaining sexual divisions within the factory. The result, a weak position for women workers, did not create a strong position for male workers. In Cynthia Cockburn's view, 'it is the most damning indictment of skilled working class men and their unions that they excluded women from membership and prevented them from gaining competencies that could have secured them a decent living'.[79]

It is clear, therefore, that male workers with the occasional assistance of employers influenced the shape of gender relations at work. The making of gender during the period of industrialisation was also influenced by the actions of the state. Legislation to regulate or protect labour had a pronounced impact on gender relations at work and at home. The Factory Acts of the 1830s and 1840s, which sought to reduce the number of hours worked by women and children in textile factories, and the Mines and Collieries Act of 1842, designed to exclude women and children from underground work in the pits, can be seen to represent increasing contemporary concern about what married women's labour meant for the working-class family and especially its children. The forces behind such protective legislation were complex. Pressure came from reformers appalled by the conditions under which women and children were forced to work, less because of concerns about exploitation than anxiety about women's morals and the future of the family.[80]

Debates surrounding mid nineteenth-century protective legislation helped to consolidate the growing consensus about gendered roles and responsibilities in the workplace and in the home. State legislation projected ideas about gender that were important to industrial development and played a part in the making of gender. Women were constructed as special kinds of workers. While men were viewed as free economic agents, who, in the prevailing spirit of *laissez-faire*, were immune from most state legislation, women were seen as dependent subjects, defined by their fitness for domesticity by 'maternal roles and maternal bodies'.[81] The legislation simultaneously placed responsibility for the welfare of babies and children on individual women and discouraged alternative policies for the provision of child care facilities. It therefore impeded women's equal and effective participation in the workplace. The Factory Acts and the Mines Acts contributed to women's lack of competitiveness but at the same time failed to protect them from their low-paid positions in the labour market. Indeed, for the poorest, the so-called 'protective' legislation probably further restricted their earning capacity.[82] The legislation to control women's employment did not exclude women completely from the public sphere of work, but rather influenced the types of paid work to which women had access and the conditions under which it was performed.[83]

The actions of the state affected men and women differently. They contributed to a situation in which male labour became more attractive to employers in the developing areas of the economy.[84] By emphasising the importance of women as providers of domestic services,[85] the actions of the state contributed to the general devaluation in the status of women's work, and further privileged men's work through the growing emphasis on occupational identity in male self-definitions.[86] The safety provisions of the 1844 Act confined machine-maintenance work to adult men and thus made a contribution to the masculine construction of work surrounding the repair and adjustment of machines.[87] Also important was the juridical distinction the Act made between the protected categories (women and children) and men, which helped to empower men as they contested and renegotiated the gender division of labour.[88] Significantly, if ironically, women were limited by protective legislation, while men 'were able to negotiate for themselves conditions far superior to the law'.[89] The legislative outcome of struggles to regulate factory hours and conditions was part of the process by which gender was constructed.[90]

The Mines and Collieries Act of 1842, the first piece of gender-specific legislation, was designed to counter the attack on physical welfare posed by mine work, but it also represented a contemporary preoccupation with moral issues. Women who worked in cramped and dirty conditions, often in close proximity to unrelated men, would be severely morally challenged. It was feared that women miners would 'lose every quality that is graceful in women, and become a set of coarse, licentious wretches, scorning all kinds of restraint and yielding themselves up, with shameless audacity to the most detestable sensuality'.[91] It was also believed that bodily deformations caused by mine work would impair women's reproductive capacities and that coal-mining women lacked appropriate maternal and other domestic skills. Mine work was likely to 'destroy that purity and delicacy of character which ought ever to invest her with a hallowed atmosphere; and to lay the foundation for a life of sensual indulgence, domestic thriftlessness, dirt, dissipation and quarrels'.[92] Joseph Kennedy, whose inspection of mines in Lancashire was recorded in the Royal Commission, was critical of mining conditions but was particularly concerned about the home situation of mineworkers. Not only were miners and their children 'exceedingly dirty' but their houses were recognisable from 'the accumulations of filth and excrement at their doors'.[93]

Despite the intention of the legislation to 'protect' women and especially to secure the well-being of the working-class family, very few feminist historians have explored the effectiveness of the Acts within these terms. Jane Humphries' analysis of the 1842 Mines Act provides an exception. Humphries does not dispute the way in which protective legislation cemented gender differences at work and generally undermined the position of women in the workplace. She believes, however, that the 1842 Act 'limited the exploitation' of a class of workers on the basis of gender, and that what matters is the way in which female and male members complemented each other in the enhancement and protection of the working class.[94] If the Act enhanced the quality of life of coal-mining families, and this is by no means certain, it did so at the expense of women's position as workers. The gendering of the working class was ultimately to women's great disadvantage.[95]

Tensions in gender relations were exacerbated as employers sought to substitute cheaper female and child labour for skilled men during the nineteenth century. The making of gender in the period of industrialisation was neither automatic nor straightforward. It was subject to a variety of contests and compromises as new techniques and organisations of production were introduced. In the early stages of industrialisation, employers hired as much female and child labour as possible. Such labour was cheap, flexible, compliant and willing to work long hours for little reward.[96] Although women were generally employed on the most unfavourable of terms, male workers envied and felt threatened by their indispensability. Industrialisation introduced individual wage earning and more formalised labour markets and in this context men felt the competition of female workers particularly keenly. Rather than seeking to minimise gender differences and establish worker solidarity, male workers attempted to distinguish themselves from women workers as much and as often as possible. With the support of male-dominated trade unions, and the, possibly, unintentional support of the state, men felt empowered as workers while women were marginalised. The making of gender, therefore, entailed emphasising gender differences. While working-class men actively encouraged such distinctions in the workplace and the labour market, middle-class men and women encouraged equivalent distinctions in the home. As women's role as worker was undermined, so their domestic position became sanctified. The actions of working-class men played straight into the hands of the employers.

This chapter has concentrated on the formal economy because that is where the processes involved in the making of gender were most perceptible. Nevertheless, the outcomes of such processes clearly impinged on those women, and men, who worked in less formal environments. The varied ways in which women, and to a lesser extent men, worked during the period of industrialisation will be explored in the following chapter.

5 Women, Work and the New Industrial Economy

The contribution of female labour to the evolving industrial economy is impossible to measure with confidence, but available evidence indicates that women – especially those who were young and single – played a vital role in early factory manufacture. It is also clear that the work of married women in particular offered a viable, labour-intensive alternative to mechanised and centralised production. In the context of industrialisation, women's outwork, and their casual and sweated labour provided a much-needed flexibility for the sometimes inefficient factory forms of production. Although often described as marginal and peripheral, this type of work was essential to the operation of the new industrial system. The deployment of cheap female labour may have generated short-term gains for the English economy, but reliance on this type of worker probably discouraged investment in improved methods of manufacture and therefore hindered long-term progress. More importantly, by confining most women to routine and unskilled work, much potential was squandered. The English economy was ultimately damaged by its failure to make effective use of its resources.

Evidence suggests that women's participation in productive activity – while subject to regional and structural heterogeneity – probably reached its numerical peak in the early stages of the Industrial Revolution, as economic growth generated employment opportunities in both old and new sectors of activity.[1] During the early decades of the nineteenth century, many women found work in the factories and large workshops of the textile trades of northern England, in metal manufacture in the Midlands, and in the potteries.[2] Larger numbers of women were also apparently occupied in agriculture and domestic service.[3] From the mid nineteenth century, however, as the range of employment opportunities for women contracted relatively to those for men, female participation rates fell. The decline in the proportion of married women who worked was particularly marked. By the first decade of the twentieth century less than 10 per cent of married women – but almost 70 per cent of single women – were in recorded employment.[4]

The work of many women did not enter official statistics during the period of industrial development. It is well known that the centralised collection of occupational data through the decennial censuses of the nineteenth century both understated the extent of women's employment and misrepresented its sectoral distribution.[5] Deficiencies existed in the historical recording of men's employment also, but these can be more readily rectified.[6] The measurement of women's work in the context of nineteenth-century industrialisation is fraught with difficulties, most of which stem from contemporary economic definitions. Deborah Valenze's analysis of the writings of early nineteenth-century political economists shows that work was identified as the source of expanding national wealth.[7] In this context, work was understood as an activity which had a quantifiable market value. Work that had only use value was both unremunerated and dismissed as unproductive.[8] For Adam Smith, wealth consisted of tangible, material goods, not the provision of services. Labour, in Smith's view, was 'productive' only if it added value to a material object or created a storable commodity.[9] The makers of the census were clearly guided by the definitions provided by contemporary economists, so the production of use values, common among married women, was deemed not to constitute gainful employment and was therefore excluded from the census.[10] 'The equation of masculine identity with an occupation', and its corollary that the feminine identity was defined by 'non-occupation', was fundamental to the making of the census in the nineteenth century.[11] Although investigation of occupations became more thorough towards the end of the century, market activity remained the basis of census categories. Women's contributions to the family and to the national economy continued to be underenumerated.[12]

The census makers of 1831 equivocated over whether females of the family should be returned as of 'no occupation or of the occupation of the adult males'. The 1841 enumerators were instructed that the 'profession of wives or of sons or daughters living with and assisting their parents . . . need not be inserted'. Because of the required blank against the names of many married women, they featured little in the occupational censuses, even when the product of their work in the home entered the market. In 1851 householders were instructed to record the occupations of women employed from home or at home, in any but domestic duties. The domestic work of women was still defined as a residual category and not to be entered.[13] The two subsequent censuses recognised the activities of women who, while unpaid, nevertheless contributed to the operation of family farms and businesses. There were, however, inconsistencies in the way in which this information was recorded. The position was clarified in 1881 when all women assisting in family enterprises without pay were categorised as 'unoccupied'.

The recording of women's employment was therefore incomplete throughout the nineteenth century. The extent of the underenumeration varied, however, between localities and decades, because instructions provided for enumerators and their interpretation of them lacked consistency. Even had an enumerator been inclined to record female occupations, it is unlikely that he[14] would have captured the diversity and dynamism of many women's livelihoods. During industrialisation as before, women were more likely than men to be multioccupied. In urban areas as in the countryside, women were rarely employed in the same occupation throughout the year, and some even migrated on a seasonal basis.[15] Part-time and casual work, as well as seasonal harvest employment, were explicitly excluded from the census. In any case it appears that the production of an accurate record of women's occupations was not a priority for the majority of enumerators. Edward Higgs believes that the occupational tables of the census were constructed by men who adopted very clear positions on gender roles. Typically women were defined as dependants whatever their productive functions, while men were carefully classified according to the nature of their labour.[16] There was no guarantee that even women working in the formal economy for wages would be included in the census. Evidence has been uncovered to suggest that some married female factory workers appeared in the census as 'wife',[17] which casts some doubt on the assumption that factory work was performed almost entirely by young single women and girls and that married women rarely worked in the public sphere. Higgs, however, whose extensive knowledge of the census is founded on many years' research, believes that in general the recording of female factory workers was reliable.[18]

By specifying the deficiencies of the census with regard to women's work it is possible partially to remedy them.[19] Apart from the general problem of under-recording – which the excessive size of the unoccupied category suggests was real – the census also greatly simplified what is now known to have been a very complex pattern of women's employment. In 1851, for example, 80 per cent of women recorded as economically active were allocated to the textiles, clothing and domestic service categories. Domestic servants alone appear to account for 40 per cent of all employed women. Not only are these proportions misleading, but the growth of the unoccupied category from 5 million in 1851 to over 11 million in 1911 both exaggerates women's 'idleness' and fails to capture the 'actuality and fluctuations' of women's work.[20]

The high level of female unemployment implied by such recording has rarely been explored by historians. Ellen Jordan has recently attempted to fill this surprising gap. Her study shows that 66 per cent of females but only 17 per cent of males over ten were returned as unoccupied in 1881. By 1901 the respective figures were 68 and 16 per cent. The explanation for this gender differential is assumed to have been a combination of poor recording and high female voluntary unemployment.[21] Jordan suggests that because of regional variations in the figures, structural unemployment was an additional relevant factor. The highest levels of female unemployment were found in counties that were predominantly agricultural or where mining and farming occupations were combined. The lowest levels of unoccupied females were in counties where textile production or putting-out in women's activities predominated.[22] It is also possible that the recording of women's participation was more complete in such districts. The large unoccupied figure needs to be treated with caution and the apparently high level of women's inactivity requires further investigation.

Recent revision of the data has suggested two particular and important shortcomings in the conventional portrayal of women's occupations in the new industrial economy. Edward Higgs believes that the nineteenth-century censuses grossly inflated the number and proportion of domestic servants and understated the number of female agricultural labourers. These two alleged deficiencies are partially related. A substantial number of women who were described as domestic servants in the census appear to have been either farm servants or general servants in rural areas. Such women were expected to milk cows and make butter and cheese. The products of their labour, therefore, entered the market economy. These so-called 'domestic servants' would more accurately be categorised as agricultural labourers. In compliance with census regulations, however, only men were to be counted as farm servants in the agricultural sector, while the female equivalents were to be described either as farm servants (indoor) or under the appropriate suborder for domestic servants according to the duties performed.[23]

The heterogeneity of domestic service and its location at the interface of the formal and the informal economy can also account for its exaggerated presence in the nineteenth-century census.[24] Several activities were categorised as domestic service not because this was necessarily an accurate description of them but rather because of the absence of a suitable alternative category. Some women who were allocated to the category of domestic servant may have been better placed elsewhere, or at least described more precisely. Although the extent of domestic service has almost certainly been exaggerated, there is little doubt that as it became feminised through the eighteenth and nineteenth centuries, the number of servants, or those classified as such, grew. The nature of service varied often according to the location of the work. The large homes of the upper and middle classes administered a hierarchy of servants which contained both men and women. It was common for relatively modest households to keep a general help – often a family member – from the early years of the nineteenth century. Many of the women described in the census manuscripts as general servants, housekeepers and nurses were related to those for whom they worked. They were typically either widows, who probably worked as part of the family economy or earned their keep by performing childminding functions, or more distant relations, often the children of overburdened families, who may have been treated as paid domestics. These findings suggest that domestic service should be seen less as an occupation and rather as a 'set of social relations from close kinship to cash nexus'.[25]

The suggestion that domestic service performed a variety of social and economic functions is not new. Many writers have attested to the attraction of urban service for rural migrants and therefore its significance as a stimulus to mobility.[26] The apprenticeship of young girls to domestic service, and the employment of pauper women as servants were forms of poor relief which became increasingly popular after the 1834 Poor Law Amendment Act. Domestic service has also been perceived by some historians as an instrument of social control, whereby the ideals of domesticity were both explicitly feminised and became acquired by working-class households.

Higgs is probably correct to conclude that nineteenth-century censuses have exaggerated the extent of domestic service although his suggested reduction of 48 per cent may itself be excessive.[27] The precise measurement of the sector is, however, less important than an understanding of the relevance of domestic service for women's social and economic position. The expansion and feminisation of domestic service served to reinforce the role of female labour in the provision of support functions and as flexible, adaptable and non-specialised workers within the new industrial economy.

Women's general abilities also featured in their contribution to the agricultural sector, which has probably been inadequately recognised. The census under-recording of both seasonal and specifically female agricultural tasks has distorted the depiction of women's participation in farm work. This problem was exacerbated by the timing of enumeration. From 1811 to 1831, the census was taken at the end of May and in 1841 in early June. Between 1851 and 1901 the census was taken consistently in late March or early April.[28] Four other sources of deficient enumeration of agricultural occupations can be identified, namely, the omission of seasonal labour,[29] the exclusion of workers without an occupational title, the removal of female relatives of farmers from the occupied population, and the placing of farm workers in categories other than agriculture. Higgs has attempted to correct for these inadequacies by including an allowance for the wives and other female relatives of male farmers and agricultural workers, who are assumed to have worked on the land for two months at harvest time. His recalculation raises the average proportion of women engaged in agriculture between 1841 and 1891 from 3.5 to 23.1 per cent.[30]

Edward Higgs is not alone in identifying the underestimation of female agricultural workers in census reports, which has perpetuated the conventional image of the agricultural labourer as male.[31] Both Ivy Pinchbeck, and more recently, Karen Sayer have drawn on the evidence of nineteenth-century Parliamentary Reports to rectify women's invisibility in historical representations of farming.[32] Throughout the nineteenth century, farmers' wives and relatives worked on small farms, female farm servants were hired by the year, and women day labourers performed tasks that varied over time and place. Pinchbeck's investigation unearthed evidence of a wide range of female farm work, which tended to be of the irregular and low-paid variety that farmers required but only women were willing to perform. Women's facility with root crops and drill husbandry was recognised by contemporaries. 'It was soon found that women could be employed to hoe turnips and other root crops at a much cheaper rate than was being paid to men for this work . . . and better than by men.'[33] Women also did the setting of crops, weeding, stone gathering, meadow dressing and market gardening. 'Their [the fruit women's] industry is unequalled in Britain or perhaps the world' it was claimed. Because of the seasonality of demand for labour, 'the farmer needed five times as many hands in summer as in winter', so the employment of women and children was crucial. 'Had they not been available, it is probable that much of the work demanded by the new cultures would have remained undone, or that the expense of employing extra men would have deterred many from adopting new methods.'[34]

Many nineteenth-century regional farming specialisms, especially those that were labour-intensive, depended on the contribution of women and children. Across the country, women were sought both for their fine motor skills and for their physical strength and stamina. In Essex, where a change in the crop mix from hops to grain led to the substitution of male for female labour, the local cultivation of saffron required unusual levels of diligence and care provided only by women. Female and child labour was also employed to raise the treble crop of teasel, caraway and coriander.[35] In pastoral farming, dairymaids and farmers' wives made butter and cheese.[36] Much female farm work could be extremely arduous.[37] In Northumberland, for example, where there were few alternative jobs for women but plenty for men, women engaged in heavy farm work until the end of the nineteenth century.[38] It was not unusual for women to care for stock, and to engage in ploughing, hedging and ditching.[39] Some women only performed functions associated with the harvest such as binding and gleaning. Although women also reaped alongside men in the early part of the nineteenth century, the majority of women employed in agriculture pieced together a steady low income throughout the year by engaging in a succession of seasonal jobs including stone picking, muck spreading, weeding, hoeing, pulling up and cutting turnips and mangolds. In some regions, market gardens and fruit picking provided summer employment for women and children.[40] Women were rarely offered regular long-term employment.[41] The marginal living that agriculture offered to many women is indicated by local Poor Law listings, where single and widowed women's wages from farming especially in the grain-growing areas were very small.[42] Women persisted in securing a livelihood – however menial – from agriculture even after the Poor Law Amendment Act of 1834. In order to avoid the work-house, many women joined gangs of field workers who travelled the countryside in search of casual work. The gang system became more prevalent after 1834, especially in the eastern counties, in order to meet irregular demand for labour on large farms.[43] Gangs were often associated with turnip singling, a traditional female occupation, generally found further north than Essex.[44]

Although the diversity of regional experience was very noticeable in agriculture, some general trends are discernible. The available evidence suggests that agriculture was a more important occupation for women than was previously believed or was indicated in the census.[45] Women participated in a variety of paid and unpaid agricultural work during the nineteenth century, although the numbers fluctuated according to season, area and period under consideration.[46] Although women's farm work varied by county and changed differentially during the nineteenth century, most of it was arduous and skilled, but was not always recognised as such.[47] There was little significant shift in the sexual division of labour through the eighteenth or nineteenth centuries. Even in the late nineteenth century women and children still comprised a large reserve pool of casual labour which was crucial to the capitalist farming system.[48] The women farm servants, farmers' wives and dairywomen, however, had largely 'passed from view'.[49]

The invisibility of female farm labour by the late nineteenth century was partly the result of middle-class reluctance to acknowledge the presence of women in an occupation that appeared to challenge both feminine ideals and working-class morals. A succession of Parliamentary Reports attempted to place women on the periphery of agricultural activity. The 1843 Report underplayed women's participation in farming, except in field work which was singled out for critical appraisal by both the commissioners and the female subjects.[50] Other contemporary work lamented the very existence of female farm labour. In a study of farming in the far north of England, the Canon of Durham complained that 'the greatest evil in our rural districts is the degradation of the female sex, by their employment in labours adapted for men . . . their skin is wrinkled, their faces burnt, their features masculine'.[51] In the 1860s women's field work was cited as a primary cause of infant death and was also condemned for offending middle-class sensibilities. Women of the fields were perceived as bold, boisterous and unchaste, but above all they were 'painfully visible'.[52] They were also said to know nothing of domestic skills and were defeminised in appearance and behaviour.[53] Thereafter women were viewed as objects of contagion rather than as victims and it became the desire of the state to remove women from the fields. Because this was impossible to achieve in reality, it was achieved through imagination. In a government investigation of 1892, women agricultural workers went 'uncounted and unwatched'.[54]

The uncomfortable juxtaposition of the feminine ideal and the masculine image of the female field worker, found a parallel in the nineteenth-century coal mines. Women who worked in the pits, like those who worked in the fields, adopted 'masculine' patterns of behaviour and appearance. According to the census of 1841, approximately 7000 women and girls were employed in mine and quarry work, of which 2350 were believed to be in coal mining. Angela John believes this to be an underestimate, and although more accurate figures were produced in 1842 by the Children's Employment Commission, these too are deficient, because of the failure of a number of coal owners to complete their questionnaires. A reasonable estimate is believed to be between 5000 and 6000.[55] Such relatively small numbers in regional and local concentrations encouraged contemporaries to legislate for exclusion of women, which had not been deemed possible in the case of agriculture.

Sufficient evidence exists to confirm that women had worked in coal mines for centuries. Wives and daughters had played a vital role in helping husbands and brothers to extract coal from easily accessible holes. Until the early nineteenth century, mine working was typically organised in family teams, in which the male hewers hired their own help.[56] During the eighteenth century, women were employed as drawers, which involved pulling baskets or tubs of coal along low passages to the bottom of the shaft for raising to the surface.[57] Although women engaged mainly in haulage work until the mid nineteenth century, in Scotland they were also bearers, and in Pembrokeshire women worked windlasses above and below ground.[58] Women continued to work in mining through the eighteenth century even as the pits became deeper and larger and as accidents became more common.[59] It was no coincidence that women were most commonly found in the mines with the poorest conditions and the worst accident rates.

Women worked in coal mines where little alternative employment for female labour existed locally. Few women worked in mining if they had the choice. Evidence collected in the 1840s revealed women's antipathy to mine work, which they nevertheless regarded as preferable to unemployment and starvation.[60] The captive position of most female mine workers was exploited by colliery owners. Cheap female labour was used a means of cost containment. Women and girls worked very long hours. Hurriers (conveyers) and drawers worked two hours per day longer than colliers; 14-hour days were not unusual in winter and night work was common.[61] Girls were found to be more amenable and less ambitious than boys. Girls made 'far better drawers than the lads, they are more steady'.[62] The existence of women made some mines profitable that otherwise would not have been, but also reduced the likelihood that conditions would be improved. In the 1841 debate on the issue of female miners, some colliery owners argued that they could ill afford to pay the wages of male miners, and that if women were to be excluded from the mines they would be forced to make costly improvements to the working environment.[63]

Although women accounted for less than 5 per cent of the total mine-working population in the early nineteenth century, they were geographically concentrated so that in some coalfields women formed an important component of the workforce.[64] In Pembrokeshire, for example, where there was no other local work for women, they comprised around 30 per cent of mine workers, and in Midlothian and East Lothian, the proportion was nearer 25 per cent. Women were also important in the other Scottish minefields, and to a lesser extent in Lancashire and Yorkshire.[65] In other areas, female miners had become less common by the early nineteenth century. The Northumberland and Durham coalfield ceased employing women around 1780. In Cumberland women's mine work became less extensive from the early nineteenth century. Women were not employed below ground in the coalfields of Gloucestershire, Staffordshire, north Somerset, Warwickshire or Leicestershire during the nineteenth century.[66]

It seems that legislation to ban the underground working of female coal miners was introduced at a time when the demand for female labour at the face was in any case declining and conditions in the mines improving.[67] The impetus for legislation was provided by the findings of the first report of the Children's Employment Commission of 1841 whose brief to investigate child labour was extended upon the discovery of women miners. The extent of subterranean horror was revealed in 1842 to an apparently shocked public.[68] Although prior ignorance appears unconvincing given the long history of traditionally accepted family group mining practices, the relative isolation and autonomous nature of mining communities may provide a partial explanation for the level of surprise. Legislation to protect women and children from the scandal of underground working was enacted with impressive speed, despite the vigorous debate that surrounded its formulation.[69]

Evasion of the 1842 Mines Act, which prohibited the employment of women and children underground, was both inevitable and relatively straightforward. Little, if any, consideration had been given to identifying alternative means of livelihood for the affected women, many of whom supported dependants.[70] The prospect of securing other work was poor. In Scotland limited employment was available for women in domestic service, seasonal field work and small textile mills. In principle, the textile industries in west Yorkshire and west Lancashire provided greater opportunities, but these were constrained in the depressed economic conditions of the 1840s.[71] While the intention of the reformers was that women should be removed from the mines to engage in domestic pursuits, in practice hundreds of women continued to work underground and many of the remainder found employment sorting coal at the surface as 'pit brow lasses'.[72] As surface workers, women encountered greater hostility from men – some of whom had been discharged to make way for the women – than they had done as underground workers. By the 1880s, opposition to pit brow women developed into a sustained challenge to women's right to work. The expression of moral and physical concerns by non-miners, redolent of the 1840s, was augmented by economic complaints of miners, who sought to remedy their own positions by the exclusion of their cheap female co-workers.[73] On this occasion women effectively resisted such action, and the Mines Act of 1888[74] permitted all females over 13 to remain at the surface. Thereafter, however, demand for such work began to decline and by the early twentieth century about 90 per cent of women employed were engaged on sorting work.[75]

It is clear that much female work in the new industrial economy failed to be officially documented. It is also apparent that a great deal of it met with profound disapproval. Women's employment that aroused male hostility and/or public concern was the most likely to be recorded if not always accurately. Factory employment was particularly relevant in this context. In the early nineteenth century, the offence caused by women and child factory workers to middle-class sensibilities matched that generated later by female farm workers and miners. In addition they engendered the antipathy of male workers.[76] Factory production was restricted to a small number of manufacturing sectors during the early industrial period. It was first introduced in textiles, especially cotton and worsted spinning.[77]

It is important to recognise the diversity of women's experience within the cotton industry. Labour-intensive activities, using cheap women and children, formed an integral part of the manufacturing of many factories. The bulk of factory spinning, following the introduction of the large mule in the 1790s, was conducted by men with the assistance of women and children, whose work as piecers and menders was often paid for out of the male spinners' wages. Many women worked in the early cotton-spinning factories, therefore, but not generally as spinners. Only for a very brief period in the late 1820s and early 1830s were small numbers of women employed in spinning, for which they were paid 50 per cent of the male piece rate. Divested of their traditional skill, some women became peripheral, support workers within the factory, for example as pickers, tenters and carders.[78] Others became home-based handloom weavers for whom there was huge, short-term demand. Having gained experience in cotton weaving, women then found employment in weaving factories following the successful application of the power loom in the 1830s. By this time the cotton industry was concentrated in Lancashire, and power loom weaving took place only in the south-east of the county.[79] Although this accounted for just a small pocket of factory employment, the shift in women's position from ancillary to core worker that power loom weaving introduced, was both unusual and significant. The security of women's position in the cotton industry was ensured as female labour became central to one of the two primary operations of the trade. By the 1840s women accounted for just under 40 per cent of all cotton weavers and slightly more than 30 per cent of workers in the industry as a whole.[80]

The distribution of factory work in worsted production was similar to that of cotton. Although women were generally consigned to less skilled operations, in worsted as in cotton, the division of labour and its gendering were subtly different, and provided women with a wider range of opportunities. Women were generally assigned labour-intensive and repetitive tasks, while men dominated supervisory and maintenance jobs. Where throstle frames were used, women were engaged in the spinning process, though men and boys usually worked the mules. Evidence suggests that women dominated the weaving sector. According to one contemporary observer, women comprised two-thirds of the power weaving workforce and young men the other third.[81] In the woollen industry, adoption of the factory system, where male labour dominated, proceeded at a slower pace. Organisation of production in the silk industry was diverse. Within factory units, of which Courtauld's Essex mill is an example, women dominated the productive labour force. In the 1830s, more than 90 per cent of the workers in the mill were women weavers. The men performed mechanical or overseeing functions.[82]

In addition to the women who worked in textile mills, smaller numbers were employed in tobacco and food processing factories. Outside of these areas, however, very few women worked in factories at all. Eric Richards suggests that at the peak of such employment in the 1830s, the total number of women employed in factories was 65 000. This amounted to a little over 10 per cent of women employees in manufacturing at the time, and under 2 per cent of the total female labour force.[83] While such figures are very approximate, they suggest that the importance of factory employment has probably been unduly emphasised in historical representations of women's work. Such exaggeration is partly the result of extensive contemporary interest in the nature of factory work. Although the protection of children was the explicit motive of the early Factory Acts, there is no doubt that the moral welfare of young women, including the sexual behaviour of the mill girl, formed the subject of intense investigation. The wide publicity allocated to such individuals captured the imagination of contemporary writers of fact and fiction. Fears that factory employment might upset the process of balanced physical development were expressed in notions of premature puberty among mill girls. According to contemporary medical opinion, the overheated atmosphere of the factory, which accelerated puberty, also caused sexual precocity.[84] Stories of factory employers seducing young mill girls in the rooms set aside at the mill 'adorned with the appliances of luxury and the conveniences of vice' realised the sexual fantasies of middle-class men about working-class girls and women.[85]

Factory work was not typical female employment in the nineteenth century, yet it had implications for the organisation of the lives of many working-class families. By moving the work of one or more members of the family out of the home, the factory transformed the nature of the family economy. Factory production directly and indirectly created new opportunities for wage-earning employment within the home. Some manufacturing processes, which were domestically based, were linked to centralised production.[86] Married women became increasingly unlikely to engage in factory employment, yet they were still affected by it. Married women's labour in production and reproduction, for example, was influenced by the change in the meaning of work that was introduced by the factory. The association of work with waged labour that the factory served to confirm, further marginalised the place of married women in particular who remained outside of this definition. Moreover, the organisation of the household became increasingly regulated by factory activity. The structure of family life was often determined by the employment in the factory of its male and child members. Finally, a large proportion of women's traditional domestic work, especially that in textiles and clothing, was taken over by the factory, although as will be illustrated below, some stages of the production process continued to be performed by women in the home.

There was therefore an interaction between factory work and domestic work in the nineteenth century. Industrialisation consisted of a growth in centralised and high productivity manufacturing industry alongside a persistent informal economy characterised by the family as a productive unit and by a growing outwork and sweating sector. As Maxine Berg has argued, 'technological change and factory production formed but one part of the route to industrialisation'.[87] The informal economy, which underpinned the industrial system, was a rural as well as an urban phenomenon. Not only was there often a manufacturing relationship between town and countryside in the nineteenth century, just as there had been in the protoindustrial era, but the distinction between them should not be exaggerated.

Although the expansion of factory production was associated with, but did not necessarily locationally correspond to, the contraction of some domestic industries in the early decades of the nineteenth century, other rural and urban industries and forms of production emerged to fill the ensuing gap. Cheap female labour became a resource for such new rural industries as lace, straw plait, hat and bonnet making, hand knitting, and button making, mainly in the south and east of the country.[88] In these areas, which have been described as industrially marginal to the manufacturing regions in the north,[89] cheap women's labour using hand or intermediate techniques 'long continued to be chosen as an alternative to mechanisation'.[90] In Essex, where rural industries developed in a 'wave like process as successive industries replaced one another',[91] silk production, commercial lace embroidery, straw plaiting, shoebinding and tailoring provided female employment for several decades in the nineteenth century following the contraction of the local woollen industry.[92] Lace embroidery expanded enormously on the basis of cheap female and child labour between 1815 and 1850 in Nottingham and Essex.[93] Although the 'partial mechanisation' of patterned lace production generated employment for women, the subsequent introduction of male-operated machines confined women and children to peripheral processes.[94]

In the early nineteenth century, silk manufacture was an important new industry that tapped child and female labour in the declining woollen regions. Hand silk throwing was performed by women and children who later, after the mechanisation of throwing, were used in repair and winding operations. Where supplies of such labour were cheap and plentiful, manually operated winding and throwing mills operated long after water- and steam-powered mills had appeared.[95] Straw plaiting was a highly localised Essex trade, which continued until the appearance of cheap Asian straw in the 1880s. From 1800, the Essex industry concentrated on the plaiting of straw rather than the making of hats, which was conducted in such specialist hat centres as Luton. In the early stages of the industry, the local farmers supplied the straw free or at a nominal rate, but as demand rose, they began to prepare straw on a commercial basis. While drawing on cheap rural labour, the straw-plaiting industry was largely organised by town-based merchants and thus provides an example of the interaction of urban and rural activity.[96]

The persistence of traditional forms of production was also a feature of the Midlands textile industries throughout the nineteenth century. It has been assumed that the family unit of manufacture became less important in the context of the organisational changes associated with industrialisation, and was further discouraged by a range of contemporary social and legislative processes. Evidence suggests, however, that although the family economy can be seen to have been restructured, it did not disappear. The shift from the household economy to the formal waged economy was slow and uneven, and exhibited pronounced regional and industrial variations. Recent research by Sonya Rose reveals how a form of family economy persisted within the Nottingham hosiery industry even after the introduction of factory-produced hose. Some of the manufacturing processes remained in the home and dovetailed with those in more centralised units. Rose analyses evidence from the censuses of 1851 and 1881 for Arnold in Nottinghamshire to show how the economic viability of households remained based on a family economy as the seaming of stockings, themselves mechanically produced in the factory, became a female-dominated outwork activity. Under the domestic system, wives and daughters sewed up the stockings made by related male framework knitters. Following the introduction of town-based hosiery factories the same women, or their daughters, were employed as waged homeworkers in seaming hose made by their husbands, or fathers, in steam-powered factories.[97] Thus a continuity of household economic arrangements was ensured as women performed the same tasks as their mothers. Even though some women engaged in factory work, the gender division of work in late nineteenth-century hosiery production resembled that of 100 years earlier when it had been equally rare for women to enter the core and well-paid activity of knitting.[98] A similar division of function and location was a feature of the Midlands lace industry, where finishing processes were performed domestically by women – often in the countryside – until well into the twentieth century.[99] As Pamela Sharpe and Stanley Chapman argue, there was no linear process by which hand-produced lace was supplanted by machine.[100] In Coventry, silk ribbon production was similarly conducted on the basis of a 'detached' family production unit.

Such instances imply that local traditions regarding family employment may have influenced the organisation of industry and determined work opportunities for women as mechanisation and centralised production progressed. In some industries, labour-intensive methods transformed the organisation of production during industrialisation as employers made use of outworkers in order to save on overhead costs. Domestic industry and labour-intensive homework were integral to the development of numerous industries in the later nineteenth century. This type of employment was also essential to the family economy. Fluctuations in trade meant that even the most skilled workers depended on other members of their households to contribute to the subsistence of the family. Family strategies adapted to industrialisation, but did not change in a uniform way.[101] Joan Scott and Louise Tilly have insisted that throughout the nineteenth century, 'the interdependence of family members . . . remained strong. The importance of family membership and family ties continued . . . the old rules of the family economy continued to operate in new contexts.'[102]

The growth of domestic work was an integral component of nineteenth-century industrial expansion. Home-based production was often generated by the increasing subdivision of tasks within the factory. Mechanisation in one part of the work process often led to the growth of homework in another. The division of labour within large factories frequently created tasks that could easily be performed at home by hand or using small machines. Where this was the case, a 25–50 per cent reduction in labour costs and large savings on overhead expenses could be achieved.[103] The success of the new industrial system depended on maintaining cheap production methods. The search for means of cost containment sometimes led to mechanisation, but it could equally result in a more intensive use of cheap labour. In some cases the outcome was a combination of both. Evidence for such symbiosis can be found in many of the urban trades of the nineteenth century.

The most telling example of the way in which outwork and homework interacted with centralised production units is provided by the garment trade.[104] Several occupations comprised the clothing industry and until the early nineteenth century, relatively small numbers of women were employed in the 'female' sectors of dressmaking and millinery, while skilled men controlled the substantial tailoring trade.[105] A high level of demand for cheap, ready-made military clothing during the Napoleonic Wars, however, stimulated changes in the organisation of tailoring. A system developed whereby cloth was given out from large warehouses to small workshop owners, who then employed cheap, and mainly female labour to make up inexpensive ready-made garments.[106] Demand for cheaper clothing then expanded and the use of subcontracting and female outworkers spread to other sectors.[107] By the mid nineteenth century, factory production of tailored items was introduced into the main clothing centres of London and Colchester, closely followed by Leeds. Rather than reducing the requirement for outwork, however, such centralisation generated expansion in alternative forms of production. Throughout the nineteenth century it was rare to find a clothing firm that did not employ women at home in addition to those in the factory and workshop.[108]

The introduction of the sewing machine was crucial in extending sweatshop and homeworking employment for women. The small and portable machine that was initially operated by foot power, permitted the clothing manufacturers to make full use of a cheap and flexible labour force at a time when the expansion in demand for ready-made clothing placed great pressure on existing methods of production. The garment trades of such centres as London, Colchester and Bristol were typically organised on the basis of outwork making use of the large female workforce in the towns and surrounding rural areas. By the later nineteenth century, when the tailoring trade was becoming increasingly concentrated in Leeds and in London,[109] the organisation had become even more complex. Manufacture was divided into three levels of production, each of which was linked by systems of contracting and subcontracting. The first level consisted of large wholesale businesses which contracted work to the second level of small factories and workshops. Homeworkers and sweated labour, who were given work by both wholesaler and contractor, comprised the third level.[110] The system was capable not only of mass output, but also of rapid expansion and contraction of production. Such flexibility of manufacture, which was more relevant to the success of the garment trade than to most others because of the extreme seasonality of demand, was provided by female labour operating in sweatshops or in their own homes. These women were typically paid below subsistence wages, and their 'marginal' work was in fact critical to the survival of many clothing enterprises.[111]

Sally Alexander's portrayal of women workers in mid nineteenth-century London provides an invaluable insight into the erratic and sweated nature of many trades in the capital, which were typical of those in other urban centres.[112] Her description of the experiences of women garment workers is particularly harrowing. The spread of factory mass production of clothing was contained by the high cost of rents and transport in London; and the large supply of cheap underemployed labour facilitated the spread of sweated outwork in the city's garment trades.[113] The women employed in such conditions were forced to alternate months of intense labour with periods of short-time working, and remained near to destitution.[114] Irregular and casual work characterised the employment of women both in the capital and elsewhere. The seasonality of employment was particularly marked in London, however, and a summer exodus of women to the market gardens and hop fields of Kent and Surrey – which resembled pre-industrial bi-employment – was essential to family survival.[115]

The bulk of married women's employment in London and other large towns and cities was provided by sweated needleworking trades. A range of other casual outwork was also available sometimes in association with quite highly mechanised industries. Outworkers often carried out a single process in the chain of production, such as pressing clothes, but sometimes, as in the case of matchbox making, they produced a complete article. Until the late nineteenth century, outworking or homeworking[116] was common in a range of important industries. The examples of the Midlands lace and hosiery trades have been discussed above. In the Birmingham nail and chainmaking trades, women worked in sheds attached to their homes. In the Northampton boot and shoe industry workers engaged in domestically based stitching,[117] and in the last quarter of the nineteenth century in Colchester, tailoring firms used rural outworkers for making-up processes.[118] Outworkers were also numerous in silk weaving, in the making of brushes and artificial flowers and in the carding of hooks and eyes, buttons and pins. The number of homeworkers increased at the end of the nineteenth century when factory and workshop regulations encouraged manufacturers to put out more work.[119] The majority of homeworkers and outworkers during the period of industrial expansion in the nineteenth century were women. The view of Duncan Bythell, who has investigated this area most thoroughly, is that 'not only were most outworkers women: until the last quarter of the nineteenth century, most of the women who worked in industry probably did so as outworkers'.[120]

Much of women's work during the nineteenth century was easily picked up and put down and could be performed in a variety of locations. Many women, especially those who were married, were employed on a part-time, casual or intermittent basis in what might be described as an 'informal' economy.[121] This included not only domestic outwork and sweatshop activity, but also a range of other forms of working by which women ensured the survival of their family as they had done in the past. Childminding, casual cleaning and washing, and accommodating lodgers are examples of such income-generating activities. Many married women were involved in some form of trading, often on a temporary, part-time or casual basis.[122] The lives of the majority of working women were 'spent in a variety of partial occupations'. The informal economy, therefore, incorporated a range of activities that were compatible with both the image of domesticity and the reality of working-class women's domestic existence. Married women, for example, 'who sold food from their back kitchens or front parlours nicely illustrate the margin of the public and the private spheres which existed in so many women's lives'.[123] Many informal activities were of a non-market variety. Neighbourhood and kinship networks of service exchange involved reciprocity and payment in kind as well as cash.[124] The piecemeal earning opportunities implied by this net-working illustrate the resourcefulness of women and their support of one another as they pursued family well-being in the face of restricted possibilities for waged work.

According to Sally Alexander, 'a mixture of washing, cleaning and charring as well as various sorts of home- or slop-work, in addition to domestic labour, occupied most women throughout their working lives'.[125] All working-class married women, whether they worked full- or part-time or did not earn a wage at all, performed work with social as well as economic value. In their domestic role, women acted as unpaid cooks, dressmakers and nurses. This production of use values provided crucial support to the industrial system. Working-class families would have faced destitution, and employers a hugely increased wage bill had such services cost their market value.[126] The relentless toil that characterised the lives of working-class women clearly failed to enter the official record through occupational censuses. The work of married women was particularly understated by census enumeration.[127] When part-time and casual wage earning[128] is allowed for it is clear that employment among married women was common.[129] The idea that working-class women accepted a notion of a separate female sphere that did not include paid work should be vigorously challenged. Sources used in this chapter are consistent with the notion that women worked hard throughout their lives and that they 'expected to earn wages whenever their other responsibilities allowed it'.[130] Evidence presented to a Parliamentary Inquiry of 1904 suggested that in areas where men's employment was scarce, 'a woman is looked upon as lazy unless she takes her share in contributing to the family income'.[131] Little support has been found for Ivy Pinchbeck's optimistic observation that as a result of industrialisation 'the home was no longer a workshop, many women were able, for the first time . . . to devote their energies to the business of homemaking and the care of their children'.[132]

The formal record misrepresents the nature and extent of women's employment in the new industrial economy. In reality, women's work exhibited elements of continuity within a changing context of industrial activity. In the early stages of industrialisation, women, as much as men, were drawn into the new core areas of manufacturing. The visible participation of women workers was short-lived, however, and their position as key members of the labour force appeared to dissolve during the new industrial age. This can be explained partly because of the nature of structural change in industry. Pinchbeck, for example, recognised that the quantity of employment for men, but not for women, increased as a result of industrialisation.[133] While traditional men's occupations had proved sluggish during the early years of the Industrial Revolution, new 'male' industries that emerged during the nineteenth century, particularly in engineering, transport, iron and steel and the utilities, proved highly productive. Female labour played only a small part in these expanding trades.[134]

In the late nineteenth century, high and rising levels of female unemployment were, according to Ellen Jordan, partly a reflection of difficulties caused for women by the sexual division of labour and by the concentration of those industries which employed women in limited geographical areas. Also relevant was the tendency for women to be denied access to the new industries of the nineteenth century.[135] Women's retraction can also be interpreted as acquiescence in the face of the backlash against women's work outside the home. The apparent strength of women's employment position during the initial period of industrialisation, as revealed in employer preference for female labour, aroused the antipathy of male workers. The antagonism between male and female workers in the labour market caused anxiety among employers and unease within society at large.[136] This concern generated legal and social responses. Factory and mine legislation was designed to restrict women's waged work and to encourage their homemaking pursuits. Such state action served to diffuse the image of the domestic woman, which was already popular among the middle class and which found further support among working men. These strategies discouraged married women from entering the labour market as much as they discouraged employers from seeking their labour.

The retreat into the home by married women was by no means total but their need to comply with socio-legal pressures, while at the same time ensuring their own or their family's survival, resulted in compromise. As women accordingly sought home-based wage-earning activities, they offered employers a cheap and flexible supply of labour. This chapter has shown that industrialisation consisted of a growth in high productivity manufacturing industry alongside an expanding informal economy which was characterised by home-work, outwork and sweating. Within the new industrial context where formal and informal activities grew in tandem, it was women who dominated the informal sector. The positions that women occupied in this sphere were not unlike those they had occupied in the previous centuries. Through the nineteenth century, therefore, women's activities, more than men's, indicated continuity with earlier times. Women's participation in informal activities, as well as those in the formal sphere of work, provided an essential service to the industrial system. Female labour contributed a vital flexibility to an economy increasingly influenced by trade cycle and other fluctuations. Unpaid domestic work ensured the reproduction of labour on a daily and a generational basis.

Some of the work of women during industrialisation has been described as marginal or peripheral. It was certainly rewarded as such. Much productive activity – even in core industries – took place at a conceptual margin. Centralised production may have generated economies of scale, yet the advantages of the factory form were not overwhelming. Mass output was not an appropriate objective of all industries. Even in cases where large-scale production was an aim, flexibility was also required because of the inherent inefficiency of the factory system. Women provided both flexibility and cheapness and thus constituted a super-exploitable pool of industrial labour. Without such labour the British economy may have achieved less short-term success, but may have been forced to become more efficient. Ironically, had women's cheap and flexible labour not been so readily forthcoming, progress in the economy may have been prolonged.

6 The Making of Gender Identities during the Period of Industrialisation

The working-class family is assumed to have been reorganised as a result of industrial change. Conventional wisdom suggests that it was transformed from an economic unit of production to one that was supported by a family wage earned outside of the home. Evidence presented in Chapter 5, however, indicates that such a transition was only partial before the late nineteenth century. Nevertheless, relationships between family members underwent a process of restructuring from the late eighteenth century, as gender roles were more sharply defined. During industrialisation, the family changed from a co-operative unit of production where all members contributed flexibly, if not equally, to the survival of the whole, to a structure in which individual functions were more rigidly and hier-archically applied. Adult males assumed positions of authority while women performed supportive, mainly domestic roles. Most children did not formally become economic assets until they approached teenage years, yet they performed childminding duties and other functions in the informal economy much earlier. It will be suggested below that although gender was a means of constituting power rela-tions, the nineteenth-century definitions of masculinity and femi-ninity can be seen to have served the interest of the working class in protecting the material position of the family.

The family played an important part in the creation of gender roles, which had extensive social, political and economic relevance during the nineteenth century. Most importantly, gender positions influenced the allocation of jobs in the new industrial economy. The primary identification of women with the home, and the gendering of work that allowed men to be constructed as breadwinners can be perceived as an outcome of industrialisation. Historians and social scientists have, in recent years, extensively but inconclusively debated the explanation for the supposed shift to these distinctive gender positions from more fluid roles in the pre-industrial period. Among the several competing strands of explanation is that which assumes the differential positions of men and women to have been reinforced through the interaction of domestic and workplace inequality. Women were marginalised both at home and at work, while men's superiority was maintained in both settings. There is disagreement about the direction of causation. It has been argued, for example, that women's labour market weakness emanated from a pre-existing domestic subordination. The possibility that struggles in the labour market were instrumental in changes in the family and in the domestic division of labour that marginalised women, has also been suggested. The domestic dependence of women in this case is seen as the outcome of the success of male workers in establishing gender segregation at work and in excluding women from a wide range of occupations. A further strand of explanation suggests that women were forced to marry or cohabit on unequal terms because their weak working position and low wages precluded an independent subsistence.

The pre-industrial and early industrial family economy certainly embodied gender divisions, but these distinctions were less pronounced than was to be the case in the industrial period. Before industrialisation or within the protoindustrial system, it was common for all members of the family to participate in production subject to ability and to be paid as a group. Within a labouring family's home, domestic tasks were limited to rudimentary cooking and basic cleaning and were performed by those whose opportunity cost was lowest at the time.[1] Recent investigation of late eighteenth-century household budgets shows that the relative contributions of members to family income varied according to region and occupation. Women and children appeared to play a particularly significant role in the case of outworkers' incomes.[2] Among artisan families in the early period of industrialisation, it was assumed that both husbands and wives would work to maintain a respectable income level. Early nineteenth-century autobiographies provide evidence that men valued the contribution of their wives. David Love, for example, recalled his first wife as a 'blooming young woman . . . excellent at working, careful and industrious'. Another described his affectionate partner as 'a wise counsellor, a model of industry'. Joseph Livesey, a Preston weaver, praised a good wife as 'sober, affectionate and industrious'.[3] Joint enterprise, however, did not imply undifferentiated gender roles. Women performed functions as both wife and worker, but the satisfaction of family requirements took precedence over work.[4] Complete interchangeability of gender roles, such as that suggested in the more optimistic descriptions of the protoindustrial family economy,[5] was rarely evident in the early industrial family, yet some flexibility of activity existed. Women were assumed to have greater responsibility for childcare, for example, but in the more marginal domestic pursuits, gender distinctions were blurred.

The working-class family economy was reformed but not ultimately weakened by the economic and social changes associated with the period of industrialisation. Previous chapters have shown, for example, that the enclosure movement restricted women's informal earning opportunities within the agricultural sector. This, together with the foreclosure of other female occupations, undermined traditional sources of family income.[6] The household production unit might have been expected to disappear as paid work for some members of the family became separated from the home. Yet there was no sudden breakdown in family relations of production as centralised manufacturing initially drew upon the combined labour of working-class family teams. All family members continued to contribute to the household unit either together in the factory, where young women and children were supervised within a kin-based network, or through a combination of factory employment and outwork. Family members were not always hired as a team for factory work, but even when members were formally hired separately, kin connections were important in providing recruitment and supervisory functions. Such family networks often extended quite widely to include uncles, nephews, nieces and cousins.[7] Factory managers relied heavily on paternal or equivalent authority to keep young people and women in line. Subcontracting systems were not confined within the factory. It was not unusual for male textile factory workers to take home piecework to be completed by their wives with the help of their children. In this case the family production unit operated between spheres.[8] Even as waged work outside of the home became more important, the working-class family economy continued to depend on the various productive contributions of all household members. The labour of families typically combined formal and informal activities through much of the early period of industrialisation and beyond. The family economy 'rarely dovetailed neatly' with a single source of employment, either in the factory or in the domestic sector, though its activities were generally influenced by the expansion of production outside of the home.[9]

The working-class family economy as a flexible and broadly co-operative unit adapted to economic changes, but its internal structure became shaped by the social and political outcomes of the process of industrialisation, the most influential of which was the rise of the middle-class ideology of separate spheres.[10] The creation of distinct functions and locations for men and women was by no means new to the eighteenth and nineteenth centuries, yet it can be argued that this period witnessed a sharpening of differences between male and female social roles.[11] Women's relative powerlessness was written into the marriage contract. According to John Stuart Mill, the legal subordination of women within a marital relationship formed the basis of their subjection in the political and economic sphere.[12] Although solemnisation of marriage was not practised widely among the working class who were deterred either by cost, anti-church feeling or for reasons of local custom,[13] pressure to establish a household with a sexual partner was irresistible. There is evidence, however, that women felt trapped by their financial reliance on a male provider because sustaining the type of stable sexual relationship that ensured such support was fraught with difficulty. Consensual unions were common in many parts of the country before 1850 and separations were also frequent.[14] A further cohabiting relationship commonly followed such separation, but the informality that such successive liaisons implied, was not an indication of equality of gender partnership.[15] Women appear to have been subordinated in the majority of heterosexual cohabiting relationships. They were forced into dependent relationships, whether marriage or cohabitation, because of low female wages and limited employment opportunities.[16] In the context of the more pervasive ideology of domesticity, women were subjugated within marriage where they retained few more legal rights than unpaid domestic servants.[17] Women's relatively weak position within a marital relationship and specifically the working-class family was recognised by radical groups in the early nineteenth century. The Owenite socialists, for example, who advocated more egalitarian structures, believed that it was 'as husbands and fathers that men oppressed women'.[18]

The family, and the operation of separate spheres, were clearly important in the making of gender identities during the new industrial age. Such identities in turn shaped men's and women's opportunities for engaging in economic and political action. The construction of clear and dichotomous conceptions of men and women in the nineteenth century built on ideas stemming from the scientific revolution of the seventeenth and eighteenth centuries, which added dubious medical explanations to the traditional Christian belief in women's inferiority.[19] Representations of women as irrational, backward and limited by their bodies were juxtaposed with portrayals of men whose rational and civilised nature was enhanced by their physical presence.[20] Such an ideology of difference, while fundamental to the practical organisation of separate spheres, did not exist unchallenged.

The sentiments of Mary Wollstonecraft, which rejected assumptions of women's mental and physical inferiority, were echoed in a 'steady stream of writing from the pens of progressive literati' in the late eighteenth century.[21] Wollstonecraft's views on women's education and women's rights provided renewed impetus to arguments for intellectual equality between the sexes. Dismissing the idea of women's naturally distinctive qualities, Wollstonecraft argued that inadequate education prevented women becoming as 'rational' as men. She also believed that women's potential was crushed by such other institutional arrangements as marriage.[22] In her *Vindication of the Rights of Woman*, she wrote that

> the most perfect education, in my opinion, is . . . to enable the individual to attain such habits of virtue as will render it independent. It is a farce to call any being virtuous whose virtues do not result from the exercise of its own reason. This was Rousseau's opinion respecting men: I extend it to women and confidently assert that they have been drawn out of their sphere by false refinement, and not by an endeavour to acquire masculine qualities.[23]

The late eighteenth-century feminist response to the ideology of difference, which challenged notions of masculinity as well as those of femininity, was branded as politically extreme. The resulting backlash generated support for the more 'moderate' separate spheres position of the evangelicals. All attempts to extend women's role beyond domestic and family activities, were presented as threats not only to the balance of sexual power within the household, but also to the balance of moral forces within the nation as a whole.[24]

By the early nineteenth century, robust challenges to the notion of women's intellectual inferiority notwithstanding, women's paramount association with the home and domesticity was generally accepted. Several decades later, despite intervening attacks on the double standard, female domesticity was barely questioned even by feminists.[25] John Stuart Mill, who lamented women's inadequate occupational and political opportunities, nevertheless shared the view of many contemporary feminists that, given the freedom to choose, most women would prefer to remain within a domestic environment.[26] Only a handful of exceptional feminist writers were willing to challenge the division of labour within the home. The freethinker Richard Carlile rejected the idea that housework was naturally women's work, and in 1832 argued that 'it is as much the proper business of the man as the woman's'.[27] Mary Leman Grimstone, a radical liberal feminist, whose writing was published in the Owenite press, argued for a reversal of roles. She was angered by the way in which society wasted women's talents. 'Shame on the world! In madness or in pride, Has woman's mental birthright been denied. Be she the weaker, kindly give her might; be she man's equal, then it is her right.'[28] Owenite socialists, at least in the early stages of the movement's existence, explicitly countered ideas of gender difference. Robert Cooper, for example, wrote that 'our females are not considered by the males, as they are generally in the old world, as their inferiors . . . mere creatures made for their sexual pleasure and indulgence; but . . . as their equals, confidential companions . . . in their moral and intellectual improvements and enjoyments . . . '.[29] Such eccentric opinions were rare and were ridiculed by society at large. They did, however, influence the thinking of later nineteenth-century feminists.[30]

During the nineteenth century gender identities were constructed by a range of processes. A number of definitions of both femininity and masculinity existed in print but, increasingly, perceptions of maleness and femaleness within the working-class family corresponded to the separate spheres model of the middle class. The adoption of separate spheres can be seen as part of a working-class strategy to harmonise domestic relationships in the context of the gender differentiation of work, and to gain the political support of social superiors by demonstrating respectable patterns of behaviour.[31] This was done by simultaneously emphasising men's dominant role as worker, undermining women's working position, and stressing female domesticity. Respectability, therefore, was a complex value system, based on specific notions of masculinity and femininity. To be manly, according to Sonya Rose, was to be honourable and respectable, which meant being brave, strong and independent. For a woman, to be honourable and respectable meant to have the virtues of sexual purity, domesticity and motherhood.[32]

The creation of a cultural identity of men as worker and breadwinner became cemented during the nineteenth century as patterns of household work changed to place greater emphasis on men's unaided labours. It occurred despite the prevalence of women's employment, and despite the importance of women's economic contribution to the family. It was designed to enhance the status of the adult male by reducing his, or his family's, dependence on female earnings.[33] The weight attached to the male as sole or main wage earner was 'reflected positively in the demand for a family wage and negatively in the humiliation of the unemployed man obliged to depend on his wife's earnings and in the anger of the skilled artisan displaced by female labour'.[34] Within this context, men experienced 'a sense of degradation in being dependent upon the manual labour of his wife for support'.[35]

As the male identity was shaped by work, and because of the growing ideological distinction and physical separation between housework and 'real' work, household chores became more feminised. As the female identity was thus shaped by domesticity, men distanced themselves from such activity. John Tosh has provided evidence to suggest that working-class husbands who helped with the housework, for example, were seen as unmanly.[36] The view of William Dodd, writing in 1842, was that 'it is quite pitiable to see these poor men taking care of the house and children, and busily engaging in washing, baking, nursing and preparing the humble repast for the wife who is wearing her life away in the factory'.[37] Such reversal of traditional roles was attacked by many contemporaries, perhaps most memorably by Frederick Engels who described the case of the factory-employed wife whose 'husband sits at home, tends the children, sweeps the room and cooks . . . *condemned* [my italics] to domestic occupations'.[38]

Separate spheres ideology was also represented within nineteenth-century economic thought, which marginalised the family economy. Historically, household relationships had been central to economic life but became excluded from consideration within the emerging discipline of economics. According to Jean Gardiner, industrialisation produced a redefinition of public and private spheres. The commercial world of the market economy was separated from the domestic morality of the family. Classical political economy generated assumptions about work, in which household economic activity was devalued. Adam Smith believed that both spheres, and the gendering of the activities within them, were necessary to the well-being of society. Women, Smith argued, occupied a sphere of social relations that were determined by morality rather than by efficiency criteria. Women were not intended to be guided by self-interest, and it was their role in the household that provided the necessary counterbalance to the individualism and materialism of the market.[39] John Stuart Mill disputed such a construction of women's marginal economic importance. He insisted that 'if women had as absolute control as men have, over their own persons . . . there would be no plea for limiting their hours of labour for themselves, in order that they might have time to labour for the husband'.[40] Although Mill's argument won favour among contemporary feminists, Smith's proposition was more representative of nineteenth-century economic analysis in which separate, gendered spheres of activity became formalised.[41]

Domesticity was clearly central to the making of femininity in the nineteenth century. Women's special responsibility for the organisation of domestic life accompanied the functional separation of home and work through the nineteenth century. The primacy of women's position in the home was further confirmed as centres of male sociability came to lie outside the home and the family.[42] The outcome of a specialised domestic role for women during industrialisation was associated with both the expansion of formal economic activity outside of the home, and the creation of an ideology of domesticity. Such an ideology was well established in Britain by the 1830s and provided a definition of women as primarily relating to the home and to the family. It formed an important component of the new industrial bourgeois culture and of middle-class consciousness. The ideology was shaped by religion and specifically by the evangelical movement, which engaged in a moral crusade to encourage a new respectability in a society where instability and decay were endemic. Women were judged to be naturally equipped to play an instrumental role in the increasingly urgent battle against sin. The duties to be performed by women, which were prescribed in great detail in contemporary conduct books, included the care of husbands and children (in that order) and the setting of moral standards for the family. Full-time domesticity for women, and the ideas that underpinned it, were particularly relevant to the middle class, yet it was also viewed as a desirable aspiration for working people. An active domestic role for working-class women was intimately associated with socialisation of children and with a robust construction of housework through which unpaid services for their husbands were performed.

The package of obligations implied by the concept of domesticity combined to restrict women's freedom to engage in other social and economic activities.[43] Nevertheless, many working-class people and organisations pursued domesticity in an attempt to enhance family living standards and material comforts. Ivy Pinchbeck perceived the opportunity for women to devote the bulk of their energies to the care of their homes and families as a beneficial, emancipatory outcome of industrialisation.[44] Some early nineteenth-century feminists likewise viewed positively women's freedom to choose a life of domesticity. John Stuart Mill, while criticising the relentless toil of domestic life, nevertheless acknowledged that *if* marriage became an equal partnership then most women would opt for either motherhood or employment rather than attempt to combine the two. 'The careful and economical application of the husband's earnings to the general comfort of the family [would constitute] not only her fair share, but usually the larger share, of the bodily and mental exertion required by their joint existence.'[45] Elizabeth Roberts' work suggests that married women who, in the later nineteenth century, were relieved of the double burden of wage earning and household responsibilities, saw themselves and were perceived by others to be more liberated than their overworked sisters.[46]

Although female domesticity operated to weaken the working position of women, it became a more powerful objective of most radical working-class movements than did the egalitarian stance of Owenism. The domestic framework of Chartism, for example, was connected to the notion of working-class respectability and male self-respect, and was expected to create better husbands and a pleasanter family life. Indirectly, therefore, domesticity was seen as a means of making the lives of working-class women easier.[47] Yet the pressure was on women to perform domestic chores adequately. It was argued that the time and effort women expended in enhancing the comforts of the home would discourage male drunkenness and increase marital happiness, implicitly blaming women's previously poor homemaking record for their husband's disagreeable behaviour.[48]

In principle, the domestic ideal acquired popularity among elements of the working class, but in practice it created tensions. Ultimately, domesticity and the separate gender spheres that it implied, placed women in a dependent and powerless position.[49] It stripped women of their identity as workers and constrained their access to employment. Many women were thus forced either into unwanted dependence on a man, or into dire poverty.[50] Domesticity created unreasonable expectations for working-class women who struggled to attain the ideal without the necessary financial resources. The inevitable failure to meet the standards imposed by such an ideology gave rise to internal conflicts and family disharmony. The notion of domesticity was presented within working-class movements as of material benefit for the family, but its successful attainment depended on agreement among members of the working-class household about their respective roles. Evidence from the nineteenth century suggests that men and women often represented divergent viewpoints, inhabited different material worlds and embodied different levels of power.[51] The tensions that such divergent positions provoked were frequently resolved through domestic violence.

This was particularly regrettable since domesticity was presented as a partial solution to the abuse that many women suffered at the hands of drunken and irresponsible husbands. Many men apparently believed that they had the right to beat their wives who in turn dreaded the working man's day off, 'Saint Monday' when 'her husband beats her and spends her savings on drink'.[52] Marital unhappiness also revealed itself in the letters of Owenite women to *The Pioneer*. One woman complained that 'if she offers the least resistance [to her husband] it is thrust down her throat with his fist'.[53] Examples of male remorse are few. Chartist T. B. Smith encouraged men to feel shame and to mend their ways. 'Look at the tattered gowns of your wives', he said, 'at the frockless and shoeless children who are crawling on the floor, at the almost coalless grate, and the near breadless cupboard, and then look at the well-filled tobacco pouch, and the flowing pint, and blush for your own delinquencies.'[54] It was believed that if women devoted themselves to the care of their home and family, men would be happier and less likely to drink. Studies of family violence in the mid nineteenth century, however, reveal both the extent to which domesticity thus far had failed to create harmonious working-class living conditions, and the degree to which the right to punish a wife physically was an indicator of the domestic power structure and especially of male dominance within the home.[55] Ironically, therefore, domesticity was a divisive instrument. It split the interests of working women and men, and divided women according to marital status.

During the nineteenth century domesticity operated in various ways but it especially served to construct femininity. The identity of women during industrialisation and its aftermath, rested squarely within the context of the family. The construction of the male identity during the same period focused on work and especially on the power to earn a wage sufficient to support a family. The breadwinner wage was designed to provide men with a more complete persona, by incorporating elements of both family responsibility and worker identity. The breadwinner ideology conveniently accommodated both the values of evangelicalism and the exclusionist strategies of organised male workers. It also neatly encapsulated expectations of gendered activities both at home and at work. The family wage idea was based on assumptions about respective responsibilities of men and women both in the labour market and in the home and served to favour men in the allocation of jobs as well as in the distribution of resources in the home.[56]

The making of the working-class family through the advocacy of the family wage, the norm of domesticity, and the marginalisation of female labour, appeared to constitute a comprehensive attack on woman's identity as worker.[57] The undermining of women's working position, however, may have been a necessary element in the struggle of the working class to protect itself through its family. The male breadwinner wage became a central feature of nineteenth-century trade union demands, although only the most skilled men earned sufficient to support their families before 1900.[58] Much debate surrounds the explanation for the rise of the family wage idea. It appeared to develop out of the challenge to men's labour market position caused by the decline of family hiring and subcontracting which provided women with an opportunity to earn an independent wage.[59] The exclusionary strategies pursued by men in response to this threat met with only limited success, and were replaced by the less overtly selfish family wage construct. It was argued in 1825 that the withdrawal of women and children from the labour market would be 'highly congenial to the feelings and habits of Englishmen, as conducive to domestic comfort and kindly affections as tending to establish the authority of father, and as making each man responsible for the comfort, respectability, and the education of his family'.[60]

The popularity of the breadwinner wage stemmed from its coincidence with Victorian moral discourse and with contemporary market economics which was generally hostile to the employment of women and children. This interpretation is broadly consistent with that of Wally Seccombe who argues that the emergence of the individual wage in place of group payment, which, he controversially believes, stemmed from an artisan tradition, was an inevitable outcome of industrialisation, but that the particular form of the male breadwinner wage was the result of the reaction of an 'increasingly conservative labour movement . . . to the very real threat of cheap female labour to skilled men's job security and wage levels'.[61]

Attempts by male workers to exclude or marginalise women workers may seem perverse given the dependence of many families – even among the comfortable artisan group – on the earnings of their female members.[62] Such efforts, firstly through exclusionary tactics and later through demands for a breadwinner wage, operated to divide the working class and thus increase its vulnerability to employer exploitation. Several authors have highlighted this apparent anomaly. According to Seccombe, the 'drive of the craft unions to exclude women and enforce a secondary labour market position under the banner of a living wage was doubly divisive'. It separated workers by both gender and skill. 'Instead of reaching out to organise women workers and improve pay', Seccombe suggests that 'most unions attempted to defend their own narrow interests by means of legislative regulation, exclusion and often intimidation and harassment of unorganised women workers . . . and made the male breadwinner norm their ideological armament.'[63] Adopting a position that was not unusual in the late 1970s, Heidi Hartmann argued that male workers were motivated by the desire for women's domestic subordination. She among others believed that male and female labour could have worked together to achieve equal pay, but that men chose a separatist position because of their desire to retain their wives' services at home.[64] Moving from an approach that emphasises patriarchal influences to one that focuses on male gender identity, Sonya Rose links the support for the breadwinner wage to a number of issues that centred on men's identity. The breadwinner ideal was central to the construction of masculinity. It was the meaning attached to wages and jobs for men that underpinned their strategies in the struggle with women for work and resulted in job segregation.[65]

While not obviously serving the interests of all members of the working class, the breadwinner wage has been interpreted by a growing number of authors as a means by which the working-class family was strengthened. Jane Humphries was one of the first exponents of this approach.[66] According to Humphries, the struggle for the breadwinner wage was based on the working-class family's need to protect its members from the rigours of industrial employment, to provide materially for its unemployed members, and to act as a mechanism for control of the labour supply. The retreat of specified family members from the labour force combined with a family wage and the labour of the (female) domestic worker, would in principle, serve to raise the standard of living of the working class as a whole. The potential material benefits to the working-class family of the breadwinner wage were clear, yet Humphries' analysis neglects the gender and intra-class divisions implied by the ideal. For example, it fails to consider explicitly the interests of women or the differential positions of sectional groups. Nevertheless, despite the masculine construction of the breadwinner wage, it remains important to consider the possibility that it served the joint interests of working-class men and women in enhancing family life. The making of differential gender identities, as reflected in the family wage and the ideal of domesticity, does not necessarily imply gender domination.

Working-class struggles which focused on the defence of the family may have been a reaction to employer oppression, as Humphries suggests, or, alternatively, a response to the actions of the state. Colin Creighton, for example, suggests that battles to defend working-class interests were 'saturated with concern for the maintenance of the working class family' in response to the Poor Law and other invasive social policies.[67] On the surface, however, it seems that state legislation – the Factory Acts as well as the Poor Law – encouraged precisely the family structure that the working class apparently perceived as its defence mechanism. Discussions surrounding nineteenth-century protective legislation reflected an increasing level of anxiety about the impact of married women's labour on the working-class family and specifically on the health of its children. Richard Oastler and other supporters of the Factory Acts believed that all members of the family would benefit both at home and at work from shorter working hours. His rhetoric clearly indicated, however, that any such gains would be distributed differentially between genders. Oastler assumed, for instance, that women's newly acquired free time would be devoted to additional housework, while men would enjoy more leisure time at home and elsewhere. The enhancement of working-class life through the family, therefore, was to be obtained by consolidating the domestic role of women.[68] The legislation helped to cement a growing consensus about the different responsibilities that marriage conferred on women and men. Individual women were held responsible for the welfare of babies and children, and alternative policies that would have given either the state or employers some obligation for infant and childcare, failed to materialise.[69]

Evidence suggests that employers, too, were instrumental in encouraging a particular family form. In the early stages of industrialisation, textile factory masters were content to employ men, women and children together in kinship groups. Their family hiring system, however, both depended on and perpetuated the authority of the father, by relying heavily on male supervision and control. Employers preserved the dominance of the male worker in the factory and, indirectly, in the home as a means of controlling textile communities through paternalism.[70] The rules of nineteenth-century factories incorporated evangelical notions of gender roles. Among the regulations of Hirst, Bramley and Co., Leeds, is an address to the burlers and other females: 'We are fearful that many of you seldom reflect upon the duties required from you, in your several relations of daughters, sisters, wives or mothers, and of the strict account which will one day have to be given, of the manner in which you have discharged the duties of these several stations.' The men meanwhile were encouraged to 'control [their] passions and to attain a higher degree of moderation'.[71] At Samuel Courtauld's silk mill in Halstead, a ruling was introduced in 1860 which prohibited the wearing of 'shockingly indecent' crinolines and urged women to dress 'with as much BECOMING NEATNESS as they can'.[72] Men received no such exhortation. In the early 1870s women, but not men, were subject to strict rules on mealtime procedures, which served to intensify the work discipline that permeated women's experiences of the factory.[73] There seems little doubt that gender distinctions formed the basis for the structuring of many industrial enterprises and were reflected in paternalistic practices. The separate spheres ideology that shaped middle-class culture, and increasingly came to determine the structure of the working-class family, influenced paternalistic factory regimes. These in turn were motivated by the problematic accommodation of the ideal of domesticity and the presence of women workers, which troubled middle-class employers.[74]

The industrial relations practices of Courtauld in the mid nineteenth century reveal how the firm's attempt to reconcile their dependency on female labour with the espousal of the domestic ideal, resulted in a form of paternalism that re-created the family in its mill.[75] Its highly segregated and vertically ranked labour force was intended to re-create the hierarchical structure of family life. Such a hierarchy was reinforced by a particular wage payment system, within which women and girls were paid very low piece rates, and by a gendered disciplinary system, whereby women but not men were fined for lateness, irregularity, misconduct and abusive language. The women in Courtauld's factory were also encouraged to acquire the principles of domesticity in out-of-work activities. Domesticity as woman's natural domain was a central theme in the organisation and practices of the Evening School, and the monthly 'maternal meetings' promoted middle-class notions of child welfare. The inaccurately named Amusement Society, membership of which 'implied a certain moral standing' concentrated its activities on bourgeois feminine accomplishments like singing, drama and piano playing. Masculinity pervaded the men's Literary and Mechanics Institute which resembled a Gentlemen's Club but without the smoking and drinking. A range of reading material was provided in order to educate men in the habits of respectability.[76] The factory provided a day nursery and a home to accommodate mill girls, but their strict regimes were rejected and both were closed within a few years from under-use.[77] Such evidence suggests that the interpretation of domesticity presented by Courtauld's did not attract their female employees, and that 'the evocation of a well-tended home as a haven from the workplace had a far greater appeal for working class men than for working class women'.[78] In this case, and despite some female resistance, the separate spheres paternalism played a central role in keeping women in a subservient position at work and at home, and in fostering the growth of a male labour elite whose patriarchal interest increasingly coincided with those of their employers.[79]

Evidence from other paternalistic employers reveals the extent to which their practices were gendered in a way that supported notions of separate spheres. At the Gregs' cotton mill in Styal, Cheshire, paternalism was directed more towards the factory children, and the gender segregation of workers was less complete than at Courtauld's. There was, nevertheless, a female society, girls but not boys were taught to sew as part of their education, and during periods of mill shutdown, men cotton operatives were found outwork on the estate, while the women operatives were rounded up into a sewing school to make garments. In non-work time, 'old and young cooperated, the daughters keeping up a close intercourse with the girls and the sons bringing home the results of their studies and their travels to the boys and men – teaching, lecturing and stimulating'.[80] Employer strategies to encourage male power in the family were extended in the later nineteenth century by the introduction of the marriage bar which embodied both a domestic ideology and the cult of mother-hood. Sonya Rose suggests that the marriage bar should be under-stood as part of a package of gendered employment practices. Industrialists' organisation of work was consistent with 'taken for granted ideas about gender difference', which were linked to an ide-ology of family life. According to Rose, paternalism grew out of a 'transposition of hierarchical and gender family relations onto class relations'.[81]

Much of the argument presented above indicates the interplay of employer interest, state legislation and working-class pursuit of respectability in the way in which the structure of its families evolved during the period of industrialisation. The definition of women as primarily domestic and men as the main wage earners may well have served the longer-term interests of employers. The priority placed on women's domestic activities ensured the repro-duction of labour on a daily and a generational basis. No wage was paid for their domestic services. Male labour was therefore made available to employers more cheaply than had the market cost of domestic chores to be met indirectly through higher wages. There is little doubt that working-class desire for acceptance through respectability was a response to early nineteenth-century economic and industrial change. The practice of a more rigid separation of domestic and public spheres by working people was an essential part of the drive for respectability, but was not the only reason for it.[82] The working-class value system already embodied honesty and decency,[83] and although in the search for the approval of their social superiors they appeared to adopt some aspect of their lifestyle, the move towards a separate spheres position was also a response to economic changes associated with industrialisation, in particular the productive basis of the family.[84] If political gains emanated from such a process, so much the better.

Working-class thought was clearly influenced by bourgeois notions of family life and organisation, which were adapted to suit particular circumstances. Pressures on family structure by the economic and social developments of the period of industrialisation varied from one group of workers to another. Working-class family life may have altered during the nineteenth century, but such change varied greatly according to region and employment patterns. Barbara Taylor points out that the emergence of the factory system in some areas resulted in the decline of home-based industry and the subsequent separation of family and home from work, whereas in other areas it was associated with the rise of the outwork system and an expansion of home-based industries employing entire families.[85] The family economy persisted through the nineteenth century and working-class life remained dominated by the harsh realities of earning a living. The home did not become a refuge from the outside world as adherents of the family wage had hoped, but remained, according to David Vincent, 'the arena in which the consequences of exploitation and inequality were experienced and battled with'.[86]

The working-class pursuit of respectability and labour movement demands for a breadwinner wage have been presented here as mechanisms by which working people attempted to protect their position, yet neither was fully realised. The outcome of the efforts to achieve these ideals was an almost complete exclusion of married women from the formal workforce and a segregation of other women into lower-paid and unskilled employment. Many men may have enjoyed better pay and job security following the removal of competitive female labour from their workplace. For much of the nineteenth century, however, the pursuit of the breadwinner ideal may be perceived as a working-class 'own goal' as families were deprived of the earning capacity of their female members long before the family wage approached reality.[87] Notions of working-class respectability did not include a wage-earning wife, yet without such a member, many working-class families would have faced destitution. By the late nineteenth century, men enhanced their masculinity through work in two ways: 'by doing physically demanding and/or difficult tasks, and/or by earning sufficient wages to support a family'.[88] Men had created for themselves a strong work identity, but before the twentieth century this was associated with an incomplete breadwinner wage structure where it was necessary for women to engage in lengthy hours of sweated labour, often within the cramped conditions of the home.[89] In the short term, separate spheres created more disadvantages than benefits for working people, especially for married women who were denied a working identity yet were forced to combined often long hours of home-based labour with greater domestic responsibilities.

Breadwinning and mothering were oppositional constructs both in their ideological representations and in the ways they were organised socially. From the mid nineteenth century, female industrial homeworkers were increasing in number as working-class poverty coincided with the public perception of motherhood and domesticity as women's primary responsibilities. Women who earned wages in this way were unlikely to be visible in the official record. Working-class budgets suggest that only a minority of working-class men were sole family providers.[90] After marriage many women were deterred from wage earning or preferred not to work, yet the family needed their income. The belief that femininity was defined by motherhood and excluded breadwinning, placed working-class women in a contradictory situation, which only homework appeared to reconcile. Homework was not simply an alternative to waged work outside of their homes but became the only option for married women on the breadline. Homework was located at the juncture of 'familial, political, cultural and economic relations', and suited employers' appetite for cheap and flexible labour as well as women's enduring capacity for self-exploitation. For employers, its profitability was dependent on the social contradiction between wage earning and mothering/domesticity, and for women, homeworking was the only way to ensure that their families were fed.[91]

During the period of industrialisation, the working-class family was subjected to a range of pressures that generated changes in its internal organisation and in its interaction with the wider economy. Many of these forces were related to the restructuring of gender roles and gender identities which created separate spheres of activity for men and for women. The actual differences in gender roles, however, were less than the ideologies suggested. The family economy adapted the new ideas in various ways to ensure working-class survival. Married women's opportunities for paid work were declining during the nineteenth century, but they continued to work in the home in activities that did not invade their domestic responsibilities too extensively.

Regional variations in employment patterns influenced the extent to which the working-class family shifted from a family economy to a family wage economy. In some areas, such as the Midlands textile districts, a family economy operated between spheres. In many large towns a symbiosis existed between the factory, the workshop and home-based sweated labour. In areas dominated by 'male' industries, women performed a range of makeshifts, and combined earnings from these activities with domestic chores. Even where men were well paid, irregularity of employment through seasonality and recession meant that supplementary income from other members of the family was essential. The poorer the family, the greater this ancillary portion was likely to be. The contribution of wives and other family members also fluctuated over the course of the family life cycle.[92] Thus for many working-class people the household economy, perhaps in a different guise, continued to function through much of the nineteenth century.

Industrialisation operated to the detriment of many working people.[93] Lives of the working class were protected to some extent from the unfavourable circumstances of industrial society by the particular gendered form that the family adopted. The advocacy of the family wage, the norm of domesticity and the marginalisation of female labour, however, attacked women's identity as workers. Women were thus deprived of choice, families were deprived of much-needed income earners, and the economy was deprived of valuable human capital.

This chapter has suggested that the family provided a site of class and gender struggle. This struggle is explored more fully in the following chapter.

7 Industrialisation and the Gendering of Class

It has been said that industrialisation unsettled class relationships. Industrial change, however, generated crises of gender relationships as well as those of class. During the period of industrialisation, the interests of gender and class sometimes converged and sometimes conflicted. This chapter will explore the responses of working men and women to the economic and social changes introduced by industrialisation, with particular reference to the nature and development of working-class associations. It will show how the construction of gender identities described in the previous chapter formed an important element of the strategy to protect working-class interests. This book has been concerned to emphasise the central role of gender in the process of industrialisation. This chapter places gender centrally in a consideration of the outcomes of that process.

Changes in the organisation and location of work, which took place from the late eighteenth century, challenged the traditional structure of household and artisanal production. As a result of the industrialisation process, industrial labour was forced to relinquish some control over its work. Such alteration in the nature of work was reflected in relationships of class and gender, neither of which was fixed but rather provided sites of 'interdependence, conflict and negotiation'.[1] From an early stage of industrialisation it was clear that the experiences of working men were to be different from those of working women. The process of industrialisation both depended on the undervaluation of women's labour and challenged traditional male crafts through potential deskilling.[2] Industrial change also threatened to undermine the working-class family and its domestic stability. Through the course of the industrialisation process working men and women became increasingly aware of a range of forces by which they were disadvantaged, and they strove together and separately to minimise the extent of their oppression. By means of such struggles, which were most prominent during the 1830s and 1840s, and which aimed to strengthen and protect the interests of the working class, a consciousness of class developed. The same contests also embodied differential gender interests and gave rise to a distinct consciousness of gender. Recent research has emphasised how gender conflict increasingly informed the class struggle, as men felt threatened by female labour in the context of capitalist deskilling. Working women's sensitivity to class exploitation was augmented by increasing oppression in gender terms. Thus the changing relationship between men and women was reflected in their response to developments in the nature of work during the period of industrialisation and beyond. The contradiction between gender consciousness and class consciousness which took shape during the third decade of the nineteenth century, became more pronounced during the second half of that century as sex oppression and class exploitation formed the basis of distinct struggles.[3]

Vigorous attempts to weaken the impact of industrial change on the working and family lives of men and women, were only partially successful. The introduction of productivity-enhancing technology from the later eighteenth century, threatened to devalue the skills and ability of both men and women. Men in particular strove to resist the shift in their position from skilled craft worker to machine operative that technical innovation implied. Women, who were conventionally perceived as less skilled than men, found their status only marginally affected by the deskilling process. They were, however, charged as agents of deskilling by artisans and skilled male workers. Industrialisation also threatened to disturb the domestic security of working people by the foreclosure of women's traditional employment and by the harsh employment conditions of women and children as well as men in the early factories. From the late eighteenth century, factory workers were subjected to long and irregular hours of work for low wages, which devalued domestic life. The process of industrial change, therefore, reduced individual determination of work and home life. Attempts to retrieve some control over these areas of existence motivated the actions of early nineteenth-century working-class movements. Their strategies were also informed by the way in which working people were perceived by other social groups. Middle-class concern for working-class morality, for example, was countered by the working-class construction of a particular brand of respectability. The articulation of middle-class notions of separate spheres was met by a politicised working-class version of domesticity.

The reactions of working people to the varied outcomes of industrial change were increasingly informed by gender. The chronological exploration of such responses which follows will be overlaid with an analysis of gender and class interaction. During the early stages of industrialisation, working men and women reacted in a unified way to challenges to their position.[4] This embryonic class action was founded on and drew strength from an approximate equality of gender. From the early years of the nineteenth century the importance of gender equity to the development of class consciousness began to fade, and probably disappeared with the collapse of Owenism, whose radical ideals had been founded on joint if not always equal participation of the sexes. From the late 1830s, a reversal of the earlier correspondence of gender and class interests became apparent. A rejection of gender equality and a divergence of gender interests seemed to become part of the working-class strategy to resist exploitation. Gender consciousness either became subsumed in class issues[5] or, within feminism, became quite separate from a consciousness of class.

The cleaving of gender identities and interests in the pursuit of class action from the later 1830s can be identified in the rhetoric of Chartism, in the campaigns for factory reform and in the struggle over employment. All these activities were founded on gendered representations of the participants. Differences in gender identities and in gender roles were structured and emphasised within working-class movements in order to achieve benefits for the working class as a whole. As women were marginalised in working-class politics, however, the working-class agenda lost not only a valuable component of its potential support, but also the opportunity to legitimate the different perspectives 'that working class women might have contributed to Victorian political discourse'.[6]

During the early stages of industrialisation, struggles of working people did not yet reveal a highly developed consciousness of class but focused on material concerns, especially food prices and narrow workplace issues. These were not overtly gendered activities but rather reflected the partnership between men and women in ensuring family survival, and their common experiences of work. Actions of working people at this early stage did not represent a shared resistance to the advance of industrialisation but rather indicated continuity with earlier disputes. Typical of these movements was the bread riot, a traditional form of protest that persisted through the age of industrialisation. Men and women joined together spontaneously in local actions against rises in food prices because of their common interest as breadwinners.[7] Some historians have argued that women played a special role in these disputes because of their position as controllers of the household purse.[8] Recent research has shown, however, that during the early stages of industrialisation, women participated equally with men as they had done in pre-industrial actions,[9] but that the breadwinning partnership represented by this shared engagement was to change in a later stage of industrialisation as class and gender interests became differentiated. From the 1830s and 1840s, therefore, women became leaders in food riots in the industrialising regions, but at this point, such protests became less significant as forms of community politics. The trade union movement, in which women played a relatively minor role, took precedence as a political form in industrial towns. At that point, women were 'relegated to the discredited sphere of crowd violence'.[10] The evolution of plebeian politics separate from household and community, corresponded to the gender division of labour that became more pronounced during industrialisation.[11]

Initially, however, industrially motivated protest revealed unity of action between men and women. Research on trade unions confirms that in the early clothing and textile trades, where women played a major role as workers, successful collective action would have been impossible without the knowledge, support and co-operation of women.[12] The first unions in the cotton industry from the 1790s had included female members, and the importance of women's part in industrial grievances and other textile trade union activities was acknowledged.[13] Contemporary newspapers remarked upon the visibility of women who were as likely as men to be arrested and prosecuted for their involvement in strikes and demonstrations.[14] Gender unity was also observed in industrial disputes in the East Midlands hosiery and ribbon industry and in the Loughborough lace trade.[15] The joint struggle of men and women in the clothing industry was evident from the later eighteenth century until the early years of the nineteenth. In the London trades, in particular, men and women went on strike and protest marches together, typically to improve wages and working conditions and their co-ordinated activity often achieved success. Misogyny soon raised its ugly head, however, when deskilling and slop clothing production threatened artisanal superiority and resulted in male strikes specifically attacking the employment of female labour.[16]

Co-operation between the sexes in early industrial disputes, however, did not preclude the formation by women of their own interest groups. It is difficult to estimate the extent of their participation yet it is clear that women protested alone in the small-scale craft industries and in the textile trades.[17] In the late eighteenth and early nineteenth centuries, women were particularly active in establishing all-female friendly or benefit societies, especially in the textile regions. Admittance to these societies required possession of some property and moral respectability and excluded women engaged in unhealthy and dishonourable trades.[18] The Female Reform Society established in 1815, agitated for the fairer representation of women in politics. The particularly active female reformers of Manchester and Blackburn saw themselves as responsible for their families and pressed for the politicisation of domestic issues.[19] The emergence of uniquely female societies reflected women's militancy as well as their undeniable organisational capabilities, but it also suggested the development of a specifically female consciousness. The influence of the contemporary feminist movement was evident in the formation of women's groups, which, however, also indicated the slackening solidarity of male and female workers from the early years of the nineteenth century.

The first decade of the nineteenth century witnessed strikes by men against women workers who were used by employers in a range of trades to introduce new machinery and to replace apprenticed and skilled male workers. Between 1806 and 1810, male hatters, calico printers, tailors and framework knitters all engaged in strike action against women's encroachment on their occupations. The tailors, whose actions through the first half of the nineteenth century mirrored stages in the development of gendered class relations more generally, protested against the threat to male skill and status by the invasion of women into the expanding unskilled sectors of the trade. Other groups of skilled male workers and artisans, namely textile warpers, weavers and cotton spinners, were among those who resisted the introduction of female competition. The objective of their actions was to exclude women completely from their trades.

For a brief period, very early in the nineteenth century, middle-class moralists and political economists opposed efforts to exclude women from gainful employment.[20] In 1804 the Society for Bettering the Condition of the Poor complained that women's traditional trades had been 'grievously and unjustly intruded upon by the other sex' and attributed many women's poverty to constraints on their employment opportunities.[21] Otherwise there was little opposition to men's attacks on female intrusion into their work. Skilled male workers were even assisted by wider community and kinship-based networks in pursuit of their exclusionary strategies. Women emerged as vocal supporters of strikes among handloom weavers in 1808 and 1818. Men gained some female approval by presenting themselves as defenders of women and children and accepting female labour provided it was in auxiliary positions.[22] Exclusion may have constituted an extreme reaction to the competition of female labour and was unlikely to succeed, yet it was pursued vigorously. When industrial action failed to achieve the desired aim, male workers approached Parliament. In 1813, skilled men vociferously opposed the proposed repeal of the Statute of Artificers, which was designed to end the legal requirement of apprenticeship, but it failed as a tactic to bar women and other unskilled workers from artisan and textile occupations.[23]

By 1820, men's exclusivist approach had become more equivocal. It remained the case that artisans wished to exclude women from their own crafts yet they had no desire to restrict them from all waged work. Instead, the trade union movement attempted to strengthen their position through control of the labour supply.[24] Male workers arrived at this approach by recognising the need to find a compromise between masculine solidarity, the material requirements of the family and the reality of women in the workforce. Various ways of achieving this uneasy accommodation were attempted. Tailors and bookbinders, for example, channelled women into non-competitive branches. Other artisans and skilled male workers used women to perform undesirable aspects of the manufacture. Hatters and shoemakers in particular shamelessly exploited women in this way and then squandered the proceeds on manly leisure pursuits.[25]

The potential incompatibility between the needs of the family and the aims of the trade unions can be illustrated by the experience of the tailors. In 1810 and again in 1814, employers had attempted to introduce female labour into their workshops at half the male wage.[26] Such women 'deprived a man of his employment, and of the means of maintaining his family'.[27] The union successfully resisted such efforts and for a short time the wages of men were sustained. The issue was later lost, however, and men were then both 'obliged to work for women's wages'[28] and forced to depend on the earning of wives for family survival. According to Barbara Taylor, 'what was at stake in the feminisation of the declining trades was not only the status of male craftsmanship but also the conventional balance of the domestic relationship'. This reflected a gendering of class development as 'the wage-earning wife, once seen as the norm in every working class household, had become a symptom and symbol of masculine degradation'.[29]

Many of the first male factory cotton spinners were former craftworkers and it appears that they adapted artisanal patterns of hostility to female labour. From the 1790s, well-organised unions aimed to control the supply of labour to the trade in order to maintain wage levels. Attempts by employers to circumvent such action by engaging women as spinners were strongly resisted by the male mule operators, whose initial success in sustaining an effectively male monopoly depended on the support of female and child auxiliary workers. Significantly, female factory workers attributed the poverty of their lives to the actions of employers rather than those of male spinners, and in doing so expressed a solidarity with male co-workers. Such support can be interpreted as a form of class consciousness. Women cotton workers certainly saw themselves playing a role in class politics and were known to behave in an 'insulting' fashion towards their 'well-behaved superiors'.[30] Because the work of women and children was complementary to that of men in the early cotton factories, the two groups were not in competition, yet neither were they equal.[31] Women were subordinate to men both at work and in workplace struggles. The class consciousness that existed, therefore, took a gendered form. The example of the early nineteenth-century cotton spinners suggests an incipient gendering of class activity.

Male textile weavers adopted a different strategy, preferring to maintain wage levels by seeking equal pay for women. In the weaving sector, in contrast to most other trades, women performed the same skilled tasks as men. In eighteenth-century silk weaving, for example, most female weavers worked in their father's or husband's workshop, and their skill was acknowledged to benefit the family enterprise. Towards the end of the century overstocking in the trade led to retrenchment by some male weavers. Anna Clark's research indicates that although attempts were made to exclude women from the better-paid branches, the Spitalfields silk weavers incorporated women from 1802.[32] They successfully lobbied for the Spitalfields Act of 1812, which allowed women to complete regular apprenticeships and to be paid on the same level as journeymen weavers. Such an equality was still apparent in the 1840s, when women wove the finest velvets and jacquard brocades and received the same piece rates as men.[33] Misogyny was equally muted in the early nineteenth-century cotton-weaving sector, where, in Lancashire at least, women were involved in weavers' struggles. Men and women participated together in riots against the power looms that were perceived to threaten the familial textile workers' economy.[34]

In the early period of industrialisation, therefore, the response of skilled male workers to the threat of cheap female labour took several forms. None entirely succeeded in sustaining their status. Neither outright exclusion nor the demand for equal pay seemed destined to protect their position. The strategy of exclusion found little support from employers or the state, and the silk weavers' claim for equal pay was blamed by some for the collapse of the trade in the mid nineteenth century.[35] Because of the failure of exclusionary strategies, activities designed to segregate men and women in the workplace became the preferred alternative approach to male labour market protection during the 1820s. Workplace segregation, which was pursued by a growing number of trade unions, was compatible with the emergent notion of separate spheres. It both facilitated and justified male dominance in the workplace and bolstered working-class respectability.

Gender divisions at work were often mirrored in the labour movement which further privileged men as workers.[36] The Grand General Union of Spinners provides an early example of a sexually segregated trade union within a sector of industry that had been founded on female labour and within which women remained well represented. On the occasion of the formation of this 'national' union, its leader, John Doherty, successfully proposed a resolution to exclude almost all girls and women from the organisation. He simultaneously encouraged women to form their own female societies in line with the pursuit of gender segregation.[37] The spinners' union succeeded in reducing the number of female spinners in the labour market, but male workers remained anxious that women's appeal as cheap labour would continue to threaten their earnings and status. The union thus moved towards an equal pay position not for reasons of equity but rather to prevent women undercutting men's wages. In the early 1830s, following the failure of several strikes and the collapse of the union, Doherty's position, or at least his rhetoric, softened. Somewhat disingenuously he expressed sympathy with women workers, and complained about the 'dastardly strategies of running women against men' and advocated instead 'the natural equality of women: include them in all your schemes of improvement . . . treat them as equals, and you will find them the strongest part of your force'.[38]

The 1830s can be seen as a decade of flux in the construction of class and gender as separate yet complementary forces. The Owenite movement recognised the relevance of gender equality to the radicalism of the working class and initially saw solidarity of the sexes as the way to restrict the relentless march of capitalism.[39] Owenism can be located at the point of transition of women's economic position from one defined at least partly by the world of work and work-oriented relationships to one more clearly directed towards homemaking and dependence. The movement initially drew on traditions of organised militancy among working-class women and explicitly supported gender equality. During the early 1830s working-class supporters of women's rights joined Owenism and influenced its ideology. Feminism was not embraced by all members but it did constitute an important strand of eclectic Owenite socialism. The formation of the Grand National Consolidated Trade Union (GNCTU) represented the apex of Owenite socialist activity. The GNCTU comprised a conglomeration of old and new unions, dominated by London craftsmen with support spreading into the Midlands textile trades, the pottery districts and the craft workshops of Lancashire. The participation of women was explicitly encouraged and many women did join. The Society of Industrious Females, established in 1832, generated lodges of industrious females in all appropriate localities. Although the formation of women's groups suggested a separateness, working-class women within the movement became extensively mobilised in settings that expressed their class interests as well as their consciousness of themselves as an oppressed sex.[40]

Other practices within Owenite socialism[41] seemed to encourage more gender equity than was apparent in society as a whole. The movement insisted on sexually integrated dining tables, for example, while the usual public arrangements either excluded or segregated women. Within the movement, women were encouraged to speak at public meetings and attend lectures and conferences. Such activities were unusual among women in the wider society. Owenism's commitment to gender equality, however, was probably more theoretical than practical and it seems that 'egalitarian principles tugged in one direction while the tightening claims of respectable femininity pulled in another'.[42] There was evidence of masculine domination of the movement despite the joint search for a better life for all working people. Although women were expected to play an equal role in the government of the movement, in fact men held the most important positions. The lack of female leadership and divided attitudes towards women's role, reflected ambiguity in Owenite thinking.[43] Education formed an important component of Owenite activities and both sexes were encouraged to take advantage of opportunities for learning. While men were directed towards cerebral pursuits, however, women were expected to follow courses of instruction that were designed to improve their wifely capabilities.[44] Such inconsistencies were compounded by misogyny within the movement, about which many women complained.[45] Female workers who joined the GNCTU found little support from men, and were encouraged to form single-sex groups to discuss domestic matters. Uncertainty about whether women should identify themselves as workers or whether their ultimate goal should be withdrawal from the workplace to support demands for a family wage, was apparently as common in Owenism as elsewhere in the labour movement at the time.

The establishment of the GNCTU in 1834 coincided with a period of economic depression and industrial unrest. The labour struggles that occurred during this turbulent year indicated the complexity of the relationship between men and women. Gender solidarity was strong within the domestic trades that both employed sexually integrated workforces and had traditions of industrial action involving both sexes. Struggles of the Derby silk workers, framework knitters and handloom weavers illustrate such solidarity.[46] Greater segregation, by contrast, was evident in the trades where mixed unions and traditional working relations were threatened by technology and organisational change. This position was reflected in a growing number of trades. The tension between men and women undermined Owenism's commitment to sexual egalitarianism, and was partly responsible for the movement's ultimate collapse. The experience of the tailors is indicative of the destructive forces generated by the conflicting interests of men and women in the trade. Women were perceived as the cause of deskilling and of other difficulties in the tailoring trade. According to one old tailor, 'masters and sweaters have sought everywhere for such hands as would do the work below regular ones. Hence the wife has been made to compete with the husband. . . . If the man will not reduce the price of his labour to that of the female, why he must remain unemployed.'[47] Gender hostility resulted in numerous protests, the most serious of which occurred in 1834, when 9000 tailors struck for higher wages, for the abolition of piecework and for an end to the female-dominated homework. To guard themselves against charges of misogyny and to raise their level of 'respectability', the tailors declared that, while sympathetic to the tailoresses, 'the terms under which they obtain employment are of a nature too gross for the public ear . . . driven from their proper sphere . . . unfeelingly torn from the maternal duties of a parent'.[48] Such disingenuous remarks which 'set a precedent in the rhetorical war of domesticity',[49] were designed to gain political support for the tailors' strike. The strategy backfired and the strike failed. The GNCTU then withdrew its support for the tailors who in turn departed from the mass union, which collapsed soon afterwards.

Towards the end of the Owenite period, working people had become more conscious of their class position and responsibilities. In order to protect working-class interests, a strategy was developed – influenced by Owenism – in which workers and their families were presented publicly as respectable and moral. Owenite socialist life was founded on self-improvement through teetotalism, education and useful recreational pursuits. While consistent with the contemporary bourgeois exhortation to self-help, the objective of these activities was entirely different. The purpose of the Smilesean philosophy was to encourage acceptance of the existing system, while Owenites sought personal improvement and respectable habits in order to gain the confidence to change the existing social and economic structure.[50] In principle, respectability within Owenism was gender-neutral. In order to achieve political goals, however, this ostensible neutrality was in practice replaced by the 'idea of a domestic . . . private women's sphere, rigidly segregated from the male sphere of work . . . [which] became for the working class, as for the middle class, central to their concept of social respectability'.[51] Respectability, therefore, required the withdrawal of married women and children from the workplace and the construction of women as domestic. Thus a convergence of class interest became associated with a divergence of gender interests.

Later in the 1830s and during the 1840s, class activities and consciousness of class were founded upon distinct gender interests. Working-class struggles during these crucial decades focused on the drive for the franchise and the protection of working conditions. Morality and respectability, which were central to the construction of the working class and to the success of class action, were emphasised through the rhetorical strategies of domesticity and male breadwinning. Working-class respectability, which was often located within the context of the family, was, as the previous chapter showed, defined by specific constructions of femininity and masculinity. Class and gender struggle was conducted in the terrain of the family[52] – in which the home-based morality of women and the breadwinning skills of men played a major role – but also in the arena of employment as gender became more deeply embedded in the structuring of paid work. Trade union activities and industrial disputes became increasingly constructed as masculine fields. Women played an essential role in what became an explicitly male labour movement, but not usually as workers, and certainly not as equal workers. Male leaders of working-class associations and actions defined workers as men and shaped their strategies accordingly. Thus gendered class relations fostered the development of working-class associations that in turn influenced images of gender. Activities designed and organised by men to cope with the political and economic disadvantage created by industrialisation gave rise to new meanings of masculinity and femininity. The essential element in these new meanings was respectability. Male respectability, achieved through work, enhanced men's bargaining position with employers. Female respectability, achieved through domesticity, enhanced less the position of women themselves than that of the working class as a whole in the eyes of the state and the middle class.

Factory reform was one of a range of campaigns of the 1830s and 1840s, which illustrate the importance of gender to the expression of class interests. Class identities and gender differences were constructed in the rhetoric of the campaigns. In the second quarter of the nineteenth century, the 'factory question' became established as part of an agenda for 'managing the consequences of economic and social change'.[53] In the early 1830s, the campaign for the Factory Acts emerged as a mass and diverse movement. Those in favour of restricting the work of women and children formed 'an uneasy and shifting coalition with Tory radicals and sanitary reformers'.[54] The organisational structure of the factory movement privileged men, and its public rhetoric symbolised women as dependants. Men formed committees and exclusively made speeches in which women were addressed, for example, as the 'mothers of innocent children and the bearers of domestic virtue'.[55] Despite the importance of women in factory work and in negotiating their children's employment, women were portrayed as beneficiaries of factory reform rather than as instruments in its pursuit. Men were represented as manly protectors of their families.[56]

In the factory debate of the 1830s, emphasis was placed on the harmful effects of factory work on the morals of children, and the significance of this for the future of society. Contemporary anxiety about child labour took a gendered form as the link between the moral and physical welfare of girls was emphasised. The fitness of girls for future marriage and motherhood became a subject of particular concern.[57] Thus the concept of morality was employed in the construction of women and femininity. The factory movement was also driven by a specific connection between male workers' demands for a shorter working day and moral campaigns for the legislative protection of 'dependent' women and juveniles.[58] All participants in factory reform argued that the work of women and children impoverished the domestic lives of factory workers. Working-class factory reformers gained the support of the governing elites by illustrating the damage inflicted by factory work on working-class family life which could be remedied if the domesticity practised by other social groups were adopted by working-class women.[59]

The factory movement of the 1830s and 1840s supported the ideal of working-class domesticity through which the male breadwinner 'reigned over women and children both at home and in the workplace'.[60] Colin Creighton argues that the evolution of the domestic ideal was not simply a residual product of the marginalisation of women in the paid workforce. The construction of female domesticity was also a response to contemporary perceptions of the pressures on family life wrought by industrialisation. Richard Oastler, for instance, a leading figure in the Ten Hours movement, strongly believed that women's ignorance of domestic skills impaired the quality of life of working-class families. Oastler's immediate concern was to eradicate the exploitation of children within the factory system, yet his desire to enhance the welfare of the working-class family was founded on a commitment to re-establish 'traditional' gender roles, especially female domesticity. 'We want to see woman in her right place . . . on her own hearth-stone', said Oastler, 'making it ready to be comfortable for her industrious husband when he returns to his house to meals, and to his bed at night.'[61] Activists in the factory reform movement stressed the importance of protecting the moral and material well-being of the family from the threats posed by industrialisation, yet suggested doing so at the expense of women's role in the workplace.

Campaigns for factory reform through the 1830s and 1840s, while ostensibly designed to improve conditions of work for all, revealed conflicting gender interests, and ambiguity in the position of women.[62] Women played a low-key role in the factory campaigns of the early 1830s. They took part in demonstrations for shorter hours in both Lancashire and Yorkshire, but overall women's participation in the factory reform movement was motivated primarily by a desire to protect their children.[63] Their engagement as mothers rather than workers was, however, more pronounced in the textile-spinning areas than in the relatively gender-unified weaving districts, where women's perceptions of rights as workers evolved through their employment as power loom operatives.[64] Following the passage of the 1844 Factory Act, which restricted the labour of women to 12 hours, female support for the Ten Hours Bill emerged.[65] A female weaver from Todmorden, Elizabeth, described the Ten Hours movement as 'this arduous and important struggle for the liberty of our sex, and the protection of our children'.[66] In the Lancashire power-weaving districts[67] only those women – young, single and low paid – whose wages would be reduced by the cut in hours, were opposed to the legislation. Those who gave it their backing apparently did so because they hoped that the reduction in working hours would leave them more time to spend with their families, in educational pursuits and above all on domestic chores.[68] Many of the same women were instrumental in successfully resisting the introduction of shift [relay] system which some employers intended to implement in the wake of the 1847 Ten Hours Act as a means of keeping men and machines at work for 12–14 hours daily. Their action, which resulted in the 1850 Act prohibiting the relay system, provides a relatively rare example of the integration of women into the working-class movement as defenders of the rights of workers. In this case, gender issues asserted themselves within class activity. While pursuing their own aims, women came to realise more fully the interest they shared with their male counterparts.[69]

The factory movement represents an early instance of the replacement of egalitarian strategies – which were constrained by sexual tensions within working-class communities – by a gendered rhetoric of domesticity in pursuit of working-class objectives. Initially advancing domesticity as a political instrument to gain Tory radical support for the breadwinner wage and broader political rights, trade unionists turned from factory reform to Chartism, while continuing to apply the rhetoric of domesticity to restrict women workers.[70] The construction of gender identities and the respectability that formed the basis of working-class strategy was largely achieved by means of rhetorical tools. Respectability was not only an important component of the making of class but also comprised a central feature of the construction of gender and the way in which the working class aimed to enhance its social and political position. As the ideology of respectability strengthened its hold on working-class political discourse, so the difference between men and women in class activity became more pronounced.

The Chartist movement, which grew out of the agitation for factory reform, illustrates the way in which the working class capitalised on the politicisation of respectability.[71] The rise of Chartism coincided with, but was largely unrelated to, the decline of Owenism, and signified the emergence of distinct struggles in response to class exploitation and sex oppression. In the early stages of Chartist activity, radicals rallied workers to demand the 'People's Charter', which incorporated a range of political reforms. In 1837–8, large numbers of Chartists – both women and men – drew on their experience of community mobilisation to riot for their rights. Such an inclusive vision of class was short-lived, however, as women in the movement became perceived as auxiliaries to their husbands. Within the Chartist movement, the replacement of egalitarianism by domesticity served as a rhetorical instrument, not only to convince the middle class of working-class respectability but also to defend working-class morality, to stress sexual differences and to assert masculinity within an economic system that appeared to challenge male control over women.

Although the focus of the movement was provided by working-class male interests, many women were nevertheless involved in Chartism and organised themselves into over 170 associations in England and Scotland. By collecting signatures for petitions, participating in strikes and exclusive dealing, and by organising tea parties and processions for the whole family, women showed their enthusiasm for the movement in its early years.[72] Most Chartist men, however, treated women as merely supportive and belittled their political intelligence. Men controlled women's own meetings, for example, by inviting visiting male speakers to pontificate at length. Some women accepted their non-political support role, but others failed to be persuaded that constructions of domesticity and the family were in their interest. Instead, they fashioned for themselves a political identity as mothers, workers and activists that differed both from the middle-class ideal of domesticity and from the male Chartist notion of women's homemaking role.[73]

As Chartism matured, through the 1840s, its use of domestic rhetoric generated ambiguity in women's place and ultimately structured the movement as masculine.[74] This meant not only that manliness became a prerequisite for public political activity, but also that the languages of class were constructed with reference to sexual difference. Within Chartism, class was offered as a universal category even though it depended on a masculine construction, which placed women and children in dependent positions.[75] Any remaining egalitarianism was submerged as the movement's dependence on women's activism conflicted with their depiction as helpless creatures in need of male protection. Chartist men claimed, for example, that they required the vote in order to protect their wives and children from the dangers of the factory.[76] The demand for female suffrage, however, was considered to be politically untenable, and fringe members making reference to women's enfranchisement were ridiculed.[77]

In Chartists' speeches, women's interests as workers were ignored as the 'manly' conduct of trade union men was commended. Male Chartists began to call for the exclusion of women from the workforce by means of factory and 'protective' legislation.[78] They encouraged activists within the factory reform movement to shift from a position where men and women were united on the demand for a reduction of hours of child labour, to one that promoted the exclusion of women from the workplace. Chartists associated such an exclusionary objective with their own demand for political representation, which in turn they linked to a masculine monopoly of occupations and the right of men to enjoy women's domestic services. 'I see no reason', wrote Robert Blakey, 'why working men, whose labour creates every necessary and luxury of life, should be denied the pleasures and comforts of home.'[79] Such sentiments underlay the representation of the family and of domesticity as a political resource for the benefit of the whole working class. Although some Chartists had criticised married women's factory work on the grounds of the hardship it involved for women themselves, other advocates of exclusion emphasised the distress inflicted by working married women on their husbands whose relaxation was disturbed by the noise of washing and cooking. Joseph Corbett's mother apparently sat up 'nearly all night for several nights together washing and mending of clothes'. Rather than interpreting this as the gross overwork of his mother, Corbett concluded that 'my father could have no comfort here . . . and sought refuge in an alehouse'.[80]

Chartist men gladly accepted political and economic leadership as a male monopoly, and prohibited women from attending their meetings. Undeterred, many women found their own way to express political opinion, but the spectacle of rioting women, which horrified middle-class observers, served to strengthen the men's case for 'respectable' political and industrial action as their own preserve. By the middle of the 1840s, Chartism had further formalised its structure, which discouraged the participation of women who then retreated into domesticity.[81] Chartism can be represented as a movement which attempted to create class consciousness by drawing initially on traditions of sexual co-operation, but which ultimately failed because of the incompatibility of egalitarian ideals and the growing distinction of gender identities. Class consciousness then became founded on distinct gender identities, but this inevitably weakened the movement. Chartism lost its mass base in the 1850s. Thereafter socialism began a period of sexual retrenchment as men organised for their own political rights.

By the 1840s, Chartism and the factory reform movement had convinced industrialists and the state of the need to regulate the work of women and children. Factory reform can be identified as the negotiated collusion of organised male workers, employers and the state to marginalise women and to construct a domestic notion of femininity. The complexity of class and gender issues which was revealed in the background to factory regulation can also be identified in the debate surrounding the 1842 Mines Act.[82] This Act was supported by an unspecified number of miners and some employers, but was not the result of the type of campaign with which factory reform was associated. Its impetus came largely from the state.[83] Jane Humphries has argued persuasively that working miners' support for the legislation can be understood neither in terms of fear of female competition, as the work that female miners performed was complementary to men's, nor because of loss of authority within the family, because this was not threatened. It was the nature of the work that women performed and the implications of moral and sexual impropriety, to which some male miners and shocked politicians apparently objected.[84] Such gender-specific protective legislation divided women, as well as causing a rift between men and women when it became a subject of debate in the 1840s and again in the 1880s.[85]

Opposition to the Act emanated both from the affected owners, who begrudged the loss of a willing supply of cheap labour, and from many colliers in the same areas for whom, because of the practice of family hiring, a reduction in family income would follow women's removal from the mine.[86] The exclusion of women in these circumstances, therefore, especially where alternative female employment was restricted, would materially disadvantage whole families and communities. A year after the passage of the Act, C. Cumming Bruce tabled a motion in the House of Commons for a relaxation of the rule banning women. He described the hardship that arose from female exclusion in some districts and presented petitions signed by hundreds of men and women.[87] Although women's voices are mainly unheard in the debate surrounding the 1842 Act, their resistance to it, through evasion and by the signing of petitions, suggests that mining women to some extent disapproved of the measure. Women gladly accepted employment at the pit surface offered in place of the prohibited underground work and clung on to it tenaciously when their work was threatened in the 1880s. Male miners, many of whom had not supported the 1842 Act, nevertheless sought gains for themselves in its aftermath. A Miners' Union was formed immediately and began to press for higher wages in order that their wives could be kept 'at home to look after their families'.[88]

By the mid nineteenth century a narrower vision of class had been established, and in pursuit of political status, men invoked domesticity and the protection of the working-class family. The interests of the working class as a whole may have been served by this explicitly gendered approach, but it did so by disempowering women and reducing their choice. Even where men and women struggled together for better pay and conditions, women were less than equal. Women's disadvantage appears to have been compounded as the new industrial society developed.[89] From 1850, working-class activity in general and trade union struggles in particular increasingly revolved around the construction of masculinity. It was therefore difficult for women to integrate into trade union structures and to protect their own status as workers. The problems faced by women in trade unions during the second half of the nineteenth century can be illustrated by their experience in the textile workers' union in the Lancashire cotton trade.

The struggles in the cotton industry during the early 1850s marked a revival of general class conflict. The major strikes of this period involved the power loom weavers, and while women participated in these because of their interests as workers, they rarely played leadership roles. The rhetoric that placed men at the centre and women at the margin of the working class can be seen in the Preston strike of 1853–4, which was precipitated by the dismissal of two women discovered collecting subscriptions for those already on strike in Stockport. Although women were to be found to be speaking at public meetings 'with all the energy . . . and loquacity of their male coadjutors',[90] the unnatural frequency of women's public speaking was juxtaposed with the more conventional content of their utterances. During the dispute, women were heard advocating a family wage for men and urging their married sisters to remain out of the labour force.[91] A leading female orator, Margaret Fletcher, lamented what she considered to be a reversal of the natural order of things which forced a woman to leave her home and family and go to work while her husband remained at home. She also made a plea for a male breadwinner wage.[92] In the major strikes that occurred in 1858–61, women's participation was again apparent and was vital to the survival of weavers' associations.[93] The value of their support notwithstanding, women weavers, as other female textile and industrial workers, were nevertheless placed in a marginal position as workers.

The way in which a gendered workforce was reflected in gendered trade union activity can be seen even more clearly in the 1878 Blackburn weavers' strike. Sonya Rose's analysis illustrates the masculine basis of industrial action in a trade in which gender differences were apparently small. A superficial inspection of the records of the strike indicates that women took an active part in the general meetings of workers and served on strike committees.[94] By adopting an approach that analyses language and rituals to understand the interaction of gender and class, Rose interprets the subtleties of the differential activities of men and women in the strike.[95] She examined a variety of data, including written texts and spoken words, to explore such elements of gender difference that were not explicitly commented upon because they were taken for granted.[96] Rose argues that gender was implicit in the struggle between employers and workers in the nineteenth century and workers' solidarity was often diffused by gender politics.

During the 1878 strike male trade union leaders used a language of respectable masculinity and dissent to bargain for a breadwinner wage and to subtly marginalise female co-workers. In the Blackburn cotton industry, weaving was performed by women and men on apparently equivalent terms,[97] yet both the union leaders and the principal orators at the strike were all men. As strike leaders attempted to generate solidarity, they expressed their vision of orderly industrial relations in the 'language of respectable manhood', and employed images of respectful family relationships. Rose's analysis of speeches made during the strike reveals that while relatively inclusive language was used by the male speakers, women were constructed at best as minor actors and at worst as an inconvenience for the union. The words of the men left no doubt that it was unusual and not respectable for women to speak in public. At a strike meeting attended by women and men, the chair asked, 'is there any gentleman in the body of the hall, or a lady either for all that, if they think proper, who wishes to make any remarks in support of this resolution or otherwise?'[98]

Because of their marginalisation in the Blackburn strike, women sought alternative forms of expression. Because women were not welcomed on to the platform to speak, for example, they engaged in disorderly heckling from the floor. Because they were excluded from the strike's decision-making processes, women sought outlets to their frustrations through street disturbances. 'Large, flinty stones were hurled through windows', stated a startled press, ' . . . and it is not a little remarkable that women took a prominent part in the rioting.' Those whose actions fell outside of the construction of 'respectable manhood and peaceful conduct', were accused of undermining the 'solidarity' of the union and of the strike. In the aftermath of the street disturbances, a placard was erected, inscribed with the words 'every factory worker who conducts himself peacefully, proves himself a man! Every factory worker who conducts himself in any other way, injures his own cause and degrades his own class.'[99] Responsibility for the ultimate failure of the strike, however, more likely rested with the strike leaders, whose refusal to embrace gender equality, and whose misplaced insistence on the masculinity of respectable protest destroyed unified action. The strike ended amid acrimony between the union leadership and the rank and file. 'The gendered style of contention practised by the trade union leaders', argues Rose, 'disregarded the actual heterogeneity of working men and women in north Lancashire whose lives were structured by the intersections of age, gender and ethnicity.'[100]

Further evidence that the differential construction of femininity and masculinity became widely accepted beyond middle-class ideology and beyond manufacturing industry, can be found in a recent study of nineteenth-century agriculture.[101] Women's farm work, which was wide-ranging, repetitive and laborious, attracted the same kind of critical middle-class attention in the mid nineteenth century as female factory employment had done a little earlier. Female dairy workers and women employed in haymaking were not seen as a problem, but women farm labourers were presented as unsexed and immoral. Milkmaids were represented as feminine English roses, and harvest workers or gleaners were accepted because of the communal nature of their work. Field women, however, were always 'tainted with a customary immorality, and heedless of the fatal results which their love of this busy and independent life is bringing on their unfortunate offspring who are pining at home'.[102] Official reports of the later nineteenth century argued strongly that they challenged dominant definitions of femininity. The language and behaviour of field workers were 'coarse, rough even to strangers . . . some of the big girls and young women returning from work were strangely bold in look and manner'. Women of the fields, therefore, possessed 'dirty and degraded habits . . . slovenly and slatternly households [and] the alienation of husbands by the discomfort of their homes'.[103]

Male farm workers, through the all-male National Agricultural Labourers Union, exploited the power of such middle-class condemnation in order to put pressure on women – who were believed to be responsible for undermining men's wages and security of employment – to leave field work.[104] The union, formed in 1872, adopted the approach that women should not work in agriculture as it took them away from their homes and children, depressed men's wages and reduced the number of male jobs. As femininity was threatened by farm work, 'dung spreading and such like work unsexes a woman', so was masculinity. If women stayed at home, their husbands could start 'living and acting like men'.[105] Although there were regional variations, recent research reveals that women farm workers only rarely contested the dominant definitions of femininity as passive domestic and apolitical through strike action.[106]

Through the period of industrialisation and beyond, the work identity of women, especially married women, was constantly under threat. Even in the textile industry where women's position was more nearly equal than in any other manufacturing sector, their subordination within the workplace, the trade union structure and in industrial action was reflected in a variety of ways. Joanna Bornat's exploration of the West Riding textile trades reveals a high level of female union membership and strike activity, yet she finds that women were poorly represented in policy making and other leadership positions in the unions.[107] Jan Lambertz's work on sexual harassment in the later nineteenth-century cotton industry also suggests an underlying inequality despite superficial appearances to the contrary. Her study indicates that it was rare for unions to fight cases of abuse of women by men, and that female exploitation was not taken seriously.[108]

The gendering of work and union activity which was central to the working-class strategy of self-protection but which rested on the subordination of women was, through the nineteenth century, confirmed by a range of ideological constructions. These included the perception of industrial action as masculine, the identification of respectable industrial protest with manliness, and the association of female protest with undesirable forms of worker resistance. On a practical level, the issues raised by trade unions in the wake of industrialisation reinforced the gendering of identities through the family wage, the marriage bar and protective legislation, and as a result women were discouraged from union participation.

This chapter has shown how the response of working people to the challenges imposed by industrialisation created a gendered working class. Gender and class constituted dynamic and interacting structures during the nineteenth century, sometimes conflicting and at other times corresponding. Gender influenced the working class, but the precise mechanism of this influence remains unclear. Initially, working-class consciousness was based on a vision of equality and community in the family as well as in the workplace. By the second half of the nineteenth century, the emergence of working-class consciousness in which politics was reserved for men, identified women unequivocally with the home.[109] The chapter has shown that class had a masculine identity even when not all the actors were male.[110] The formulation of class consciousness in a masculine frame took place over several decades and passed through a number of distinct phases. The sexual crisis of the early stage of industrialisation, when male artisans feared female competition, was replaced – through Owenism – by a radical move to class and gender equality. This, in turn, was rejected in the late 1830s and 1840s when the masculinisation of trade unionism and working-class political activity took hold. The process became more intense after 1850 as the maleness of industrial protest was confirmed and as men's ambivalence to women both in the workplace and in industrial protest became more overt. Although the issues pursued by the trade unions can be said to have served the interests of the working class, they appeared to have benefited men at the expense of women whose worker identity was undermined as a result. Ultimately, the subordination of women and the adoption of middle-class values of respectability were the costs of the partial empowerment and social integration of working-class men.[111]

8 Conclusion. A Gendered Industrial Society

By the late nineteenth century, English society was defined by both industry and gender. The process of industrialisation and the responses to it had created a gendered industrial society. Industrialisation can be seen as a social and cultural process through which gender issues and relationships were contested and negotiated. It is true that gender divisions at work and in the home were not new to the period of industrialisation. It is also the case that the construction of gender identities which placed emphasis on man's role as worker and woman's primary concern with domestic activities was not peculiar to the nineteenth century, even though the meaning and purpose attached to such definitions may have become more specific during this period. The marginal position of women in economic, social and political activity was broadly continuous from the fifteenth century. The traditional basis of the gender hierarchy was, however, undermined by changes in the organisation of production and work introduced during the course of industrialisation. The nature of industrial change created an opportunity for the realignment of gender relationships. The introduction of new industries, and innovation in older trades and processes, permitted a novel deployment of labour. In principle, it was possible, for example, for men and women to be perceived as equivalent labour units, or even that they be employed according to individual merit rather than socially determined aptitudes and talents. In practice this never happened.

This book has analysed the process of industrialisation and the making of industrial society through the lens of gender. The gendering of work and the relationship between gender, the organisation of production, and ways of working, have been essential areas of exploration. The first part of the book pursued the theme that gender, especially the gender of labour, was important in determining the nature of manufacturing and of industrial change. In other words, it interpreted industrialisation as a gender-made

138

process. The theme of the second part of the book, especially Chapters 6 and 7, was that industrialisation was also a process that 'made' gender. Specific notions of masculinity and femininity were constructed during the course of industrialisation which have served as the basis of gender identities since then.

Before the onset of industrialisation, gender inequalities existed in work and at home. Although some historians have noted a lessening of the differences between working men and women during the eighteenth century, especially in the context of the protoindustrial family economy, evidence for this is insufficient. Male and female activities were complementary and there may have been some co-operation between the sexes in the production process, yet work in the pre- and protoindustrial period was divided along gender lines. Before industrialisation, women were more likely than men to be generalists in their work, to engage in several occupations within a short period of time, and to work flexibly. The priority of both men and women during the pre-industrial period was family survival, yet women more than men took ultimate responsibility for closing the gap between subsistence and destitution. It was typically women who sat up at night to complete orders and who, often with small children in tow, scavenged the neighbouring commons for berries and firewood. The experience of poverty also distinguished the sexes. Eighteenth-century records indicate that women were more likely to be poor and in receipt of poor relief, mainly because of the absence – through death or desertion – of a male partner. By the late eighteenth century, the poverty of women met with the profound disapproval of those who earlier in the century had praised their industriousness.

During the eighteenth century, some changes occurred in the way in which women were perceived, which typically emphasised their domestic responsibilities and underplayed their working role. At the same time, incongruously, early industrial development made a special use of female labour. Women's flexibility, diligence, patience and cheapness, were well recognised during the pre-industrial period, and these attributes were key determinants in the making of the early industrial labour force. It was believed that women adapted well to novelty in manufacturing methods and in conditions of work. It was women, therefore, who provided the labour for many of the first factories and on whom early textile technologies were tested. Men and women shared in the expansion of manufacturing industry, yet their contributions were quite different. Initially, female labour was crucial to the development of the new and high productivity industries especially cotton spinning, while men's association with traditional, lower value-added trades continued. This differentiation was temporary, however, and although women remained important in factory textile production, female labour became more significant for its encouragement of hand and intermediate techniques and the continuation of old-established ways of working.

Manufacturing practices varied according to region and industry, and an important feature of industrialisation to which the gender of labour was relevant, was the range of scale, location and organisation of production forms that remained efficient. Economies of scale are assumed to have emanated from the large, centralised factory, yet such forms of organisation were neither commonplace nor were they necessarily more cost effective than small-scale manufacturing units making intensive use of cheap female and child labour. Furthermore, large units of production failed to offer the flexibility of production appropriate to the erratic requirements of the new consumer markets, nor were they well suited to the vagaries of the trade cycle. Units of production using variable quantities of female labour met many of the needs of early manufacturing. Women were valuable to English industrialisation, but they were at best undervalued and at worst shamefully exploited. Male labour was by no means immune to low pay and unemployment, but was generally less poorly treated than female labour. Men and women workers were used in quite different ways during industrialisation and beyond.

Such differentiation was neither automatically achieved nor did it reflect a simple continuity with the pre-industrial structure. The rigid gender division of work that was sustained by the process of industrialisation, was the result of contests and negotiations that were conducted in different regions and industries through much of the nineteenth century. Men and women had been distinguished as workers before industrialisation, but there was no intrinsic reason why such distinctions should continue. Because industrialisation was a novel process, it introduced the potential for social and economic relationships to be reshaped. Such a possibility posed a challenge to men's pre-existing superiority. Male workers, through their trade unions and often with the tacit or explicit support of the state and paternalistic employers, negotiated a continuation of their position of strength. The dissenting, or even the supportive voice of women was largely unheard. The outcome of most – but not all – individual industry struggles over the allocation of work, was a hierarchy of labour in which women were located in the lower skilled positions. Men continued to be perceived as more skilled and more capable as industrial workers. Gender then became deeply embedded in the structuring of employment, in the use of machines and in the condition of work to the extent that industrialisation could be seen to have developed as a gendered set of practices.

The recording of women's employment through the period of industrialisation was inconsistent and partial. No information was collected officially before the nineteenth century, and the census of occupations, first taken reasonably systematically in 1841, adopted a measure of work that excluded much that female labour performed. Nevertheless, sources exist that allow the variegated picture of women's employment to emerge. The official view that women were employed overwhelmingly in domestic service, dress and textile production, has been replaced recently by one that recognises additional categories especially in agriculture and in the informal economy. In the industrial as in the pre-industrial period, many women, especially those who were married with dependent children and/or husbands, engaged in several intertwining occupations. In the eighteenth century, women without secure employment exploited the resources that the common land had to offer, grew kitchen crops and reared small animals. In the nineteenth century, women, especially those who were married and without formal employment, accommodated lodgers, took in washing and made food for sale. For many working women, industrialisation did little to reduce the sheer drudgery of their lives.

In the early years of industrialisation, the ways in which people lived and worked and related to one another were unstable. Relationships between employers and workers were negotiated and renegotiated during the Industrial Revolution. Equally, relations between men and women in the workplace and in the home, which had been disturbed in the course of industrial change, were potentially open to restructuring. The workplace and the home became physically more distinct in the context of industrial developments. Although the functional separation of domestic and manufacturing activity was not as complete as conventionally assumed,[1] gendered positions in each context were formulated with reference to the other. Within the working-class family, changes occurred in the roles of its members. The newly created functions implied a hierarchy in which men became the main or, occasionally sole income earners and assumed positions of authority, and where women performed supportive, mainly domestic roles. Gender constructions were not necessarily hierarchical, however, and it has been suggested in this book that particular definitions of masculinity and femininity were used to serve the interest of the working class by protecting the material situation of its family. This does not mean that definitions of masculinity and femininity were uncontested. Gender identities were constructed by a range of processes during the course of nineteenth-century industrial developments, and they were, like the related constructions of gender divisions at home and in the workplace, targets of struggle. The combined outcome of such struggles was a gendered workplace and a gendered home which appeared to be complementary and mutually reinforcing.

During the period of industrialisation, the working-class family changed as the restructuring of gender roles and gender identities created separate spheres of activity for men and for women. In practice, however, the differences in gender positions were less pronounced than the ideologies suggested. The distinct breadwinning function for men and the domestic role for women were inappropriate for many working-class families. The tensions created by these unrealistic expectations can be seen in the persistence of domestic violence – which female domesticity had promised to reduce – and in the employment of married women. Although their opportunities for paid work were declining during the nineteenth century, and despite the working-class acceptance of the norm of domesticity, it was necessary for most married women to earn some income. Typically, they did this by working in the home in activities that did not prevent the fulfilment of domestic obligations.

For much of the nineteenth century, many working people continued to operate within a household economy redolent of the pre-industrial period. Nevertheless the idea of different gender roles and specific constructions of masculinity and femininity were promoted by the working class to enhance their status of respectability and to further class objectives. The construction of gender, therefore, was used in the making of class.

This book has argued that during the period of industrialisation, the interests of gender and class sometimes converged and some-times conflicted. Through the nineteenth century, working people struggled against the unfavourable conditions imposed on them by industrialisation. Disputes were particularly prominent during the 1830s and 1840s, when a shift took place in the relationship between gender and class. At the beginning of this period, a consciousness of class was influenced by ideas of gender equity. By the end of the 1840s, the distinct interests of men and women formed the basis of working-class action. The divergence of gender identities in the fur-therance of class interests was particularly visible in later Chartism, and in struggles over employment conditions, in which working-class men saw the interests of their class, and incidentally their own, to be best served by adhering to a notion of respectability based on dis-tinct notions of masculinity and femininity. Class identities and gender differences were constructed in the rhetoric of political cam-paigns and labour movements. The language of respectable manhood became fundamental to public political action, as a narrow, male, vision of class replaced egalitarianism. Women's role in the masculine political project became at best peripheral and at worst a nuisance. The contradiction between gender consciousness and class consciousness became more pronounced during the second half of the nineteenth century as sex oppression and class exploitation formed the basis of distinct struggles. A gendered work-force, a gendered home and a gendered labour market were there-fore contested outcomes of industrialisation. Industrialisation was not only a gendered process, but gender was located at the centre of the outcomes of industrial change.

Industrialisation may have threatened the 'natural order of things' but by the later nineteenth century this had been created, re-created and restored through political struggle. The extent to which gender divisions were deeply embedded in late nineteenth-century English industrial society can be seen by the persistent gendering of work through the period of renewed restructuring in the economy. Between 1870 and 1914 two broad changes took place in economic activity. The first was the result of the emergence and expansion of new industries, and the relative, but limited decline in the traditional trades during the 'second industrial revolution'. The second was the expansion of the service sector, which was an inevitable outcome of the maturation of the English economy. The implications of these quite major changes were different for women and for men, but they did little to upset the hierarchical gendering of the labour market, or to undermine the ideology of domesticity which largely excluded married women from the formal economy.

The industries that emerged towards the end of the nineteenth century, which included electrical engineering, automobile and bicycle production, pharmaceuticals and the manufacture of soap and chocolate, offered few employment opportunities to women. Evidence of late nineteenth-century female unemployment indicates that there was a huge shortfall of work available for women willing to enter the labour market.[2] High levels of unemployment among young women and very low levels of participation among married women, reflected both the existence of a gendered industrial society in which married women played a limited public role, and the shortage of paid work available to women for structural reasons. Research by Ellen Jordan shows that unemployment among women increased through the period of industrialisation because of the nature of the gender division of work, which gave a higher proportion of tasks to men, and because women were confined to a narrow range of trades for which the labour market was overstocked. In the late nineteenth century, therefore, structural changes in industry further disadvantaged women.

The growth of the service sector, by contrast, appeared to generate new jobs for women losing out through changes in the manufacturing sector. The revolution in retailing, for example, which led to the growth of high street chain shops and department stores, absorbed large numbers of young, single women as shop assistants who might previously have found employment in domestic service. Of most significance, however, was the expansion of clerical work. Not only did office work proliferate in the 30 years before the outbreak of the First World War, but it became dominated by women. Before the late nineteenth century, clerical work was located mainly in law and accountancy firms, and was considered a male occupation. As the sector expanded, women performed more of the work, especially that of a routine nature. On the surface, the 'white blouse revolution' symbolised the positive nature of the proliferation of office employment available to women from the 1880s, but closer inspection reveals two features of clerical work that disadvantaged women.

In the first place, a gendered hierarchy of labour was created which ensured that women continued to operate in the less skilled and lower-paid grades of work. This was supported by the way in which the typewriter, initially gender-neutral, became feminised upon its association with shorthand. By the early years of the twentieth century, shorthand typists earned no more than domestic servants or employees in a low-paid manufacturing activity. Female subordination in the clerical sector was designed to protect male workers in the same way that the gendering of work in manufacturing in the earlier nineteenth century had done. According to Ellen Jordan's investigation of 'lady clerks' at the Prudential insurance company, vertical segregation by sex was introduced by the management to preserve the male career ladder in the face of a vast expansion of routine office work.[3] The second area of disadvantage within the clerical sector was the introduction of a 'marriage bar' whereby women were expected to resign their jobs on marriage. Such a requirement not only prevented married women from gaining employment, but it also ensured that all work defined as 'female' would be constructed as temporary and without career prospects. Low status clerical work performed by women, with little chance of promotion, implied that the male career path was to be preserved at the expense of women. The continuity with the earlier nineteenth-century experience is striking. Jane Lewis argues that the nature and conditions of women's clerical work should be considered as part of the construction of masculinity and femininity. As before, male employers and workers had firm ideas about women's proper place as wives and mothers.[4]

The opening of a new sector of employment, therefore, did nothing to undermine the construction of women as essentially domestic, and whose association with the workplace was merely transitory. For much of the nineteenth century, such a construction had been embodied in domestic service in which employment began to decline as girls and young women took positions as clerks and shop assistants. There may have been a change in employment structure, therefore, but there was continuity in the way in which women were perceived.[5]

The nature of girls' training and employment in the later nineteenth century provides evidence that the subordination of women in the labour market and the specific gendering of work established during industrialisation was set to continue. In the county of Lancashire, where gender inequality at work especially in the textile trades was probably less pronounced than in other English regions, and where female participation was higher than elsewhere, girls were paid a much lower wage than boys in the later nineteenth century and had less opportunity for career advancement.[6] Outside of the textile towns, girls who worked were restricted to a small number of occupations, including domestic service and dressmaking, which were recognised as 'women's work'. The majority of girls, but few boys, undertook unpaid, invisible work within their family homes, which was considered to be suitable training in household skills for later life.[7] Girls were less likely than boys to receive training in industrial skills, and were more commonly found working in unregulated environments. Later in the nineteenth century, therefore, the expectation that a girl's place would be in the home and not in the workplace was prevalent.[8] There was little sign that the next generation of women would enjoy a more equal experience of work than their mothers.

The rewriting of the past in terms of the 'preoccupations of the present' is apparent in the recent reinterpretations of industrialisation presented in this book. In the last decade, gender has become central to analyses of social and cultural change. In the same period, industrialisation has become identified as a key instance of such social and cultural change. The understanding of the past has been enhanced by exploring the way in which men and women interacted with one another in social, political and economic contexts. Gender history, and women's history, have succeeded in breaking out of their original position as subdisciplinary specialisms. The positioning of women, and men, and gender relations, within the mainstream of historical thought has begun to challenge conventional views. Traditional periodisations in historical scholarship have not yet been replaced by specifically gendered alternatives. Yet gender history offers – at the very least – novel perspectives on conventional chronologies. This has been particularly successful in the case of interpretations of industrialisation. Until recently, the Industrial Revolution was viewed as an economic process. Its cultural and social dimensions are now becoming more sharply drawn as an explicitly gendered analysis of the industrialisation process has been achieved.

Gender was important to the making of industrialisation. Equally, industrialisation was important to the making of gender. Historians have learned more about the process of industrialisation and the construction of gender by examining their interaction. This book has attempted to show how an understanding of industrialisation and the emergence of industrial society have been enriched by developments within gender and feminist history. Analyses of the nature of industrialisation and the main strands of women's history and gender history have increasingly converged. This book has reflected the two main strands in the historiography, namely that women's specific activities played a key role in industrialisation, and that industrialisation was a gendered process with gendered outcomes. It has shown how every aspect of the history of industrialisation has a gendered component, each of which was vital to the operation of the whole process. A gendered society may not have been unprecedented, but each element of the new industrial society was negotiated from a novel starting point. The outcome, which was not inevitable, was at some cost to the long-term position of women and to long-term economic and social progress.

Notes

1 Feminist History and the Historiography of the Industrial Revolution

1. David Cannadine, 'The Present and the Past in the English Industrial Revolution 1880–1980', *Past and Present*, 103 (1984), p. 131, citing the view of many historians from B. Croce onwards.

2. Quoted in Sally Alexander, *Becoming a Woman and Other Essays in 19th and 20th Century Feminist History* (London, Virago, 1994), p. 276.

3. Alexander, *Becoming a Woman*, pp. 366–7.

4. See, for example, the debate between Bridget Hill and Judith Bennett. Bridget Hill, 'Women's History: a Study in Change, Continuity or Standing Still?', *Women's History Review*, 2 (1993) pp. 5–22; Judith M. Bennett, 'Women's History: a Study in Continuity and Change', *Women's History Review*, 2 (1993), pp. 173–84.

5. Alexander, *Becoming a Woman*, p. 272.

6. Judith M. Bennett, 'Feminism and History', *Gender and History*, 1 (1989), p. 254.

7. Elizabeth Fox-Genovese, 'Placing Women's History in History', *New Left Review*, 133 (1982) p. 6.

8. Fox-Genovese, 'Placing Women's History', p. 15.

9. For example, Judith M. Bennett, *Women in the Medieval English Countryside. Gender and Household in Brigstock before the Plague* (Oxford, OUP, 1987); Susan Cahn, *Industry of Devotion. The Transformation of Women's Work in England 1500–1660* (New York, Columbia UP, 1987); Mary Prior (ed.), *Women in English Society 1500–1800* (London, Methuen, 1985).

10. Joan W. Scott, 'Women in History: the Modern Period', *Past and Present*, 101 (1983), p. 152.

11. Barbara Taylor, *Eve and the New Jerusalem. Socialism and Feminism in the Nineteenth Century* (London, Virago, 1983); and Gareth Stedman Jones, 'Rethinking Chartism' in Gareth Stedman Jones, *Languages of Class: Studies in English Working Class History, 1832–1982* (Cambridge, CUP, 1983), pp. 90–178 are excellent examples of this approach.

12. Scott, 'Women in History', p. 155.

13. Marilyn Boxer and Jean Quataert (eds), *Connecting Spheres. Women in the Western World, 1500 to the Present* (Oxford, OUP, 1987), p. 13.

14. Catherine Hall, *White, Male and Middle Class. Explorations in Feminism and History* (Cambridge, Polity, 1992), p. 7.

15. Bennett, 'Feminism and History', p. 259.

16. Bennett, 'Feminism and History', pp. 266–7 and 'Continuity and Change' which restates her support for the historical understanding of oppression through patriarchy.

17. Hall, *White, Male*, p. 12.

18. Hall, *White, Male*, pp. 1–2.

19. Gisela Bock, 'Women's History and Gender History: Aspects of an International Debate', *Gender and History*, 1 (1989), p. 19.

20. Joan Scott, *Gender and the Politics of History* (New York, Columbia UP, 1988), p. 6.

21. Scott, *Gender*, p. 10.

22. Hannah Barker and Elaine Chalus (eds), *Gender in Eighteenth Century England. Roles, Representations and Responsibilities* (London, Longman, 1997), p. 5.

23. Jean Gardiner, *Gender, Care and Economics* (Basingstoke, Macmillan, 1997), p. 123.

24. Although Scott is clearly an exponent, one of her staunchest critics has pointed out that she has not yet produced a researched scholarly work based on her own or on modified post-structural theories. Joan Hoff, 'Gender as a Post-modern Category of Paralysis', *Women's History Review*, 3 (1994), p. 27. Gisela Bock has also seemingly embraced the new way at least partly because of her belief that by such means the marginalisation of women's history could be terminated.

25. Hoff, 'Gender as a Post-modern Category', p. 150.

26. June Purvis, 'Women's History and Post-structuralism', *Women's History Review*, 5, 1 (1996), p. 6. In Hoff's view, therefore, post-structuralism is regressive and forms part of the backlash against both radical and mainstream feminism, Hoff, p. 154.

27. Catherine Hall, 'Politics, Post-structuralism and Feminist History', *Gender and History*, 3 (1991), p. 209. Michel Foucault is one of a group of French post-structuralists which also includes Jacques Derrida and Jacques Lacan, whose impact on the methodology has been huge.

28. Barker and Chalus, *Gender*, p. 7.

29. Pamela Sharpe, 'Continuity and Change: Women's History and Economic History in Britain', *Economic History Review*, 48, 2 (1995), p. 353.

30. Jane Humphries, 'Mainstreaming Women's History', unpublished contribution to 'Towards a New History of Industrialisation in Britain' at the annual conference of the Economic History Society, University of Nottingham, 8–10 April 1994.

31. Ibid.

32. Pat Hudson, 'Introduction', unpublished contribution to 'Towards a New History of Industrialisation in Britain' at the annual conference of the Economic History Society, University of Nottingham, 8–10 April 1994.

33. Research on women and work has probably progressed furthest among both historians and social scientists.

34. Maxine Berg and Pat Hudson, 'Rehabilitating the Industrial Revolution', *Economic History Review*, 45 (1992), pp. 24–50. Relevant individual work includes Maxine Berg, 'What Difference did Women's Work Make to the Industrial Revolution?', *History Workshop Journal*, 35 (1993), pp. 22–44. Pat Hudson, *The Industrial Revolution* (London, Edward Arnold, 1992).

35. See Sara Horrell and Jane Humphries, 'Women's Labour Force Participation and the Transition to the Male-breadwinner Family, 1790–1865', *Economic History Review*, 48 (1995), pp. 89–117.

36. Jan de Vries, 'Between Purchasing Power and the World of Goods', in Pamela Sharpe (ed.), *Women's Work. The English Experience 1650–1914* (London, Arnold, 1998), pp. 214–31.
37. Sharpe, 'Continuity', p. 353.
38. Sharpe, 'Continuity', p. 354.
39. Robert Gray, *The Factory Question and Industrial England, 1830–1860* (Cambridge, CUP, 1996), p. 1.
40. Maxine Berg, 'Women's Work, Mechanisation and the Early Phases of Industrialisation in England', in Patrick Joyce (ed.), *The Historical Meanings of Work* (Cambridge, CUP, 1987), p. 96.
41. Jordan Goodman and Katrina Honeyman, *Gainful Pursuits. The Making of Industrial Europe 1600–1914* (London, Edward Arnold, 1988), pp. 76 and 206.
42. Goodman and Honeyman, *Gainful Pursuits*, pp. 205 and 209.
43. Berg and Hudson, 'Rehabilitating', p. 31.
44. Raphael Samuel, 'The Workshop of the World', *History Workshop Journal*, 3 (1977), p. 28.
45. Samuel, 'Workshop', pp. 33–5.
46. Kristine Bruland, 'The Transformation of Work in European Industrialisation', in Peter Mathias and John Davis (eds), *The First Industrial Revolutions* (Oxford, Basil Blackwell, 1990), p. 158.
47. Berg and Hudson, 'Rehabilitating', p. 44.
48. Robert B. Shoemaker, *Gender in English Society, 1650–1850. The Emergence of Separate Spheres?* (London, Longman, 1998), p. 169.
49. Berg, 'Women's Work', pp. 95–6.
50. Goodman and Honeyman, *Gainful Pursuits*, pp. 112–14.
51. This aspect is explored in James A. Schmiechen, *Sweated Industries and Sweated Labour. The London Clothing Trades* (Urbana, University of Illinois, 1984). See also Goodman and Honeyman, *Gainful Pursuits*, pp. 104 and 111.
52. Hudson, *Industrial Revolution*, p. 226.
53. Goodman and Honeyman, *Gainful Pursuits*, p. 115.
54. Gray, *Factory Question*, p. 23.
55. John Smail, 'Manufacturer or Artisan? The Relationship between Economic and Cultural Change in the Early Stages of the Eighteenth Century Industrialisation', *Journal of Social History*, 25 (1991–2), p. 791.
56. It was also crucial to the long-term lack of progress. In Britain as in many other countries, employers failed to make full use of the skills of women and failed to invest in the development of those skills. This ultimately disadvantaged both individual enterprises and the performance of the overall economy.
57. See especially Ivy Pinchbeck, *Women Workers and the Industrial Revolution 1750–1850* (London, Routledge, 1930) [reprinted 1969].

2 Gender and Work before Industrialisation

1. See Maxine Berg, *A Woman in History. Eileen Power 1889-1940* (Cambridge, CUP, 1996), which focuses on the life and work of Eileen Power but vividly portrays the influence of other women on the development of economic history during the inter-war years.

2.   At least one of the pioneers, however, expressed dissatisfaction with the progress made by these later generations. Certainly, there was a lag of some 30 years before any significant follow-up work appeared. See Ivy Pinchbeck's preface to the 1969 edition of her *Women Workers in the Industrial Revolution 1750–1850* (London, Routledge, 1930).

3.   A view to which the notion of protoindustrialisation has provided some conceptual rigour.

4.   Olwen Hufton, 'Women in History: Early Modern Europe', *Past and Present*, 101 (1983), p. 26.

5.   This is exemplified in the debate between Bridget Hill and Judith Bennett, which also raises substantial historiographical and methodological issues. Bridget Hill, 'Women's History: a Study in Change, Continuity and Standing Still?', *Women's History Review*, 2 (1993), pp. 5–22; Judith M. Bennett, 'Women's History: a Study in Continuity and Change', *Women's History Review*, 2 (1993), pp. 173–84.

6.   Mary Prior (ed.), *Women in English Society 1500–1800* (London, Methuen, 1985), p. 96 shows not only how women held everything together, but that it was 'important to good order that this was never recognised'. This underlines women's relatively low status.

7.   Merry E. Weisner, *Women and Gender in Early Modern Europe* (Cambridge, CUP, 1993), p. 83.

8.   Alice Clark, *Working Life of Women in the Seventeenth Century* (New York, Dutton, 1919) [reprinted London, Routledge and Kegan Paul, 1982], *passim*. Berg, *A Woman* describes the context within which the book was written.

9.   Clark, *Working Life*, p. 9 .

10.   Clark, *Working Life*, pp. 292–4.

11.   Joan Thirsk, 'Foreword' to Prior (ed.), *Women in English Society*, pp. 9–12. Clark, however, failed to consider the position of women who did not belong to a family.

12.   Dorothy George, *London Life in the Eighteenth Century* (London, Kegan Paul, Trench, Trubner, 1925), p. 172, quoted in Robert B. Shoemaker, *Gender in English Society, 1650–1850. The Emergence of Separate Spheres?* (London, Longman, 1998). p. 179.

13.   Maxine Berg, 'Women's Work, Mechanisation and the Early Phases of Industrialisation in England' in Patrick Joyce (ed.), *The Historical Meanings of Work* (Cambridge, CUP, 1987), pp. 66–7.

14.   Thirsk, 'Foreword', p. 7.

15.   Such a distribution closely resembled that suggested by the census for the same area in the mid nineteenth century. Peter Earle, 'The Female Labour Market in London in the Late Seventeenth and Early Eighteenth Century', *Economic History Review*, 42 (1989), pp. 339–44.

16.   The work of both Peter Earle and Merry Weisner confirms that women were forced to seize opportunities wherever they could, and that they did. See Earle, 'The Female Labour Market' and Weisner, *Women and Gender*.

17.   Chris Middleton, 'Women's Labour and the Transition to Pre-industrial Capitalism', in Lindsey Charles and Lorna Duffin (eds), *Women and Work in Pre-industrial England* (London, Croom Helm, 1985), pp. 182–3.

18. Middleton, 'Women's Labour', p. 184.
19. Ibid.
20. Maxine Berg, 'Markets, Trade and European Manufacture' in Maxine Berg (ed.), *Markets and Manufacture in Early Industrial Europe* (London, Routledge, 1991), pp. 4–5.
21. Jordan Goodman and Katrina Honeyman, *Gainful Pursuits. The Making of Industrial Europe 1600–1914* (London, Edward Arnold, 1988), p. 77. See also Peter Kriedte, Hans Medick and Jurgen Schlumbohm, *Industrialisation before Industrialisation* (Cambridge, CUP, 1981).
22. Shani D'Cruze, 'Care, Diligence and "Usfull Pride" [*sic*]: Gender, Industrialisation and the Domestic Economy, c.1770–c.1840', *Women's History Review*, 3 (1994), p. 1 citing Tilly and Scott, and Medick.
23. Hans Medick, 'The Proto-industrial Family Economy' in Kriedte *et al.*, *Industrialisation*, p. 61.
24. Medick, 'The Proto-industrial Family', p. 62. This emphasis on gender equality implies a protoindustrial golden age.
25. R. A. Houston and K. Snell, 'Protoindustrialisation, Cottage Industry, Social Change and the Industrial Revolution', *Historical Journal*, 27 (1984), p. 487.
26. Pat Hudson, *The Industrial Revolution* (London, Edward Arnold, 1992), p. 227.
27. Berg, 'Women's Work', p. 68.
28. Berg, 'Women's Work', p. 76.
29. Hudson, *Industrial Revolution*, p. 227. There is much evidence, therefore, to suggest that during this period, the association of women's industrial work with low wages was cemented, as Pinchbeck and others suggested several decades ago.
30. Hudson, *Industrial Revolution*, p. 228.
31. Louise A. Tilly and Joan W. Scott, *Women, Work and Family* (New York, Holt, Rinehart and Winston, 1978), e.g. p. 45; Goodman and Honeyman, *Gainful Pursuits*, pp. 113–14.
32. Hannah Barker and Elaine Chalus (eds), *Gender in Eighteenth Century England. Roles, Representations and Responsibilities* (London, Longman 1997), p. 12.
33. They were subordinated in other ways also as reflected in evidence of wife-beating. See Margaret Hunt, 'Wife-beating, Domesticity and Women's Independence in Eighteenth-century London', *Gender and History*, 4 (1992), pp. 10–33.
34. Judith M. Bennett, 'Medieval Women, Modern Women: across the Great Divide' in David Ares (ed.), *Culture and History 1350-1600: Essays on English Communities, Identities and Writing*, (London, Harvester Wheatsheaf, 1992), p. 153 citing the words of L. F. Salzman.
35. Bridget Hill, *Women, Work, and Sexual Politics in Eighteenth Century England* (Oxford, Basil Blackwell, 1989), p. 45.
36. Elizabeth C. Sanderson, *Women and Work in Eighteenth Century Edinburgh* (Basingstoke, Macmillan, 1996), p. 168.
37. Women were prominent protesters against rising food prices. Deborah Valenze, *The First Industrial Woman* (Oxford, OUP, 1995), pp. 115–16.

38.   John Bohstedt, 'Gender, Household and Community Politics: Women in English Riots 1790–1810', *Past and Present*, 120 (1988), pp. 92–3.

39.   Bohstedt, 'Gender, Household', p. 97. In what might be perceived as a transitional period, rioting was a dominant mode of collective popular politics, which focused on the welfare of local communities and the defence of the family economy. Women participated in them along with all other family members.

40.   Valenze, *The First*, p. 3.

41.   Valenze, *The First*, p. 17.

42.   Valenze, *The First*, pp. 14 and 25.

43.   Valenze, *The First*, p. 8.

44.   Valenze, *The First*, p. 159. This may have been less true in the northern counties. A preliminary investigation of late eighteenth-century apprentice-ship records in the Halifax area reveals less restricted opportunities for girls.

45.   Deborah Simonton, 'Apprenticeship: Training and Gender in Eighteenth-century England', in Berg, *Markets and Manufacture*, p. 237.

46.   Simonton, 'Apprenticeship', p. 230.

47.   Hill, *Women, Work*, p. 101. This was also the case in the early nine-teenth century. See Mary Rose, *The Gregs of Quarry Bank Mill. The Rise and Decline of a Family Firm, 1750–1914* (Cambridge, CUP, 1986), pp. 30–1; and Michael Winstanley (ed.), *Working Children in Nineteenth-century Lancashire* (Preston, Lancashire County Books, 1995), p. 28.

48.   Simonton, 'Apprenticeship', p. 245.

49.   Peter Rushton, 'The Matter in Variance: Adolescents and Domestic Conflict in the Pre-industrial Economy of Northeast England, 1600–1800', *Journal of Social History*, 25 (1991–2), p. 97. He also finds a similar per-centage in Wetherby in 1776. The discrepancies can be partly attributed to regional variations in occupational structure.

50.   Simonton, 'Apprenticeship', p. 250.

51.   Simonton, 'Apprenticeship', p. 245. She also shows that girls were apprenticed on the same conditions as brothers.

52.   Simonton, 'Apprenticeship', p. 254.

53.   Hill, *Women, Work*, p. 102.

54.   Simonton, 'Apprenticeship', p. 255.

55.   This was at least partly because of the 1777 tax on servants. See John Chartres, 'English Landed Society and the Servants Tax of 1777' in Negley Harte and Roland Quinault (eds), *Land and Society in Britain, 1700–1914. Essays in Honour of F. M. L. Thompson* (Manchester, Manchester UP, 1996), pp. 34–56.

56.   Valenze, *The First*, p. 158.

57.   D. A. Kent, 'Ubiquitous but Invisible. Female Domestic Servants in Mid-eighteenth Century London', *History Workshop Journal*, 8 (1989), *passim*. Male servants were better paid and more likely to enjoy a career path.

58.   The training of the children of the poor as servants was the main objective of much eighteenth-century philanthropy. Hill, *Women, Work*, pp. 100 and 128.

59.   Hill, *Women, Work*, p. 173. See also Bridget Hill, *Servants. English Domestics in the Eighteenth Century* (Oxford, Clarendon, 1996), *passim*.

60.   Valenze, *The First*, p. 45. See also Jane Humphries, 'Enclosures, Common Rights and Women: the Proletarianisation of Families in the Late Eighteenth and Early Nineteenth Centuries', *Journal of Economic History*, 50 (1990), *passim*. The loss of common rights affected women more than men because it had provided them with the opportunity for productive work.

61.   Valenze, *The First*, p. 45.

62.   The scientific revolution of the seventeenth and eighteenth centuries appeared to provide medical explanations for the male/female dichotomy. Women were represented as irrational, backward and limited by their physical bodies, while men were considered to be rational, civilised and enhanced by their physical bodies. The physical qualities of men, namely strength and intelligence, only gave them capabilities. In the contemporary conduct books, female virtues were primarily concerned with qualities associated with emotion. Men had the larger share of reason. Shoemaker, *Gender*, Ch. 2, especially pp. 18–21.

63.   Valenze, *The First*, pp. 49, 54–9 and 67. There is evidence of a similar process taking place 150 years later in Sweden. See Lena Sommestad, 'Creating Gender: Technology and Femininity in the Swedish Dairy Industry', in Gertjan de Groot and Marlou Shrover (eds), *Women Workers and Technological Change in Europe in the Nineteenth and Twentieth Centuries* (London, Taylor & Francis, 1995), pp. 151–69.

64.   Valenze, *The First*, pp. 16–20.

65.   Richard Connors, 'Poor Women, the Parish and the Politics of Poverty' in Barker and Chalus, *Gender*, pp. 127–8.

66.   Connors, 'Poor Women', p. 136.

67.   Connors, 'Poor Women', pp. 137–41.

68.   D'Cruze, 'Care', *passim*, reveals how the domestic economy of the working class remained one of expedient through the nineteenth century and beyond. It also reveals how women were central in the organisation of the web of community credit. This feature is also identified by Elizabeth Sanderson. Sanderson also emphasises the shared experiences of men or women in work and life. Sanderson, *Women and Work*, p. 168.

69.   Hill, *Women, Work*, p. 259.

70.   Valenze, *The First*, p. 182.

71.   Valenze, *The First*, p. 42.

72.   Valenze, *The First*, p. 129.

73.   Especially spinning, knitting, garment making and buttonmaking. Valenze, *The First*, p. 130.

74.   Adam Smith, *Wealth of Nations*, Vol. 1, cited in Valenze, *The First*, p. 131.

75.   Cited in Valenze, *The First*, p. 23.

76.   Malthus was influential in this change of attitude.

77.   Especially through persistent reproduction in the context of poverty.

78.   Valenze, *The First*, pp. 136–9. The separate spheres ideology, which it has been argued, became a central theme in the making of middle-class consciousness, was clearly not new to the nineteenth century. Amanda Vickery has argued that 'separate spheres' could be applied to almost any century and almost any culture. See Amanda Vickery, 'Golden Age to

Separate Spheres? A Review of the Categories and Chronologies of English Women's History', *Historical Journal*, 36 (1993), p. 400.

79. Valenze, *The First*, pp. 129 and 140.

80. Barker and Chalus, *Gender*, p. 24.

81. Bennett, 'Medieval Women, Modern Women', pp. 162–4. See also Bennett, 'Women's History', pp. 173–84.

82. Some historians argue that change and the reason for change are what history is all about, while others argue that continuity also requires explanation. This methodological distinction also forms part of the difference between the positions of Bennett and Hill. See Bennett, 'Women's History' and Hill, 'Standing Still?'

83. For Bennett such an explanation rests on patriarchy, while Hill is more interested in economic issues.

84. Vickery, 'Golden Age', p. 413.

85. Such factual elusiveness is compatible with the continuity position of Judith Bennett who acknowledges that economic factors may have shifted over time, but suggests that they did so within the framework of patriarchy. Barker and Chalus, *Gender*, p. 15.

86. Judith M. Bennett, 'Feminism and History', *Gender and History*, 1 (1989), p. 262.

3   Women and the Making of Industrialisation

1. In order to achieve more output, equivalent increments to inputs, especially of labour were necessary.

2. The policing of the manufacturing process was a particular problem, as embezzlement became common. See for example, John Styles, 'Embezzlement, Industry and the Law in England 1500–1800' in Maxine Berg, Pat Hudson and Michael Sonenscher (eds), *Manufacture in Town and Country before the Factory* (Cambridge, CUP, 1983), pp. 179–211.

3. The work of Nicholas Crafts suggests that during this phase, agriculture not only became more efficient but achieved higher productivity than manufacturing. See N. F. R. Crafts, *The British Economy in the Eighteenth Century* (Oxford, Clarendon, 1985), p. 84.

4. Pat Hudson, *The Industrial Revolution* (London, Edward Arnold, 1992), p. 101.

5. Pamela Sharpe, *Adapting to Capitalism. Working Women in the English Economy, 1700–1850* (Basingstoke, Macmillan, 1996), p. 38.

6. During industrialisation labour was skilled, unskilled and semi-skilled. Labour embodied traditional skills and new ones. It worked in factories, workshops and homes. It worked according to a regular time discipline imposed by the demands of the factory system. It also worked irregularly according to the seasonal demands of the market. Labour was employed on a full-time or on a part-time basis. It worked at one occupation or at several.

7. Ivy Pinchbeck, *Women Workers and the Industrial Revolution 1750–1850* (London, Routledge, 1930) [reprinted 1969], *passim*.

8. These positions are expanded by Eric Richards, 'Women in the British Economy since about 1700; an Interpretation', *History*, 59 (1974), pp. 342–3.

9.   Richards, 'Women in the British Economy', pp. 338 and 343.

10.   Richards, 'Women in the British Economy', p. 338. He explains this in terms of the contemporary occupational framework, which favoured female labour during the eighteenth century and again from the early twentieth century. In the intervening period, Richards suggests, the range of opportunities for women was very limited and served to create a reserve army of labour. .

11.   Whatever the merits of such work, the generalisations produced are inappropriate not only because of the very sketchy evidence, but also because our limited knowledge suggests that women, as well as men, were subject to heterogeneous experiences. The approach that encourages general conclusions, therefore, underplays the diversity of experience based on region, class and life cycle. Hudson, *Industrial Revolution*, p. 231. Janet Thomas suggests that the resolution of a pessimist/optimist debate is intractable, for theoretical rather than empirical reasons. See Janet Thomas, 'Women and Capitalism: Oppression or Emancipation? A Review Article', *Comparative Studies in Society and History*, 30 (1988), pp. 545–7.

12.   Deborah Valenze, *The First Industrial Woman* (Oxford, OUP, 1995), *passim*, especially pp. 29–47.

13.   Pinchbeck, *Women Workers*, p. 63.

14.   Mechanisation was assumed to have been associated with large-scale centralised production and that together they pursued a linear path towards more efficient and progressive forms as they replaced traditional and less efficient forms. It was further assumed that while not all manufacturing industries and processes were transformed by technological and organisational changes they eventually would be. The existence of traditional methods of production was interpreted as a sign of incomplete transformation.

15.   Maxine Berg and Pat Hudson, 'Rehabilitating the Industrial Revolution', *Economic History Review*, 45 (1992), pp. 32–5.

16.   Berg and Hudson, 'Rehabilitating', p. 34. See also Maxine Berg, 'What Difference did Women's Work Make to the Industrial Revolution?', *History Workshop Journal*, 35 (1993), pp. 22–44 .

17.   Such gains were more difficult to measure than those associated with more conventional notions of technology.

18.   Maxine Berg, 'Technological and Organisational Change during the Industrial Revolution; New Questions', unpublished contribution to 'Towards a New History of Industrialisation in Britain' at the annual conference of the Economic History Society, University of Nottingham, 8–10 April 1994.

19.   Maxine Berg, *The Age of Manufactures: Industry, Innovation and Work in Britain 1700–1820* (London, Fontana, 1985), p. 82.

20.   Berg, *Age of Manufactures*, pp. 85–6.

21.   As handloom weavers' wages fell, many families became dependent on women and children to work in factories, though John Lyons has suggested that the availability of factory work for some family members alongside domestic industry made the decline of handloom weaving much more protracted. J. S. Lyons, 'Family Response to Economic Decline: Handloom

Weavers in Early Nineteenth Century Lancashire', *Research in Economic History*, 12 (1989), cited in Hudson, *Industrial Revolution*, p. 120.
22.　Hudson, *Industrial Revolution*, pp. 120–1.
23.　See Katrina Honeyman, *Origins of Enterprise. Business Leadership in the Industrial Revolution* (Manchester, Manchester UP, 1982), for more discussion on this point.
24.　Hudson, *Industrial Revolution*, pp. 115–20.
25.　Maxine Berg, 'Women's Work, Mechanisation and the Early Phases of Industrialisation in England' in Patrick Joyce (ed.), *The Historical Meanings of Work* (Cambridge, CUP, 1987), p. 70.
26.　Judy Lown, *Women and Industrialisation. Gender at Work in Nineteenth Century England* (Cambridge, Polity, 1990), p. 18.
27.　This was a particular feature of the Coventry silk ribbon trade. See Jordan Goodman and Katrina Honeyman, *Gainful Pursuits. The Making of Industrial Europe 1600–1914* (London, Edward Arnold, 1988), pp. 130–1.
28.　Berg, *Age of Manufactures*, p. 84.
29.　Maxine Berg, 'Factories, Workshops and Industrial Organisation' in R. Floud and D. N. McCloskey (eds), *The Economic History of Britain since 1700*, second edition (Cambridge, CUP, 1994), Vol. 1, p. 150. See pp. 123–50 for more detail.
30.　Generated by the demand for uniforms during the Napoleonic Wars. See Beverly Lemire, *Dress, Culture and Commerce. The English Clothing Trade before the Factory, 1660–1800* (London, Macmillan, 1997), pp. 9–41.
31.　Sharpe, *Adapting to Capitalism*, pp. 67–8.
32.　See Katrina Honeyman, 'Gender Divisions and Industrial Divide: the Case of the Leeds Clothing Industry 1850–1970', *Textile History*, 28 (1997), pp. 47–66.
33.　James A. Schmiechen, *Sweated Industries and Sweated Labour. The London Clothing Trades* (Urbana, University of Illinois, 1984), *passim*.
34.　C. Sabel and J. Zeitlin, 'Historical Alternatives to Mass Production', *Past and Present*, 108 (1985), pp. 133–76. Maxine Berg, 'Small Producer Capitalism in Eighteenth-century England', *Business History*, 35 (1993), pp. 17–39.
35.　Hudson, *Industrial Revolution*, pp. 123–4.
36.　Sharpe, *Adapting to Capitalism*, pp. 59–67.
37.　It is also possible that cheap labour may have retarded labour-saving innovation and more rapid technical development.
38.　Berg, 'Women's Work, Mechanisation', p. 71.
39.　The specific economic, social and cultural conditions of the Industrial Revolution which required large quantities of female labour, apparently ceased to exist from the mid nineteenth century.
40.　Crafts, *British Economic Growth*, p. 22. Women's contribution to the high productivity sector was located mainly in cotton spinning, but not only in centralised production units. The division and specialisation of labour and the intensification of work were also instrumental. When traditional women's industries declined, women shifted into new industries, domestic service or unemployment. New industries would locate where female unemployment existed so their traditionally cheap labour could be obtained even more cheaply. See Berg, 'What Difference?' especially pp. 29–31.

41. Hudson, *Industrial Revolution*, p. 164.

42. For example, the free labour of women in the household, combined with women's own low wages in the workforce, kept male wages lower and profits higher.

43. Berg, 'Women's Work, Mechanisation', p. 65; Hudson, *Industrial Revolution*, p. 226.

44. Maxine Berg, 'Women's Work and the Industrial Revolution', *Refresh*, 12 (1991), pp. 1–4.

45. Pinchbeck, *Women Workers*, p. 100.

46. The 1844 Factory Commissioner quoted in Robert B. Shoemaker, *Gender in English Society, 1650–1850. The Emergence of Separate Spheres?* (London, Longman, 1998), p. 167.

47. Manchester muslin manufacturer, quoted in cotton weavers' petitions 1808.

48. Cited in Anna Clark, *The Struggle for the Breeches. Gender and the Making of the British Working Class* (Berkeley, University of California Press, 1995), p. 126.

49. Pinchbeck, *Women Workers*, p. 252.

50. Quoted in Pinchbeck, *Women Workers*, p. 252.

51. Pinchbeck, *Women Workers*, p. 264. In discussions surrounding the 1842 Mines and Collieries Act, it was suggested that the removal of women would lead to improvements in working conditions.

52. Shoemaker, *Gender in English Society*, p. 200.

53. Hudson, *Industrial Revolution*, p. 163.

54. Sharpe, *Adapting to Capitalism*, pp. 149–50.

55. Information from household budgets is supplemented by data from a range of other contemporary documents. Sara Horrell and Jane Humphries, 'Old Questions, New Data, and Alternative Perspectives: Families' Living Standards in the Industrial Revolution', *Journal of Economic History*, 52 (1992), pp. 867 and 873; and Sara Horrell and Jane Humphries, 'Women's Labour Force Participation and the Transition to the Male Breadwinner Family, 1790–1865', *Economic History Review*, 48 (1995), pp. 101 and 105.

56. Married women in particular helped to make ends meet by taking in washing or childminding, often on a shared neighbourhood or community basis.

57. Pinchbeck, *Women Workers*, p. 20.

58. Pinchbeck, *Women Workers*, p. 21.

59. Pinchbeck, *Women Workers*, p. 22.

60. Development economists, however, have engaged in techniques that generated production estimates for largely subsistence economies. Humphries suggests that economic historians could adapt such techniques in order to assess the value of women's activities, a large proportion of which were outside the formal market economy.

61. Pinchbeck, *Women Workers*, p. 22.

62. Leigh Shaw-Taylor, 'The Hammond–Neeson Thesis Revisited', paper presented to the Economic History Society Conference, Leeds, 1998.

63. Pinckbeck, *Women Workers*, p. 2.

64. Sharpe, *Adapting to Capitalism*, p. 82.
65. Pinchbeck, *Women Workers*, p. 22.
66. Cited in Sharpe, *Adapting to Capitalism*, p. 82.
67. Deborah Simonton, *A History of European Women's Work 1700 to the Present* (New York, Routledge, 1998), p. 22.
68. Jan de Vries, cited by Pat Hudson, 'Introduction', unpublished contribution to 'Towards a New History of Industrialisation in Britain' at the annual conference of the Economic History Society at the University of Nottingham, 8–10 April 1994. Money wages constituted only part of total earnings of working-class families.
69. Hudson, *Industrial Revolution*, p. 178. See also Beverly Lemire, 'Consumerism in Pre-industrial and Early Industrial England: the Trade in Secondhand Clothes', *Journal of British Studies*, 27 (1988), pp. 1–24.
70. Hudson, *Industrial Revolution*, p. 176.
71. Neil McKendrick, 'Home Demand and Economic Growth: a New View of the Role of Women and Children in the Industrial Revolution' in Neil McKendrick (ed.), *Historical Perspectives: Studies in English Thought and Society* (London, Europa, 1974), p. 187.
72. McKendrick, 'Home Demand', p. 199.
73. McKendrick, 'Home Demand', pp. 201–2.
74. McKendrick, 'Home Demand', p. 209.
75. Berg, 'Women's Work', pp. 95–6.
76. Hudson, *Industrial Revolution*, pp. 163–4.
77. Berg and Hudson, 'Rehabilitating', pp. 35–6.
78. Ibid.

4 Industrialisation and the Making of Gender at Work

1. Samuel Smiles, *Self Help* (1856) is a classic work invoking such a view.
2. Sonya O. Rose, *Limited Livelihoods. Gender and Class in Nineteenth Century England* (London, Routledge, 1992), p. 18 and *passim*.
3. Anna Clark, *The Struggle for the Breeches. Gender and the Making of the British Working Class* (Berkeley, University of California Press, 1995), p. 265.
4. Though a hierarchy of labour could operate to provide stability for the capitalist system.
5. Even unskilled men were superior to women.
6. Sylvia Walby, *Patriarchy at Work. Patriarchal and Capitalist Relations in Employment* (Cambridge, Polity, 1986), p. 69.
7. Textile weaving can be identified as one of the few occupations in which men and women shared a working environment, and even a skill.
8. This is apparent in Judy Lown's study of Courtauld's silk factory, for example. See Judy Lown, *Women and Industrialisation. Gender at Work in Nineteenth Century England* (Cambridge, Polity, 1990), especially pp. 95–135. As will be discussed further in Chapter 6, the marriage bar can be identified as one of a range of gendered employment practices which took for granted ideas about gender difference and which were linked to an ideology of family life. Rose, *Limited Livelihoods*, p. 8.
9. Deborah Valenze, *The First Industrial Woman* (Oxford, OUP, 1995), p. 129.

10. Malthus and others believed that the labouring classes should accord the male worker a central position. Valenze, *The First*, pp. 137–8 and 141.

11. Valenze, *The First*, p. 9.

12. Valenze, *The First*, p. 11.

13. Valenze, *The First*, pp. 89, 91–4 and 109.

14. This labour occupied a distinct hierarchical position within the labour force. Women's work tended to be routine with little scope for mobility. Lown, *Women and Industrialisation*, p. 49.

15. Lown, *Women and Industrialisation*, pp. 105–8. Such a gendered pattern of rewards and punishment was found in other industries as late as the early twentieth century. See for example, Katrina Honeyman, *Well Suited. A History of the Leeds Clothing Industry, 1850–1990* (Oxford, OUP, 2000). This issue will be discussed further in Chapter 6.

16. Sylvia Walby, 'Patriarchal Structures: the Case of Unemployment' in Eva Garmarnikow *et al.* (eds), *Gender, Class and Work* (Aldershot, Gower, 1983), p. 151.

17. Joyce Burnette, 'An Investigation of the Female–Male Wage Gap during the Industrial Revolution in Britain', *Economic History Review*, 50 (1997), p. 260.

18. Burnette accepts that this was not a biological trait but was rather a type of human capital that women acquired in the long hours spent in such household tasks as spinning, sewing and knitting. See 'An Investigation', pp. 262–5, 268 and 272–3.

19. Burnette, 'An Investigation', pp. 273–5.

20. Jane Humphries, ' " . . . The Most Free From Objection . . . ". The Sexual Division of Labour and Women's Work in Nineteenth Century England', *Journal of Economic History*, 50 (1987), pp. 947–8.

21. Clark, *The Struggle*, pp. 2 and 61–2.

22. This contrasts with the hierarchical differences between men and women in the eighteenth century, when women were seen as 'flawed' versions of men rather than totally different. Clark, *The Struggle*, p. 2.

23. Clark, *The Struggle*, p. 3.

24. According to Cynthia Cockburn, 'machinery offered men as a sex opportunities that were not open to women'. See Cynthia Cockburn, 'Technology, Production and Power' in Gill Kirkup and Lauries Smith Keller (eds), *Inventing Women. Science, Technology and Gender* (Cambridge, Polity, in association with the Open University, 1992), p. 202. The appropriation of technical skill, however, played an important part in the reproduction of inequality among men as well as between men and women. Judy Wajcman, *Feminism Confronts Technology* (Cambridge, Polity, 1991), p. 39.

25. Cockburn, 'Technology, Production', p. 208.

26. Gertjan de Groot and Marlou Shrover, *Women Workers and Technological Change in Europe in the Nineteenth and Twentieth Centuries* (London, Taylor & Francis, 1995), p. 2.

27. De Groot and Shrover, *Women Workers*, p. 12.

28. Clark, *The Struggle*, pp. 120–4.

29. Clark, *The Sruggle*, p. 24.

30. In the 1780s, apparently, a female jenny spinner could earn as much as a male weaver.

31. Clark, *The Struggle*, p. 19.

32. More recent writers have questioned this assumption. Catherine Hall, for example, is critical of the circularity of the arguments that men develop the strength that they do because of the kind of work that they do. Women were encouraged to develop their manual dexterity because it was seen as a feminine attribute. Catherine Hall, 'The Home Turned Upside Down? The Working Class Family in Cotton Textiles 1780–1850' in Elizabeth Whitelegg (ed.), *The Changing Experience of Women* (Oxford, Martin Robertson in association with the Open University, 1982), pp. 17–29.

33. Hall, 'The Home', pp. 21–2.

34. Many of these spinners attempted to maintain features of artisanal status as they shifted into factory employment. They were among the first textile workers to adopt the family wage ideal, for example.

35. Deirdre Busfield, 'Job Definitions and Inequality: the 'Unskilled' Women Workers of the West Riding Textile Industry, 1850–1914', *Textile History*, 19 (1988), p. 72.

36. Tine Bruland, 'Industrial Conflict as a Source of Technical Innovation', *Economy and Society*, 11 (1992), p. 100.

37. Busfield, 'Job Definitions', p. 72.

38. Bruland, 'Industrial conflict', pp. 101–2.

39. Evidence of Richard Roberts to the House of Lords Select Committee of 1851, quoted in Wajcman, *Feminism Confronts Technology*, p. 44.

40. Upon its foundation, the union stipulated that '. . . no person . . . be learned or allowed to spin except the son, brother or orphan nephew of the spinners'.

41. For socially constructed reasons, women were automatically excluded from any position that required supervision of or authority over men.

42. William Lazonick, 'Industrial Relations and Technical Change: the Case of the Self-acting Mule', *Cambridge Journal of Economics*, 3 (1979), pp. 236 and 245.

43. Mary Freifeld, 'Technological Change and the "Self-acting" Mule; a Study of Skill and the Sexual Division of Labour', *Social History*, 11 (1986), pp. 324–8. She draws on the evidence of the machine manuals to support her argument.

44. Freifeld, 'Technological Change', pp. 321, 324, 332–3 and 337–9. Freifeld's position is broadly supported by the work of Harold Catling, *The Spinning Mule* (Newton Abbott, David & Charles, 1970).

45. Clark, *The Struggle*, pp. 20–2; Robert B. Shoemaker, *Gender in English Society 1650–1850. The Emergence of Separate Spheres?* (London, Longman, 1998), p. 166.

46. Although men tended to be allocated to the better jobs where these existed. Walby, *Patriarchy at Work*, p. 94. See also Rose, *Limited Livelihoods*, pp. 154–7.

47. Walby, *Patriarchy at Work*, p. 94.

48. Walby, *Patriarchy at Work*, p. 133. In this way, employers could have skilled weaving at cheap prices. Nineteenth-century legislation to restrict women's hours of work failed to dislodge women weavers.

49. Clark, *The Struggle*, p. 126.
50. Clark, *The Struggle*, p. 131. Catherine Hall maintains that more women remained in relatively skilled work in the textile industry than in any other branch of manufacturing. Hall, 'The Home', p. 27.
51. Clark, *The Struggle*, p. 139.
52. Anne Phillips and Barbara Taylor, 'Sex and Skill: Notes towards a Feminist Economics', *Feminist Review*, 6 (1980), p. 79.
53. Judy Wajcman, 'Patriarchy, Technology and Conceptions of Skill', *Work and Occupations*, 18 (1991), p. 33.
54. Therefore, to understand fully gender divisions at work it is necessary to recognise both the ideological and the real material aspects of skill. There are important connections between women's relative lack of power and their lack of technical skills. This is also constructed. The appropriation of technical skills plays an important part in the reproduction of inequality between men and women, as well as among men. Wajcman, 'Patriarchy', pp. 38–9.
55. 'The segregation of women's work from men's, conceals from many men workers the ways in which we are all becoming women workers'. Phillips and Taylor, 'Sex and Skill', pp. 86–7.
56. Also, by extending the gap between men's work and women's work, skilled men were in a position to reduce the distance between themselves and their employers.
57. See Katrina Honeyman and Jordan Goodman, 'Women's Work, Gender Conflict, and Labour Markets in Europe, 1500–1900', *Economic History Review*, 44 (1991), pp. 619–21.
58. The fact that many women engaged in heavy manual work that revealed their not inconsiderable strength, did nothing to alter the inherent maleness of physical strength. This is implicit in much of Pinchbeck, *Women Workers*. See also Leonore Davidoff, *Worlds Between: Historical Perspectives on Gender and Class* (Cambridge, Polity, 1995), pp. 135–9 and 197–200.
59. Maxine Berg, *The Age of Manufactures: Industry, Innovation and Work in Britain 1700–1820* (London, Fontana, 1985), p. 152.
60. But was typically justified in terms of women's alleged physical or mental weakness.
61. Textile weaving was probably one of those rare instances.
62. Some employers implicitly recognised women's capability but failed to reflect this in the wages paid. De Groot and Schrover, *Women Workers*, p. 6.
63. Busfield, 'Job Definitions', pp. 63–5.
64. Karl Ittman, *Work, Gender and Family in Victorian England* (Basingstoke, Macmillan, 1995), p. 48.
65. Ittman, *Work, Gender*, pp. 49–50.
66. Ibid.
67. Busfield, 'Job Definitions', p. 78.
68. The gendering of such disputes is explored in Chapter 7.
69. Rose, *Limited Livelihoods*, pp. 157–60.
70. Sonya O. Rose, 'Gender Segregation in the Transition to the Factory; the English Hosiery Industry, 1850–1910', *Feminist Studies*, 13 (1987), pp. 164, 170–4 and 178–80.

71.   The issues surrounding the Cotton Patent machine, used in the hosiery industry, resembled very closely those that arose in the context of the introduction of the self-acting mule. Rose, 'Gender Segregation', pp. 172–3.

72.   Rose, *Limited Livelihoods*, p. 110.

73.   Rose, *Limited Livelihoods*, pp. 102–119.

74.   The making of gender was a social process. 'The construction of men as strong and capable, manually able and technologically endowed and women as technically and physically incompetent' is a social process. Cynthia Cockburn, *Brothers. Male Dominance and Technological Change* (London, Pluto, 1983), p. 203.

75.   Women were employed in bookbinding, however, but this was clearly regarded as a lower skilled activity.

76.   Cockburn, *Brothers*, p. 150.

77.   Cockburn, *Brothers*, p. 26.

78.   Quoted in Cockburn, *Brothers*, p. 184.

79.   Cockburn, 'Technology, Production and Power' in Kirkup and Keller, *Inventing Women*, p. 208.

80.   Angela Coyle, 'The Protection Racket?', *Feminist Review*, 6 (1980), p. 3.

81.   Sonya O. Rose, 'Protective Labor Legislation in Nineteenth Century Britain: Gender, Class and the Liberal State' in Laura L. Frader and Sonya O. Rose (eds), *Gender and Class in Modern Europe* (Ithaca, Cornell UP, 1996), p. 194; Rose, *Limited Livelihoods*, p. 55.

82.   Coyle, 'The Protection Racket', p. 4.

83.   Walby, *Patriarchy at Work*, p. 130; Shoemaker, *Gender in English Society*, p. 206.

84.   Walby, *Patriarchy at Work*, p. 130.

85.   The actions of the state laid the theoretical basis for the family wage by constructing women as dependent. Pamela Sharpe (ed.), *Women's Work. The English Experience 1650–1914* (London, Arnold, 1998), p. 10.

86.   Shoemaker, *Gender in English Society*, p. 207.

87.   Robert Gray, 'Factory Legislation and the Gendering of Jobs in the North of England, 1830–1860', *Gender and History*, 5 (1993), p. 75. B. L. Hutchins and A. Harrison, *A History of Factory Legislation* (Westminster, P. S. King, 1903), p. 85.

88.   Gray, 'Factory Legislation', p. 75.

89.   Coyle, 'The Protection Racket', p. 5.

90.   Gray, 'Factory Legislation', p. 68.

91.   Richard Ayton, *A Voyage round Great Britain in the Summer of 1813* (1814), pp. 152–60, quoted in Angela John, *By the Sweat of their Brow. Women Workers at Victorian Coal Mines* (London, Routledge & Kegan Paul, 1984), p. 31.

92.   *Union*, no. 2, 1 May 1842, quoted in John, *By the Sweat*, p. 46.

93.   Quoted in Adam Booker *et al.*, 'Child Slaves? Working Children during the Industrial Revolution, c.1780–1850' in Michael Winstanley (ed.), *Working Children in Nineteenth-century Lancashire* (Preston, Lancashire County Books, 1995), p. 41.

94.   Jane Humphries, 'Protective Legislation, the Capitalist State, and Working Class Men: the Case of the 1842 Mines Regulation Act', *Feminist Review*, 7 (1981), pp. 1–32, especially pp. 15–20.

95. See also Jane Humphries, 'Class Struggle and the Persistence of the Working Class Family', *Cambridge Journal of Economics*, 1 (1977), pp. 241–58, which similarly interprets male exclusionary strategies in terms of support for the working-class family. This is explored in Chapter 6.

96. Shoemaker, *Gender in English Society*, p. 167.

5 Women, Work and the New Industrial Economy

1. Eric Richards, 'Women in the British Economy since about 1700; an Interpretation', *History*, 59 (1974), pp. 338 and 346.

2. Maxine Berg, 'Women's Work and the Industrial Revolution', *Refresh*, 12 (1991), p. 3.

3. Some doubt surrounds this point, however, as will be illustrated later in this chapter.

4. Berg, 'Women's Work'; Joan W. Scott and Louise A. Tilly, 'Women's Work and the Family in Nineteenth-century Europe', *Comparative Studies in Society and History*, 17 (1975), reprinted in Alice H. Amsden (ed.), *The Economics of Women and Work* (New York, St Martin's Press, 1980), p. 96. Marital status was first indicated in the census of 1911.

5. According to the census of 1851, for example, over 50 per cent of women in London were apparently 'with no occupation'. As Alexander points out, it would have been necessary for the majority of these to make a contribution to their family's income. Sally Alexander, 'Women's Work in Nineteenth Century London. A Study of the Years 1820–60s' in *Becoming a Woman and Other Essays in 19th and 20th Century Feminist History* (London, Virago, 1994), p. 7.

6. The early censuses were not primarily concerned to identify the occupational structure of the nation. Their agenda was demographic and their purpose specifically to identify trends in and causes of mortality. Once mortality rates had been seen to have reached secular decline from 1880, attention was directed to an analysis of national economic and social structure. See Bridget Hill, 'Women, Work and the Census: a Problem for Historians of Women', *History Workshop Journal*, 35 (1993), p. 86.

7. See Deborah Valenze, *The First Industrial Woman* (Oxford, OUP, 1995), especially pp. 6–7 for a discussion of this issue.

8. The Classical School of economics was concerned with the production, distribution and exchange of wealth.

9. Jean Gardiner, *Gender, Care and Economics* (Basingstoke, Macmillan, 1997), p. 23.

10. Hill, 'Women, Work and the Census', p. 81.

11. Leonore Davidoff and Catherine Hall, *Family Fortunes: Men and Women of the English Middle Class, 1780–1850* (London, Routledge, 1987), p. 135.

12. Hill, 'Women, Work and the Census', pp. 82–3.

13. Edward Higgs, 'Women, Occupations and Work in Nineteenth Century Censuses', *History Workshop Journal*, 23 (1987), p. 63. In 1851 instructions were also given that 'if a wife or daughter of a farmer was working on the farm, she was to be described as farmer's wife or farmer's daughter. Equivalent instructions were not given in the case of shopkeepers or lodging house keepers (p. 68).

14.   All enumerators were men in the nineteenth century. Women were not permitted to be employed as enumerators until 1891 and even then prospective female applicants were informed that their services were not required. Higgs, 'Women, Occupations and Work', p. 62.

15.   See Alexander, 'Women's Work', pp. 52–3.

16.   Higgs, 'Women, Occupations and Work', pp. 62–3 and 72.

17.   Higgs, 'Women, Occupations and Work', p. 64, citing the work of John Holley and Patricia Branca. Such blatant misrepresentation reflected the depth of the contemporary perception that housewife was the proper occupation of a married women whatever her actual occupation in the factory or elsewhere.

18.   Edward Higgs, *Making Sense of the Census. The Manuscript Returns for England and Wales, 1801–1901* (London, HMSO, 1989), p. 82. Higgs also points out that the recording of children's employment was inadequate. Children often made a financial contribution to the household, typically with casual and part-time employment or helping in the family shop, but increasingly parents were inclined to hide this, especially in the context of workplace regulation and compulsory schooling. Higgs, *Making Sense*, pp. 82–4.

19.   Hill's suggestion for redressing the balance is to exercise vigilance when using the census data and to incorporate it with other historical and literary evidence. Hill, 'Women, Work and the Census', p. 92. Higgs, however, makes a direct attempt to rework the figures. His revisions are discussed below. Edward Higgs, 'Occupational Censuses and the Agricultural Workforce in Victorian England and Wales', *Economic History Review*, 48 (1995), pp. 700–16.

20.   It is possible that as many as one-third of all women workers were not counted in the occupational categories. Angela V. John, *Unequal Opportunities. Women's Employment in England 1800–1918* (Oxford, Basil Blackwell, 1986), pp. 36–7.

21.   Ellen Jordan, 'Female Unemployment in England and Wales 1851–1911: an Examination of the Census Figures for 15–19 Year Olds', *Social History*, 13 (1988), p. 176.

22.   Jordan, 'Female Unemployment', pp. 180–1.

23.   Higgs, 'Women, Occupations and Work', p. 71.

24.   Domestic service has also been described as a disguised form of underemployment. Richards, 'Women in the British Economy', p. 348.

25.   Higgs, 'Women, Occupations and Work', p. 69.

26.   Scott and Tilly, for example, argued that domestic service was the chief resort of most rural girls. Scott and Tilly, 'Women's Work and the Family' in Amsden (ed.), *The Economics of Women and Work*, p. 111. Pamela Sharpe believes it was by far the most common reason for women's mobility. See Pamela Sharpe, *Adapting to Capitalism. Working Women in the English Economy 1700–1850* (Basingstoke, Macmillan, 1996), p. 102.

27.   Higgs suggests that the average proportion of women engaged in domestic service between 1841 and 1891 should be reduced from 45.7 to 20.9 per cent. Higgs, 'Women, Occupations and Work', pp. 74–5.

28.   Higgs, *Making Sense*, p. 45.

29.   Other writers have noted this omission. Angela John, for example, suggested that a number of female day-labourers who worked for at least one-third of the year were omitted from the census returns for 1871–91. John, *Unequal Opportunities*, pp. 3–4.

30.   Higgs, 'Occupational Censuses', pp. 700–2. His reworking of census figures to increase the size of the agricultural workforce by 30–40 per cent, however, raises questions about the high labour productivity in agriculture and therefore its role in industrialisation.

31.   See, for example, Eve Hostettler, 'Gourlay Steell and the Sexual Division of Labour', *History Workshop Journal*, 4 (1977), p. 98.

32.   Ivy Pinchbeck, *Women Workers in the Industrial Revolution 1750–1850* (London, Routledge, 1930); Karen Sayer, *Women of the Fields. Representations of Rural Women in the Nineteenth Century* (Manchester, Manchester UP, 1993). See also John, *Unequal Opportunities*, pp. 3–4.

33.   Pinchbeck, *Women Workers*, p. 59.

34.   Pinchbeck, *Women Workers*, p. 66. In other contexts it is shown that women were often preferred because they were better at those activities that required repetition, manipulative quickness and hard work, p. 100.

35.   Sharpe, *Adapting to Capitalism*, pp. 90–2.

36.   John, *Unequal Opportunities*, p. 3; Sayer, *Women of the Fields*, pp. 56–8.

37.   A point made by both Pinchbeck, *Women Workers* and Valenze, *The First, passim*.

38.   Elizabeth Roberts, *Women's Work, 1840–1940* (Basingstoke, Macmillan, 1988), p. 43.

39.   Sayer, *Women of the Fields*, p. 6.

40.   Sharpe, *Adapting to Capitalism*, pp. 94–5. Fruit picking was also a summer option for urban women who were otherwise underemployed. See Alexander, 'Women's Work', pp. 52–3.

41.   The only women to be employed by the year were farm servants and dairymaids. The latter declined in numbers through the nineteenth century. Sometimes men did the work but typically the farmer's wife took on the tasks associated with the dairy as part of her unpaid labour. Sayer, *Women of the Fields*, p. 6.

42.   Sharpe, *Adapting to Capitalism*, p. 88.

43.   Pinchbeck, *Women Workers*, p. 86.

44.   Sharpe, *Adapting to Capitalism*, p. 96.

45.   Conventional views on the subject failed to change much, if at all, in the light of Pinchbeck's findings.

46.   Sayer, *Women of the Fields*, p. 5. Sayer confirms Higgs' view that women's farm employment is difficult to quantify since the census was taken in April when, because many women worked casually and because their labour varied regionally, relatively few women would have been employed. Sayer, *Women of the Fields*, p. 8.

47.   Except by male farm labourers who became very hostile to the competition of women and used the power of contemporary constructions to put pressure on women to leave field work. Karen Sayer, 'Field-faring Women: the Resistance of Women who Worked in the Fields of Nineteenth-century England', *Women's History Review*, 2 (1993), p. 186.

48.   Sharpe, *Adapting to Capitalism*, p. 100.

49.   Sayer, *Women of the Fields*, p. 137, citing evidence of the Royal Commission on Labour 1892.

50.   Sayer, *Women of the Fields*, pp. 56–9.

51.   Canon of Durham, W. S. Gilly, *The Peasantry of the Border* (1842), p. 20 cited in Sayer, *Women of the Fields*, p. 61.

52.   Sayer, *Women of the Fields*, pp. 67–8, 74–6 and 92. The report of 1863 generated the 1867 Gangs Act. More evidence on the contemporary portrayal of women farm workers as unsexed and immoral can be found in Sayer, 'Field-faring Women', pp. 185–98.

53.   Sayer, *Women of the Fields*, p. 61.

54.   The 1892 Royal Commission on Labour, quoted in Sayer, *Women of the Fields*, pp. 61,100 and 147.

55.   Angela V. John, *By the Sweat of their Brow. Women Workers at Victorian Coal Mines* (London, Routledge & Kegan Paul, 1984), pp. 24–5.

56.   Robert B. Shoemaker, *Gender in English Society, 1650–1850. The Emergence of Separate Spheres?* (London, Longman, 1998), pp. 165 and 169.

57.   John, *By the Sweat*, p. 20.

58.   This was allegedly because the men refused to do such work as they found it too difficult. John, *By the Sweat*; see also Angela V. John, *Coalmining Women. Victorian Lives and Campaigns* (Cambridge, CUP, 1984).

59.   Pinchbeck, *Women Workers*, p. 241.

60.   Pinchbeck, *Women Workers*, p. 265; John, *By the Sweat*, p. 42. Similar antipathy was recorded in the context of the pit brow disputes in the 1870s.

61.   Pinchbeck, *Women Workers*, p. 255; John, *Coalmining Women*, p. 8.

62.   Contemporary opinion quoted in Pinchbeck, *Women Workers*, p. 252.

63.   Pinchbeck, *Women Workers*, p. 264.

64.   Only small numbers of women were employed in Ayrshire and Lanarkshire, however.

65.   John, *Coalmining Women*, p. 6.

66.   John, *By the Sweat*, p. 21. The decline in female pit labour in the context of the expansion of the coal-mining industry nationally coincided with regional changes in alternative female employment. By 1841, women rarely worked in pits near to Leeds and Sheffield, for example, nor in east Lancashire (p. 24).

67.   John, *By the Sweat*, p. 23; John, *Coalmining Women*, p. 5.

68.   John, *By the Sweat*, p. 12; John, *Coalmining Women*, pp. 8–10.

69.   A. J. Heesom, 'The Northern Coal Owners and the Opposition to the Coal Mines Act of 1842', *International Review of Social History*, 25 (1980), pp. 236–7.

70.   Lord Ashley, for example, believed that the vacancies in pitwork created by the exclusion of women would provide opportunities for the unemployed [*sic*]. Heesom, 'Northern Coal Owners', p. 237.

71.   John, *By the Sweat*, p. 53.

72.   In 1911, there were 2843 women coal workers in England and 2396 in Scotland, which represented very little change from the estimated numbers working in the 1840s. Roberts, *Women's Work*, p. 56; John, *By the Sweat*, p. 25. Janice Adams and Stella Clarkson, 'Work Fit for Girls' in

Michael Winstanley (ed.), *Working Children in Nineteenth-century Lancashire* (Preston, Lancashire County Books, 1995), p. 115.

73. John, *By the Sweat*, pp. 59, 135 and 200. As in the 1840s, the employers worried about the financial implications of such exclusion. One manager calculated that female exclusion would result in a 30–40 per cent increase in wages being paid to 10 per cent of the colliery workforce.

74. In contrast to the Bill put to the House of Commons in the previous year.

75. John, *Coalmining Women*, p. 39.

76. While the relevant legislation of the 1830s and 1840s reflected a primary concern to protect children from physical and moral damage, their mothers received indirect consideration.

77. Although the factory manufacture of cotton was particularly striking, its break with more traditional forms of work organisation was incomplete. The nature of the early technical inventions permitted production in small factories and domestic workshops. Home-produced yarn and woven cloth, using a mainly female labour force, continued for many years alongside the factories. The size and structure of cotton mills varied greatly. Purpose-built factories were initially rare. More common were premises converted from other uses. Many factory units were subdivided and rented.

78. Carol E. Morgan, 'Women, Work and Consciousness in the Mid-nineteenth Century English Cotton Industry', *Social History*, 17 (1992), p. 25.

79. Mainly in Stockport, Preston and Blackburn.

80. Morgan, 'Women, Work and Consciousness', pp. 30–1.

81. Karl Ittman, *Work, Gender and Family in Victorian England* (Basingstoke, Macmillan, 1995), pp. 49–53.

82. Judy Lown, *Women and Industrialisation. Gender at Work in Nineteenth Century England* (Cambridge, Polity, 1990), p. 45.

83. Calculated from estimates of B. R. Mitchell, *European Historical Statistics, 1750–1975* (London, Macmillan, 1981), p. 163; and figures in John, *Unequal Opportunities*, p. 38.

84. Mills were described by contemporaries as 'incubators of vice'. Sonya O. Rose, 'Protective Labor Legislation in Nineteenth-century Britain: Gender, Class and the Liberal State', in Laura L. Frader and Sonya O. Rose (eds), *Gender and Class in Modern Europe* (Ithaca, Cornell UP, 1996), p. 201.

85. Robert Gray, 'Medical Men, Industrial Labour and the State in Britain, 1830–50', *Social History*, 16, 1 (1991), pp. 38–9. See also Valenze, *The First*, p. 99.

86. Marilyn Boxer and Jean Quataert (eds), *Connecting Spheres. Women in the Western World, 1500 to the Present* (Oxford, OUP, 1987), p. 101.

87. Maxine Berg, *The Age of Manufactures: Industry, Innovation and Work in Britain, 1700–1820* (London, Fontana, 1985), p. 145.

88. Pinchbeck, *Women Workers*, pp. 202–26 and 306.

89. Pamela Sharpe and Stanley D. Chapman, 'Women's Employment and Industrial Organisation: Commercial Lace Embroidery in Early Nineteenth Century Ireland and England', *Women's History Review*, 5 (1996), p. 343.

90. Berg, *Age of Manufactures*, p. 146.
91. Sharpe, *Adapting to Capitalism*, p. 69.
92. Sharpe, *Adapting to Capitalism*, p. 38.
93. Pinchbeck describes lace making as a highly exploitative form of employment for children in particular. She believes that conditions in the lace schools were worse than those in factories. Children began to work 12 hours per day at the age of four or five. Pinchbeck, *Women Workers*, p. 232.
94. Sharpe, *Adapting to Capitalism*, pp. 53–5; Sharpe and Chapman, 'Women's Employment', p. 340.
95. Berg, *Age of Manufactures*, p. 149. This provides one of the many examples of industries where even when new techniques were invented, alternative labour-intensive techniques were used, or even invented to make use of a large cheap female labour force. Berg, *Age of Manufactures*, p. 146.
96. Sharpe, *Adapting to Capitalism*, pp. 62–3.
97. Sonya O. Rose, 'Gender Segregation in the Transition to the Factory: the English Hosiery Industry, 1850–1910', *Feminist Studies*, 13 (1987), pp. 181–3.
98. Harriet Bradley, *Men's Work, Women's Work. A Sociological History of the Sexual Division of Labour in Employment* (Cambridge, CUP, 1989), pp. 137–8.
99. Rose, 'Gender Segregation', p. 169.
100. Sharpe and Chapman, 'Women's Employment', pp. 342–3.
101. Rose, 'Gender Segregation', p. 182.
102. Scott and Tilly, 'Women's Work', p. 104.
103. Honeyman and Goodman, 'Women's Work', p. 618; Shoemaker, *Gender in English Society*, p. 168.
104. See James Schmiechen, *Sweated Industries and Sweated Labour. The London Clothing Trades* (Urbana, University of Illinios, 1984) for an exemplary account of such symbiosis.
105. It was not unusual, however, for a handicraft tailor to engage members of his family in such finishing processes as buttoning and button-holing. See Beverly Lemire, *Dress, Culture and Commerce. The English Clothing Trade before the Factory, 1660–1800* (London, Macmillan, 1997), pp. 11–22.
106. This was the case in London and in Colchester where Hyams, who owned a London-based operation, gave work out to small masters who in turn employed largely untrained men and women in their own homes and in sweatshops. Sharpe, *Adapting to Capitalism*, p. 66.
107. Barbara Taylor, *Eve and the New Jerusalem. Socialism and Feminism in the Nineteenth Century* (London, Virago, 1983), pp. 101–8.
108. Honeyman and Goodman, 'Women's Work', p. 616.
109. Leeds specialised in men's tailoring while London also contained a large women's garment-making sector.
110. Jenny Morris, 'The Characteristics of Sweating: the Late Nineteenth Century London and Leeds Tailoring Trade' in John, *Unequal Opportunities*, p. 117.
111. See Schmiechen, *Sweated Industries*, *passim*; Honeyman and Goodman, 'Women's Work', p. 617.
112. She wrote 'Women Workers' in frustration with the conclusion of Ivy Pinchbeck that modern industry had improved the lives of married

women by taking the work out of the home, and of unmarried women by offering them an independent wage. Sally Alexander, *Becoming a Woman*, p. xiii.

113.   Alexander, 'Women Workers', p. 23.

114.   The casual labour of their husbands in the dockyards or construction industries served to exacerbate their dire economic circumstances. Alexander, 'Women Workers', p. 27.

115.   Alexander, 'Women Workers', p. 52.

116.   Where the worker was supplied with raw material by the employer and where exploitation was particularly marked.

117.   Roberts, *Women's Work*, p. 40; Duncan Bythell, *The Sweated Trades: Outwork in Nineteenth-century Britain* (London, Batsford, 1987), pp. 108–16.

118.   Sharpe, *Adapting to Capitalism*, p. 68.

119.   The Factory and Workshop Acts of 1891 and 1895 particularly restricted activities in sewing and tailoring workshops. Roberts, *Women's Work*, pp. 41–2.

120.   Bythell, *The Sweated Trades*, p. 145.

121.   Employment of this kind was not formally recorded and until recently has failed to enter the historical accounts.

122.   Alexander, 'Women Workers', p. 9; Roberts, *Women's Work*, p. 37. Wives of shopkeepers who worked in the shop were excluded from the census.

123.   Roberts, *Women's Work*, p. 17.

124.   Ellen Ross, *Love and Toil: Motherhood in Outcast London 1870–1918* (New York, OUP, 1993), p. 288. See also Ellen Ross, 'Survival Networks: Women's Neighbourhood Sharing in London before World War I', *History Workshop Journal*, 23 (1983), pp. 4–27.

125.   Alexander, 'Women Workers', p. 9.

126.   Roberts, *Women's Work*, p. 50.

127.   Andrew August, 'How Separate a Sphere? Poor Women and Paid Work in Late Victorian London', *Journal of Family History*, 19 (1994), p. 289.

128.   Including the ubiquitous keeping of lodgers which escaped direct recording by census enumerators.

129.   Elizabeth Roberts, *A Woman's Place. An Oral History of Working Class Women, 1890–1940* (Oxford, Basil Blackwell, 1984) p. 227; August, 'How Separate', p. 290.

130.   August, 'How Separate', p. 306.

131.   Report of the Interdepartmental Committee on Physical Deterioration BPP 1904 quoted in Margaret Hewitt, *Wives and Mothers in Victorian Industry* (London, Rockliff, 1958), p. 193.

132.   Pinchbeck, *Women Workers*, p. 307. Pinchbeck also believed, erroneously, that this would be allowed because of the assumption that 'men's wages should be paid on a family basis', p. 313.

133.   Pinchbeck, *Women Workers*, p. 314–15.

134.   Shoemaker, *Gender in English Society*, p. 171.

135.   Jordan, 'Female Unemployment', p. 185.

136.   Pat Hudson, *The Industrial Revolution* (London, Edward Arnold, 1992), p. 236.

6 The Making of Gender Identities during the Period of Industrialisation

1.   Male family members were conceivably if intermittently in this category.

2.   Sara Horrell and Jane Humphries, 'Women's Labour Force Participation and the Transition to the Male-breadwinner Family, 1790–1865', *Economic History Review*, 48 (1995), p. 101.

3.   Quoted in Anna Clark, *The Struggle for the Breeches. Gender and the Making of the British Working Class* (Berkeley, University of California Press, 1995), pp. 64–5.

4.   Barbara Taylor, *Eve and the New Jerusalem. Socialism and Feminism in the Nineteenth Century* (London, Virago, 1983), pp. 77–9.

5.   See, for example, Hans Medick, 'The Proto-industrial Family Economy' in Peter Kriedte, Hans Medick and Jurgen Schlumbohm, *Industrialisation before Industrialisation* (Cambridge, CUP, 1981), pp. 38–73, especially pp. 60–3.

6.   Especially the masculinisation of dairying as shown in Deborah Valenze, *The First Industrial Woman* (Oxford, OUP, 1995), pp. 341–2.

7.   Robert Gray, *The Factory Question and Industrial England, 1830–1860* (Cambridge, CUP, 1996), p. 27.

8.   Wally Seccombe, *Weathering the Storm. Working Class Families from the Industrial Revolution to the Fertility Decline* (London, Verso, 1993), pp. 32–3, 39–40.

9.   Gray, *The Factory Question*, p. 26.

10.   Valenze, *The First*, p. 341.

11.   Robert B. Shoemaker, *Gender in English Society, 1650–1850. The Emergence of Separate Spheres?* (London, Longman, 1998), p. 6.

12.   For more detail on the political economy of women's domestic position, see Jean Gardiner, *Gender, Care and Economics* (Basingstoke, Macmillan, 1997), pp. 21–38.

13.   Jane Rendall, *The Origins of Modern Feminism. Women in Britain, France and the United States, 1780–1860* (Basingstoke, Macmillan, 1984), p. 194.

14.   See Pamela Sharpe, 'Bigamy among the Labouring Poor in Essex, 1754–1857', *The Local Historian*, 24 (1994), pp. 139–44 for an interesting discussion of this point.

15.   Taylor, *Eve*, pp. 193–6.

16.   The large proportion of single women in the population during the second half of the nineteenth century, however, indicates a reluctance on their part to enter a union based on inequality, and the possibility that there were other ways of ensuring personal survival.

17.   Property laws, which were clearly more relevant to the middle class than to the working class, accorded women very few rights, although the recent work of Maxine Berg and Jill Liddington suggests a refinement of such a position. See Maxine Berg, 'Women's Property and the Industrial Revolution', *Journal of Interdisciplinary History*, 24 (1993), pp. 233–50; and Jill Liddington, 'Beating the Inheritance Bounds: Anne Lister (1791–1840) and her Dynastic Inheritance', *Gender and History*, 17 (1995), pp. 260–74.

18.   Taylor, *Eve*, p. 32.

19.   Many identifiable qualities of women were viewed as positive, yet they were still constructed as inferior.
20.   Shoemaker, *Gender in English Society*, Ch. 2, especially pp. 20–1, reveals how eighteenth-century conduct books assigned characteristic vices and virtues to each sex. Female virtues were mainly to do with emotion, while men possessed the larger share of reason.
21.   Taylor, *Eve*, p. 1.
22.   Shoemaker, *Gender in English Society*, p. 51.
23.   Mary Wollstonecraft, *A Vindication of the Rights of Men* (1790), and *A Vindication of the Rights of Woman* (1792), edited by Sylvana Tomaselli (Cambridge, CUP, 1995), pp. 89–90.
24.   Taylor, *Eve*, p. 14. Ironically, by identifying women's rights with sexual libertarianism, infidelism and social revolution, such aspects of radical thought coalesced in the minds of the feminist opponents to new conservatism, p. 15.
25.   Criticism of the notion of masculinity, to which the domestic conception of femininity was set in opposition, was widespread. The definition of assault that permitted husbands to physically discipline their wives and the iniquitous divorce laws were specifically criticised. Shoemaker, *Gender in English Society*, p. 52.
26.   Shoemaker, *Gender in English Society*, p. 54; Rendall, *Origins of Modern Feminism*, p. 190.
27.   *The Isis*, 3 March 1832, cited in Taylor, *Eve*, p. 81.
28.   Cited in Catherine Barmby, 'The Demand for the Emancipation of Woman, Politically and Socially', reprinted in Taylor, *Eve*, p. 392. See also Shoemaker, *Gender in English Society*, p. 56.
29.   Richard Cooper, *A Contrast between the New Moral World and the Old Immoral World* (1838), p. 8, cited in Taylor, *Eve*, p. 53.
30.   Shoemaker, *Gender in English Society*, pp. 54–6; Rendall, *Origins of Modern Feminism*, p. 321.
31.   The view of Anna Clark cited in Shoemaker, *Gender in English Society*, p. 8.
32.   Sonya O. Rose, *Limited Livelihoods: Gender and Class in Nineteenth-century England* (London, Routledge, 1992), p. 15.
33.   Men's identity was seen to be threatened by such dependence.
34.   Shoemaker, *Gender in English Society*, p. 68.
35.   Rose, *Limited Livelihoods*, p. 135, quoting a remark made during the 1884 Kidderminster carpet weavers dispute.
36.   Cited in Shoemaker, *Gender in English Society*, p. 119.
37.   William Dodd, *The Factory System Illustrated* (1842), pp. 63–4, quoted in Clark, *The Struggle*, p. 238.
38.   Frederick Engels, *The Condition of the Working Class in England* (London, Panther, 1969), p. 173.
39.   Gardiner, *Gender*, pp. 24–5.
40.   Gardiner, *Gender*, p. 28.
41.   Gardiner, *Gender*, pp. 21–38.
42.   Rendall, *Origins of Modern Feminism*, p. 205.
43.   Taylor, *Eve*, pp. 124–5.

44.   Ivy Pinchbeck, *Women Workers and the Industrial Revolution 1750–1850* (London, Routledge, 1930), p. 4.

45.   Quoted in Gardiner, *Gender*, p. 30. See also Rendall, *Origins of Modern Feminism*, p. 190.

46.   Elizabeth Roberts, *A Woman's Place. An Oral History of Working Class Women 1890–1940* (Oxford, Blackwell, 1984), pp. 135–48.

47.   Clark, *The Struggle*, p. 218.

48.   Clark, *The Struggle*, p. 231.

49.   Clark, *The Struggle*, p. 263.

50.   Michele Barrett and Mary McIntosh, 'The "Family Wage": Some Problems for Socialists and Feminists', *Capital and Class*, 11 (1980), quoted in Elizabeth Roberts, *Women's Work 1840–1940* (Basingstoke, Macmillan, 1988), pp. 24–5. It is estimated that about 30 per cent of women of working age were unmarried in the second half of the nineteenth century.

51.   Ellen Ross, '"Fierce Questions and Taunts": Married Life in Working Class London, 1870–1914', *Feminist Studies*, 8 (1982), pp. 575–602.

52.   Clark, *The Struggle*, pp. 73 and 82. See also Anna Clark, *Women's Silence, Men's Violence: Sexual Assault in England, 1770–1845* (London, Pandora, 1987) for a vivid portrayal of the depths of marital misery that many women endured in the late eighteenth and early nineteenth centuries.

53.   *The Pioneer*, 12 April 1834, cited in Clark, *The Struggle*, p. 187.

54.   Clark, *The Struggle*, p. 249.

55.   See Nancy Tomes, '"A Torrent of Abuse": Crimes of Violence between Working Class Men and Women in London, 1840–1858', *Journal of Social History*, 11 (1978), pp. 328–45. See also Rendall, *Origins of Modern Feminism*, p. 199; and Ross, 'Fierce Questions'.

56.   Hilary Land, 'The Family Wage', *Feminist Review*, 6 (1980), pp. 59 and 74.

57.   Katrina Honeyman and Jordan Goodman, 'Women's Work, Gender Conflict, and Labour Markets in Europe, 1500–1900', *Economic History Review*, 44 (1991), p. 622.

58.   Colin Creighton, 'The Rise of the Male Breadwinner Family: a Reappraisal', *Comparative Studies in Society and History*, 38 (1996), p. 310. In other groups, the shortfall in earnings was made up by children, which appeared not to undermine the pride of the man as much as the employment of the spouse. Wally Seccombe, 'Patriarchy Stabilised: the Construction of the Male Breadwinner Wage Norm in Nineteenth Century Britain', *Social History*, 11 (1986), p. 54.

59.   Honeyman and Goodman, 'Women's Work', p. 623.

60.   Within the family wage construct, women's economic role was undermined, but less overtly than was the case in their exclusionary strategies, as men demanded wages sufficiently high to keep their wives at home. Clark, *The Struggle*, p. 199.

61.   Seccombe, 'Patriarchy Stabilised', p. 55.

62.   Clark, *The Struggle*, p. 198. Anna Clark rejects the artisan roots of the breadwinner wage and suggests that the wife of an artisan would be expected to work and that artisan status rested on his place in the fraternity of skilled men rather than on his ability to keep his wife at home.

63. Seccombe, 'Patriarchy Stabilised', p. 74.
64. Heidi Hartmann, 'The Unhappy Marriage of Marxism and Feminism: towards a More Progressive Union', *Capital and Class*, 8 (1979), pp. 1–33. See also Heidi Hartmann, 'Capitalism, Patriarchy, and Job Segregation by Sex', *Signs*, 1 (1976), pp. 137–69.
65. Rose, *Limited Livelihoods*, pp. 138–41.
66. Jane Humphries, 'Class Struggle and the Persistence of the Working Class Family', *Cambridge Journal of Economics*, 1 (1977), pp. 241–58.
67. Creighton, 'The Rise of the Male', pp. 331–2. Such policies served to intensify the impact of economic change on family life.
68. This view is consistent with that of Mariana Valverde that the factory movement of the 1830s and 1840s made a significant contribution to the ideal of working-class domesticity where the male breadwinner reigned over both women and children both at home and in the workplace. Mariana Valverde, 'Giving the Female a Domestic Turn: the Legal, Social and Moral Regulation of Women's Work in British Cotton Mills, 1820–1850', *Journal of Social History*, 21 (1988), pp. 619–34. See more discussion in Colin Creighton, 'Richard Oastler, Factory Legislation and the Working Class Family', *Journal of Historical Sociology*, 5 (1992), pp. 292–320.
69. Rose, *Limited Livelihoods*, pp. 72–3.
70. Clark, *The Struggle*, p. 269.
71. Quoted in Gray, *The Factory Question*, p. 123.
72. Judy Lown, *Women and Industrialisation. Gender at Work in Nineteenth-century England* (Cambridge, Polity, 1990) p. 112.
73. Lown, *Women and Industrialisation*, pp. 125–6.
74. Gray, *The Factory Question*, p. 123. More complex methods of re-inforcing gender roles and family structure within the workplace were introduced by a number of nineteenth-century paternalist employers. Paternalism was an integral part of the social experience of the propertied middle class before it became transposed for use as a special strategy of industrial relations, p. 122.
75. Lown, *Women and Industrialisation*, p. 8. See also Judy Lown, 'Not so Much a Factory, More a Form of Patriarchy: Gender and Class during Industrialisation' in Eve Garmarnikov *et al.* (eds), *Class, Gender and Work* (Aldershot, Gower, 1983), pp. 28–45, especially pp. 33–6.
76. Lown, *Women and Industrialisation*, pp. 142–52.
77. Lown, *Women and Industrialisation*, pp. 98, 144–6 and 148–52.
78. Lown, *Women and Industrialisation*, p. 165. While separate spheres may not have appealed to all or even most working-class women, it is also possible that men were equally unpersuaded. John Tosh, for example, has suggested that separate spheres also placed fatherhood in an awkward position. See John Tosh, 'Authority and Nurture in Middle Class Fatherhood: the Case of Early and Mid-Victorian England', *Gender and History*, 8 (1996), pp. 48–64.
79. Lown, *Women and Industrialisation*, p. 200.
80. Mary Rose, *The Gregs of Quarry Bank Mill. The Rise and Decline of a Family Firm, 1750–1914* (Cambridge, CUP, 1986), pp. 107, 116–17. The paternalist activities of the firm of Cadbury also drew upon and reinforced

family authority. See Leonore Davidoff and Catherine Hall, *Family Fortunes. Men and Women of the English Middle Class 1780–1850* (London, Routledge, 1987), *passim*.

81. Rose, *Limited Livelihoods*, p. 47.
82. Keith McClelland, 'Some Thoughts on Masculinity and the "Representative Artisan"' in Britain, 1850–1880', *Gender and History*, 1 (1989), p. 173.
83. This is best articulated in Sonya O. Rose, 'Respectable Men, Disorderly Others: the Language of Gender and the Lancashire Weavers' Strike of 1878 in Britain', *Gender and History*, 5 (1993), especially pp. 383–4.
84. Taylor, *Eve*, p. 264.
85. Taylor, *Eve*, p. 244.
86. Rendall, *Origins of Modern Feminism*, p. 198.
87. A compromise family wage, establishing the adult male as the principal but not necessarily the sole breadwinner, may have been a more suitable option. Given the importance of the earnings of all employable family members, the interests of adult men were more likely to be expressed in the hierarchy of pay and status in the workplace than in the exclusion of women from it. Gray, *The Factory Question*, p. 36.
88. Rose, *Limited Livelihoods*, p. 130.
89. Rose cited in Theodore Koditschek, 'The Gendering of the British Working Class', *Gender and History*, 9 (1997), pp. 345–6.
90. Sara Horrell and Jane Humphries, 'Women's Labour Force Participation and the Transition to the Male-breadwinner Family, 1790–1865', *Economic History Review*, XLVIII (1995), pp. 89–117.
91. Rose, *Limited Livelihoods*, p. 101.
92. Seccombe, *Weathering the Storm*, p. 31. The point is also made in his study of London by Andrew August, 'How Separate a Sphere? Poor Women and Paid Work in Late Victorian London', *Journal of Family History*, 19 (1994), pp. 296, 300 and 306.
93. Although the standard of living debate is still far from resolution, there is little doubt about who benefited least from the process of industrialisation.

7   Industrialisation and the Gendering of Class

1. Robert Gray, *The Factory Question and Industrial England, 1830–1860* (Cambridge, CUP, 1996), p. 27. See also Judy Lown, *Women and Industrialisation. Gender at Work in Nineteenth Century England* (Cambridge, Polity, 1990), p. 210.
2. Anna Clark, *The Struggle for the Breeches. Gender and the Making of the British Working Class* (Berkeley, University of California Press, 1995), p. 265.
3. This is argued by Barbara Taylor in her analysis of Owenism, a socialist movement that was partly informed by gender equality. See *Eve and the New Jerusalem. Socialism and Feminism in the Nineteenth Century* (London, Virago,1983), *passim*.
4. This can be interpreted as embryonic class action.
5. Barbara Taylor, 'Socialist Feminism: Utopian or Scientific?' in Raphael Samuel, *People's History and Socialist Theory* (London, Routledge &

Kegan Paul, 1981) p. 159, reveals how gender issues were attacked as bourgeois in later nineteenth-century socialist movements.

6.   Ruth L. Smith and Deborah M. Valenze, 'Mutuality and Marginality: Liberal Moral Theory and Working Class Women in Nineteenth-century England', *Signs*, 13 (1988), p. 290.

7.   John Bohstedt and Dale E. Williams, 'The Diffusion of Riots: the Patterns of 1766, 1795 and 1801 in Devonshire', *Journal of Interdisciplinary History*, 19 (1988), pp. 1–24 show how food riots typically occurred in the wake of poor harvests and consequent price rises. Such actions were sometimes associated with radicalism. In Manchester, for example, women dominated food riots and 'bitterly' defied troops. Clark, *The Struggle*, p. 151.

8.   Women were also perceived to possess a mutinous temperament. Such ideas are discussed in John Bohstedt, 'Gender, Household and Community Politics: Women in English Riots 1790–1810', *Past and Present*, 120 (1988), pp. 88–9.

9.   Bohstedt, 'Gender, Household', pp. 89 and 94.

10.   Clark, *The Struggle*, p. 151.

11.   In other words, the changing perception of food riots suggests that industrialisation resulted in the relative depoliticisation of women. Bohstedt, 'Gender, Household', p. 113 .

12.   Sheila Lewenhak, *Women and Trade Unions: an Outline History of Women in the Trade Union Movement* (London, E. Benn, 1977), p. 17. See also Clark, *The Struggle*, pp. 121 and 131–3.

13.   Malcolm I. Thomis and Jennifer Grimmett, *Women in Protest 1800–1850* (London, Croom Helm, 1982), p. 73. See also Lewenhak, *Women and Trade Unions*, pp. 18–24 and 27.

14.   Lewenhak, *Women and Trade Unions*, p. 22.

15.   Jane Rendall, *The Origins of Modern Feminism: Women in Britain, France and the United States, 1780–1860* (Basingstoke, Macmillan, 1984), p. 164.

16.   Taylor, *Eve*, pp. 106–7; Lewenhak, *Women and Trade Unions*, p. 17.

17.   Rendall, *Origins of Modern Feminism*, pp. 164–5.

18.   Clark, *The Struggle*, p. 37; Lewenhak, *Women and Trade Unions*, pp. 18–20.

19.   Clark, *The Struggle*, p. 163. Although the focus of these societies was not initially industrial action, they had much in common with the general unions of the late nineteenth century. .

20.   Clark, *The Struggle*, p. 120. A similar argument is presented by Deborah Valenze, *The First Industrial Woman* (Oxford, OUP, 1995), pp. 128–40.

21.   Clark, *The Struggle*, p. 121.

22.   Clark, *The Struggle*, p. 266.

23.   Clark, *The Struggle*, p. 120.

24.   This encouraged the expansion of the pool of low-paid female labour. Clark, *The Struggle*, p. 269.

25.   Clark's work indicates that the 1810s and early 1820s was a time when skilled men abused and exploited women while demeaning their position as workers. The court records confirm shoemakers as wifebeaters. Clark, *The Struggle*, pp. 121–4.

26. Taylor, *Eve*, p. 106.
27. Taylor, *Eve*, p. 107.
28. Quotation from *The Pioneer*, 5 April 1834, in Taylor, *Eve*, p. 107.
29. Taylor, *Eve*, pp. 110–11.
30. *Report on Children in Manufacturers*, p. 239, testimony of Nathaniel Gould, cited in Clark, *The Struggle*, p. 135.
31. Clark, *The Struggle*, pp. 133–9.
32. Clark, *The Struggle*, p. 126.
33. Their total earnings were probably less; however, domestic responsibilities ensured that women worked fewer hours. Clark, *The Struggle*, p. 127.
34. Clark, *The Struggle*, p. 131.
35. The real cause of the collapse was foreign competition, but the trade's failure clearly deterred others from pursuing an inclusive strategy. Clark, *The Struggle*, p. 128.
36. Radicals in the labour movement began to exclude women, arguing that their acceptance of low wages undercut the efforts of an all-male workforce. Smith and Valenze, 'Mutuality', p. 288.
37. After the failure of strikes in 1829 and 1830 and the collapse of the spinners' consolidated trade union, Doherty established the National Regeneration Society in which the shift from misogynist rhetoric towards a display of consideration for women workers was more a rhetorical strategy than a change of heart. Clark, *The Struggle*, pp. 209–10.
38. Editorial in *Herald of the Rights of Industry* (1834), quoted in Clark, *The Struggle*, p. 210.
39. Although Owenism has often been perceived as a minority and short-lived 'Utopian' movement, its activities did indicate the extent to which gender equality was possible within the context of an industrialising society. Owenites believed that by organising against the process of proletarianisation they could short-circuit capitalist social relations. Taylor, 'Socialist Feminism', p. 161.
40. Taylor, *Eve*, p. 89.
41. Which continued in a more Utopian form following the collapse of its economic activities.
42. Taylor, *Eve*, pp. 217 and 221.
43. Taylor, *Eve*, pp. 218 and 237.
44. Feminists within the movement, however, demanded education precisely to free women from narrow domestic concerns. Taylor, *Eve*, p. 234.
45. The problem of sex prejudice within the radical working class was a common theme on the women's page of the Owenite newspaper. Taylor, 'Socialist Feminism', p. 159.
46. Taylor, *Eve*, pp. 91–2.
47. Henry Mayhew, *London Labour and the London Poor*, Vol. 2, p. 314, quoted in Sally Alexander, 'Women's Work in Nineteenth-century London: a Study of the Years 1820–60s', *Becoming a Woman and Other Essays in Nineteenth and Twentieth Century Feminist History* (London, Virago, 1994), pp. 81–2.
48. Taylor, *Eve*, p. 202.
49. Taylor, *Eve*, p. 203.
50. Taylor, *Eve*, p. 222.

51. Taylor, *Eve,* p. 263.
52. Which was also seen to be the site of the solution to class struggle, as material disadvantage caused by industrialisation was potentially resolved within the family.
53. Gray, *The Factory Question,* pp. 22 and 163.
54. Clark, *The Struggle,* p. 215.
55. Gray, *The Factory Question,* p. 29.
56. Gray, *The Factory Question,* pp. 27 and 31.
57. Robert Gray, 'The Languages of Factory Reform in Britain, c.1830–1860' in Patrick Joyce (ed.), *The Historical Meanings of Work* (Cambridge, CUP, 1987), pp. 150–1; and Gray, *The Factory Question,* p. 34.
58. Gray, *The Factory Question,* p. 237.
59. Radical working men, conservative male trade unionists and Tory radicals alike colluded in depicting factory women as passive victims rather than active agents capable of organising themselves. Clark, *The Struggle,* pp. 216–17.
60. This is the argument of Mariana Valverde quoted in Colin Creighton, 'Richard Oastler, Factory Legislation and the Working Class Family', *Journal of Historical Sociology,* 5 (1992), p. 293.
61. Quoted in Creighton, 'Richard Oastler', p. 301.
62. Carol E. Morgan, 'Women, Work and Consciousness in the Mid-nineteenth-century English Cotton Industry', *Social History,* 17 (1992), p. 27.
63. Rendall, *Origins of Modern Feminism,* p. 178.
64. Morgan, 'Women, Work', pp. 28–9.
65. Designed to restrict the labour of women and young persons to ten hours per day.
66. Quoted in Gray, *The Factory Question,* p. 30. Gray emphasises that this was a very rare example of a woman expressing an opinion on the issues involved in factory reform. Typically, women's views were presented in summary form if at all.
67. Padiham, Burnley and Blackburn.
68. Morgan, 'Women, Work', pp. 34–5. It is possible that women mentioned this in response to questions from government officials, because they felt defensive about alleged deficiencies in the domesticity department.
69. Morgan, 'Women, Work', pp. 38 and 41.
70. Clark, *The Struggle,* p. 219.
71. This had also featured in Owenism and other socialist movements.
72. Anna Clark, 'Manhood, Womanhood, and the Politics of Class in Britain, 1790–1845' in Laura L. Frader and Sonya O. Rose (eds), *Gender and Class in Modern Europe* (Ithaca, Cornell UP, 1996), p. 275.
73. This is described by Anna Clark as 'militant domesticity'. Clark, *The Struggle,* p. 228.
74. Recent research by Fulcher provides a case study of a woman engaged in radical politics during the 1830s and 1840s which confirms Sonya Rose's conclusions about the maleness of working-class action in the later nineteenth century. Jonathan Fulcher, 'Gender, Politics and Class in the Early Nineteenth-century English Reform Movement', *Historical Research,* 67 (1994), pp. 57–74. Sonya O. Rose, 'Respectable Men,

Disorderly Others: the Language of Gender and the Lancashire Weavers' Strike of 1878 in Britain', *Gender and History* , 5 (1993), pp. 382–97.

75.   For expansion of this point, see Joan Scott, 'On Language, Gender and Working Class History' in Lenard R. Berlanstein (ed.), *The Industrial Revolution and Work in Nineteenth-century Europe* (London, Routledge, 1992), pp. 170 and 172; and Joan Scott, *Gender and the Politics of History* (New York, Columbia UP, 1988), p. 60 .

76.   Clark, 'Manhood, Womanhood', p. 278.

77.   At a Chartist meeting in east London in 1842, for example, a socialist Chartist who raised the issue was laughed down by the audience. Taylor, *Eve*, p. 270.

78.   Clark, *The Struggle*, pp. 232 and 236.

79.   Quoted in Clark, *The Struggle*, p. 237.

80.   Quoted in Clark, *The Struggle*, pp. 238–9.

81.   Clark, *The Struggle*, p. 245.

82.   This is discussed in Jane Humphries, 'Protective Legislation, the Capitalist State and Working Class Men: the Case of the 1842 Mines Regulation Act', *Feminist Review*, 7 (1981), pp. 1–32; Gray, *The Factory Question*, p. 8; Rendall, *Origins of Modern Feminism*, p. 171 .

83.   Factory reform also played into the hands of the middle class and was only successful because the middle class supported it.

84.   Rendall, *Origins of Modern Feminism*, p. 171.

85.   Angela John, *By the Sweat of Their Brow. Women Workers at Victorian Coal Mines* (London, Routledge & Kegan Paul, 1984), *passim*, especially Chs 2 and 6.

86.   Humphries, 'Protective Legislation', especially pp. 19–20. Men and women were not in competition for work as their tasks were complementary. Only when there was a shortage of male labour did women become hewers themselves. John, *By the Sweat*, p. 24.

87.   *Hansard* 1843, cited in Jane Mark-Lawson and Anne Witz, 'From "Family Labour" to "Family Wage"? The Case of Women's Labour in Nineteenth Century Coalmining', *Social History*, 13 (1988), p. 163.

88.   John, *By the Sweat*, p. 57. Such immediate pressure for the breadwinner wage appears to support the hypothesis of Jane Humphries that any support that miners had for the legislation was the result of class interest and not gender hostility.

89.   Women were used as cheap, flexible and expendable labour by employers before they were forced into distasteful jobs out of economic necessity only to then be forced out of them by male co-workers.

90.   Quoted in Morgan, 'Women, Work', p. 33.

91.   Elizabeth Roberts, *Women's Work 1840–1940* (Basingstoke, Macmillan, 1988), p. 58.

92.   Morgan, 'Women, Work', p. 39.

93.   Morgan, 'Women, Work', p. 34.

94.   Morgan, 'Women, Work', p. 40.

95.   Scott, 'On Language', p. 170.

96.   Sonya O. Rose, *Limited Livelihoods: Gender and Class in Nineteenth Century England* (London, Routledge, 1992), p. 7.

97.   Though women were in fact disadvantaged wherever possible.
98.   Rose, 'Respectable Men', pp. 386–7.
99.   Rose, 'Respectable Men', p. 390.
100. Rose, 'Respectable Men', p. 393.
101. Although the interaction of class and gender was as complex in the countryside as in the urban industrial areas, in rural society new forms of working-class respectability were relatively late to evolve. Karen Sayer, *Women of the Fields. Representations of Rural Women in the Nineteenth Century* (Manchester, Manchester UP, 1993), p. 51.
102. Sayer, *Women of the Fields*, pp. 70, 106 and 109.
103. Sayer, *Women of the Fields*, pp. 73 and 76.
104. Karen Sayer, 'Field-faring Women: the Resistance of Women who Worked in the Fields of Nineteenth-century England', *Women's History Review*, 2 (1993), p. 186.
105. Sayer, *Women of the Fields*, p. 125.
106. Sayer, 'Field-faring Women', p. 194, provides an analysis of one of the few examples of a strike mounted by women in their own interests.
107. Joanna Bornat, 'Lost Leaders: Women, Trade Unionism and the Case of the General Union of Textile Workers, 1875–1914' in Angela V. John, *Unequal Opportunities. Women's Employment in England 1800–1918* (Oxford, Basil Blackwell, 1986), pp. 211–16.
108. Jan Lambertz, 'Sexual Harassment in the Nineteenth Century English Cotton Industry', *History Workshop Journal*, 19 (1985), pp. 39 and 48–52.
109. Clark, *The Struggle*, p. 264.
110. Joan Scott, cited in Theodore Koditschek, 'The Gendering of the British Working Class', *Gender and History*, 9 (1997), p. 333.
111. Koditschek, 'The Gendering', p. 344.

8 Conclusion. A Gendered Industrial Society

1.   Nor were the two as integrated before industrialisation as was traditionally believed.
2.   Ellen Jordan, 'Female Unemployment in England and Wales 1851–1911: an Examination of the Census Figures for 15–19 Year Olds', *Social History*, 13 (1988), p. 190.
3.   Ellen Jordan, 'The Lady Clerks at the Prudential: the Beginning of Vertical Segregation by Sex in Clerical Work in Nineteenth-century Britain', *Gender and History*, 8,1 (1996), p. 78.
4.   Jane E. Lewis, 'Women Clerical Workers in the Late Nineteenth and Early Twentieth Centuries' in Gregory Anderson (ed.), *The White-blouse Revolution. Female Office Workers since 1870* (Manchester, Manchester UP, 1988), pp. 44–5.
5.   Teresa M. McBride, *The Domestic Revolution. The Modernisation of Household Service in England and France 1820–1920* (London, Croom Helm, 1976), pp. 16–17.
6.   Janice Adams and Stella Clarkson, 'Work Fit for Girls' in Michael Winstanley (ed.) *Working Children in Nineteenth-century Lancashire* (Preston, Lancashire County Books, 1995), p. 115.

7. Adams and Clarkson, 'Work Fit for Girls', p. 117.
8. Adams and Clarkson, 'Work Fit for Girls', p. 134.

Bibliography

Alexander, Sally, *Becoming a Woman and Other Essays in Nineteenth and Twentieth Century Feminist History* (London, Virago, 1994)

Alexander, Sally, 'Feminist History' in *Becoming a Woman*, pp. 275–8

Alexander, Sally, 'Women's Work in Nineteenth-century London: a Study of the Years 1820–60s' in *Becoming a Woman*, pp. 3–55

Alexander, Sally and Taylor, Barbara, 'In Defence of Patriarchy' in *Becoming a Woman*, pp. 271–4

Alexander, Sally *et al.*, 'Labouring Women: a Reply to Eric Hobsbawm', *History Workshop Journal*, 8 (1979), pp. 174–82

Anderson, Gregory (ed.), *The White-blouse Revolution. Female Office Workers since 1870* (Manchester, Manchester UP, 1988)

August Andrew, 'How Separate a Sphere? Poor Women and Paid Work in Late Victorian London', *Journal of Family History*, 19 (1994), pp. 285–309

Barker, Hannah and Chalus, Elaine (eds), *Gender in Eighteenth Century England. Roles, Representations and Responsibilities* (London, Longman, 1997)

Barrett, Michele and McIntosh, Mary, 'The "Family Wage": Some Problems for Socialists and Feminists', *Capital and Class*, 11 (1980), pp. 51–72

Bennett, Judith M., 'Feminism and History', *Gender and History*, 1 (1989), pp. 251–72

Bennett, Judith M., 'Medieval Women, Modern Women: across the Great Divide' in Davis Ares (ed.), *Culture and History 1350–1600: Essays on English Communities, Identities and Writing* (London, Harvester Wheatsheaf, 1992), pp. 147–75

Bennett, Judith M., *Women in the Medieval English Countryside. Gender and Household in Brigstock before the Plague* (Oxford, OUP, 1987)

Bennett, Judith M., 'Women's History: a Study in Continuity and Change', *Women's History Review*, 2 (1993), pp. 173–84

Berg, Maxine, *The Age of Manufactures: Industry, Innovation and Work in Britain 1700–1820* (London, Fontana, 1985)

Berg, Maxine, 'Factories, Workshops and Industrial Organisation' in Roderick Floud and Donald McCloskey (eds), *The Economic History of Britain since 1700*, Vol. 1, second edition (Cambridge, CUP, 1994), pp. 123–50

Berg, Maxine (ed.), *Markets and Manufacture in Early Industrial Europe* (London, Routledge, 1991)

Berg, Maxine, 'Markets, Trade and European Manufacture' in *Markets and Manufacture*, pp. 3–28

Berg, Maxine, 'Small Producer Capitalism in Eighteenth-century England', *Business History*, 35 (1993), pp. 17–39

Berg, Maxine, 'Technological and Organisational Change during the Industrial Revolution: New Questions', unpublished contribution to 'Towards a New History of Industrialisation in Britain' at the annual conference of the Economic History Society at the University of Nottingham, 8–10 April 1994

Berg, Maxine, 'What Difference did Women's Work Make to the Industrial Revolution?', *History Workshop Journal*, 35 (1993), pp. 22–44

Berg Maxine, *A Woman in History. Eileen Power 1889–1940* (Cambridge, CUP, 1996)

Berg, Maxine, 'Women's Property and the Industrial Revolution', *Journal of Interdisciplinary History*, 24 (1993), pp. 233–50

Berg, Maxine, 'Women's Work, Mechanisation and the Early Phases of Industrialisation in England' in Patrick Joyce (ed.), *The Historical Meanings of Work* (Cambridge, CUP, 1987), pp. 64–98

Berg, Maxine, 'Women's Work and the Industrial Revolution', *Refresh*, 12 (1991), pp. 1–4

Berg, Maxine and Hudson, Pat, 'Rehabilitating the Industrial Revolution', *Economic History Review*, 45 (1992), pp. 24–50

Berlanstein, Lenard R. (ed.), *The Industrial Revolution and Work in Nineteenth Century Europe* (London, Routledge, 1992)

Bock, Gisela, 'Women's History and Gender History: Aspects of an International Debate', *Gender and History*, 1 (1989), pp. 7–30

Bohstedt, John, 'Gender, Household and Community Politics: Women in English Riots 1790–1810', *Past and Present*, 120 (1988), pp. 88–122

Bohstedt, John and Williams, Dale E., 'The Diffusion of Riots: the Patterns of 1766, 1795 and 1801 in Devonshire', *Journal of Interdisciplinary History*, 19 (1988), pp. 1–24

Bornat, Joanna, 'Lost Leaders: Women, Trade Unionism and the Case of the General Union of Textile Workers, 1875–1914' in Angela John (ed.), *Unequal Opportunities. Women's Employment in England 1800–1918* (Oxford, Basil Blackwell, 1986), pp. 207–33

Boxer, Marilyn J. and Quataert, Jean H. (eds), *Connecting Spheres. Women in the Western World, 1500 to the Present* (Oxford, OUP, 1987)

Bradley, Harriet, *Men's Work, Women's Work. A Sociological History of the Sexual Division of Labour in Employment* (Cambridge, CUP, 1989)

Branca, Patricia, 'Image and Reality: the Myth of the Idle Victorian Woman' in Mary S. Hartman and Lois Banner (eds), *Clio's Consciousness Raised. New Perspectives on the History of Women* (New York and London, Harper and Row, 1974), pp. 179–91

Brewer, John and Porter, Roy (eds), *Consumption and the World of Goods* (London, Routledge, 1993)

Bruland, Kristine, 'The Transformation of Work in European Industrialisation' in Peter Mathias and John Davis (eds), *The First Industrial Revolutions* (Oxford, Basil Blackwell, 1990), pp. 154–69

Bruland, Tine, 'Industrial Conflict as a Source of Technical Innovation', *Economy and Society*, 11 (1992), pp. 91–112

Burnette, Joyce, 'An Investigation of the Female–Male Wage Gap during the Industrial Revolution in Britain', *Economic History Review*, 50 (1997), pp. 257–81

Busfield, Deirdre, 'Job Definitions and Inequality: the "Unskilled" Women Workers of the West Riding Textile Industry, 1850–1914', *Textile History*, 19 (1988), pp. 61–82

Busfield, Deirdre, 'Skill and the Sexual Division of Labour in the West Riding Textile Industry, 1850–1914' in J. A. Jowitt and A. J. McIvor (eds), *Employers and Labour in the English Textile Industries 1850–1939* (London, Routledge, 1988), pp. 153–70

Bythell, Duncan, *The Sweated Trades: Outwork in Nineteenth Century Britain* (London, Batsford, 1987)

Cahn, Susan, *Industry of Devotion. The Transformation of Women's Work in England 1500–1660* (New York, Columbia UP, 1987)

Cannadine, David, 'The Present and the Past in the English Industrial Revolution 1880–1980', *Past and Present*, 103 (1984), pp. 131–72

Catling, Harold, *The Spinning Mule* (Newton Abbott, David and Charles, 1970)

Charles, Lindsey and Duffin, Lorna (eds), *Women and Work in Pre-industrial England* (London, Croom Helm, 1985)

Chartres, John, 'English Landed Society and the Servants Tax of 1777' in Negley Harte and Roland Quinault (eds), *Land and Society in Britain, 1700–1914. Essays in Honour of F. M. L. Thompson* (Manchester, Manchester UP, 1996), pp. 34–56

Clark, Alice, *Working Life of Women in the Seventeenth Century* (New York, Dutton, 1919) (reprinted London, Routledge and Kegan Paul, 1982)

Clark, Anna, 'Manhood, Womanhood, and the Politics of Class in Britain, 1790–1845' in Laura L. Frader and Sonya O. Rose (eds), *Gender and Class in Modern Europe* (Ithaca, Cornell UP, 1996), pp. 263–79

Clark, Anna, 'The Rhetoric of Chartist Domesticity: Gender, Language and Class in the 1830s and 1840s', *Journal of British Studies*, 31 (1992), pp. 62–88

Clark, Anna, *The Struggle for the Breeches. Gender and the Making of the British Working Class* (Berkeley, University of California Press, 1995)

Clark, Anna, *Women's Silence, Men's Violence: Sexual Assault in England 1770–1845* (London, Pandora, 1987)

Cockburn, Cynthia, *Brothers. Male Dominance and Technological Change* (London, Pluto, 1983)

Cockburn, Cynthia, 'Forum: Formations of Masculinity. Introduction', *Gender and History*, 1 (1989), pp. 159–63

Cockburn, Cynthia, *Machinery of Dominance: Women, Men and Technical Know-how* (London, Pluto, 1985)

Cockburn, Cynthia, 'Technology, Production and Power' in Gill Kirkup and Lauries Smith Keller (eds), *Inventing Women. Science, Technology and Gender* (Cambridge, Polity, in association with the Open University, 1992), pp. 196–211

Coyle, Angela, 'The Protection Racket?' *Feminist Review*, 6 (1980), pp. 1–12

Crafts, N. F. R., *British Economic Growth during the Industrial Revolution* (Oxford, Clarendon, 1985)

Creighton, Colin, 'Richard Oastler, Factory Legislation and the Working Class Family', *Journal of Historical Sociology*, 5 (1992), pp. 292–320

Creighton, Colin, 'The Rise of the Male Breadwinner Family: a Reappraisal', *Comparative Studies in Society and History*, 38 (1996), pp. 310–37

Davidoff, Leonore, *Worlds Between: Historical Perspectives on Gender and Class* (Cambridge, Polity, 1995)

Davidoff, Leonore and Hall, Catherine, *Family Fortunes: Men and Women of the English Middle Class, 1780–1850* (London, Routledge, 1987)

Davin, Anna, 'Feminism and Labour History' in Raphael Samuel (ed.), *People's History and Socialist Theory* (London, Routledge and Kegan Paul, 1981), pp. 176–81

D'Cruze, Shani, 'Care, Diligence and "Usfull pride" [*sic*]: Gender, Industrialisation and the Domestic Economy, c.1770–c. 1840', *Women's History Review*, 3 (1994), pp. 315–45

De Groot, Gertjan and Shrover, Marlou, *Women Workers and Technological Change in Europe in the Nineteenth and Twentieth Centuries* (London, Taylor and Francis, 1995)

Delphy, Christine, 'Rethinking Sex and Gender', *Women's Studies International Forum*, 16 (1993), pp. 1–9

De Vries, Jan, 'Between Purchasing Power and the World of Goods: Understanding the Household Economy in Early Modern Europe' in John Brewer and Roy Porter (eds), *Consumption and the World of Goods* (London, Routledge, 1993). Reprinted in Pamela Sharpe (ed.), *Women's Work. The English Experience 1650–1914* (London, Arnold, 1998), pp. 209–39

Earle, Peter, 'The Female Labour Market in London in the Late Seventeenth and Early Eighteenth Centuries', *Economic History Review*, 42 (1989), pp. 328–53

Fletcher, Anthony, *Gender, Sex and Subordination, 1500–1800* (New Haven and London, Yale UP, 1995)

Fox-Genovese, Elizabeth, 'Placing Women's History in History', *New Left Review*, 133 (1982), pp. 5–29

Frader, Laura L. and Rose, Sonya O. (eds), *Gender and Class in Modern Europe* (Ithaca, Cornell UP, 1996)

Freifeld, Mary, 'Technological Change and the "Self-acting" Mule: a Study of Skill and the Sexual Division of Labour', *Social History*, 11 (1986), pp. 319–43

Fulcher, Jonathan, 'Gender, Politics, and Class in the Early Nineteenth-century English Reform Movement', *Historical Research*, 67 (1994), pp. 57–74

Gardiner, Jean, *Gender, Care and Economics* (Basingstoke, Macmillan, 1997)

George, Dorothy, *London Life in the Eighteenth Century* (London, Kegan Paul, Trench, Trubner, 1925)

Goodman, Jordan and Honeyman, Katrina, *Gainful Pursuits. The Making of Industrial Europe 1600–1914* (London, Edward Arnold, 1988)

Gray, Robert, 'Factory Legislation and the Gendering of Jobs in the North of England, 1830–1860', *Gender and History*, 5 (1993), pp. 56–80

Gray, Robert, *The Factory Question and Industrial England, 1830–1860* (Cambridge, CUP, 1996)

Gray, Robert, 'The Languages of Factory Reform in Britain, c. 1830–1860' in Patrick Joyce (ed.), *The Historical Meanings of Work* (Cambridge, CUP, 1987), pp. 143–79

Gray, Robert, 'Medical Men, Industrial Labour and the State in Britain, 1830–50', *Social History*, 16 (1991), pp. 19–43

Hall, Catherine, 'The Home Turned Upside Down? The Working Class Family in Cotton Textiles 1780–1850' in Elizabeth Whitelegg (ed.), *The Changing Experience of Women* (Oxford, Martin Robertson in association with the Open University, 1982), pp. 17–29

Hall, Catherine, 'Politics, Post-structuralism and Feminist History', *Gender and History*, 3 (1991), pp. 204–10

Hall, Catherine, *White, Male and Middle Class. Explorations in Feminism and History* (Cambridge, Polity, 1992)

Harrison, Brian, 'Class and Gender in Modern British Labour History', *Past and Present*, 124 (1989), pp. 121–58

Hartmann, Heidi, 'Capitalism, Patriarchy and Job Segregation by Sex', *Signs*, 1 (1976), pp. 137–69

Hartmann, Heidi, 'The Unhappy Marriage of Marxism and Feminism: towards a More Progressive Union', *Capital and Class*, 8 (1979), pp. 1–33

Heesom, A. J., 'The Northern Coal Owners and the Opposition to the Coal Mines Act of 1842', *International Review of Social History*, 25 (1980), pp. 236–71

Hewitt, Margaret, *Wives and Mothers in Victorian Industry* (London, Rockliff, 1958)

Higgs, Edward, 'Domestic Servants and Households in Victorian England', *Social History*, 8 (1983), pp. 201–10

Higgs, Edward, *Making Sense of the Census. The Manuscript Returns for England and Wales, 1801–1901* (London, HMSO, 1989)

Higgs, Edward, 'Occupational Censuses and the Agricultural Workforce in Victorian England and Wales', *Economic History Review*, 48 (1995), pp. 700–16

Higgs, Edward, 'Women, Occupations and Work in the Nineteenth Century Censuses', *History Workshop Journal*, 23 (1987), pp. 59–80

Hill, Bridget, *Servants. English Domestics in the Eighteenth Century* (Oxford, Clarendon, 1996)

Hill, Bridget, 'Women, Work and the Census: a Problem for Historians of Women', *History Workshop Journal*, 35 (1993), pp. 78–94

Hill, Bridget, *Women, Work and Sexual Politics in Eighteenth Century England* (Oxford, Basil Blackwell, 1989)

Hill, Bridget, 'Women's History: a Study in Change, Continuity or Standing Still?' *Women's History Review*, 2 (1993), pp. 5–22

Hoff, Joan, 'Gender as a Postmodern Category of Paralysis', *Women's History Review*, 3 (1994), pp. 149–68

Hoff, Joan, 'A Reply to my Critics', *Women's History Review*, 5 (1996), pp. 25–30

Honeyman, Katrina, 'Gender Divisions and Industrial Divide: the Case of the Leeds Clothing Industry 1850–1970', *Textile History*, 28 (1997), pp. 47–66

Honeyman, Katrina, *Origins of Enterprise. Business Leadership and the Industrial Revolution* (Manchester, Manchester UP, 1982)

Honeyman, Katrina, *Well Suited. A History of the Leeds Clothing Industry 1850–1990* (Oxford, OUP, 2000)

Honeyman, Katrina, 'Women, Work and the Industrial Labour Market, 1500–1800' in Amanda Devonshire and Barbara Wood (eds), *Women in Industry and Technology from Prehistory to the Present Day. Current Research and the Museum Experience* (London, Museum of London, 1996), pp. 115–24

Honeyman, Katrina and Goodman, Jordan, 'Women's Work, Labour Markets and Gender Conflict in Europe 1500–1900', *Economic History Review*, 44 (1991), pp. 608–28

Horrell, Sara and Humphries, Jane, 'Old Questions, New Data, and Alternative Perspectives: Families' Living Standards in the Industrial Revolution', *Journal of Economic History*, 52 (1992), pp. 849–81

Horrell, Sara and Humphries, Jane, 'Women's Labour Force Participation and the Transition to the Male-breadwinner Family, 1790–1865', *Economic History Review*, 48 (1995), pp. 89–117

Hostettler, Eve, 'Gourlay Steell and the Sexual Division of Labour', *History Workshop Journal*, 4 (1977), pp. 95–100

Houston, R. A. and Snell, K., 'Protoindustrialisation, Cottage Industry, Social Change and the Industrial Revolution', *Historical Journal*, 27 (1984), pp. 473–92

Howell, Martha C., *Women, Production and Patriarchy in Late Medieval Cities* (Chicago, University of Chicago Press, 1986)

Hudson, Pat, 'Introduction', unpublished contribution to 'Towards a New History of Industrialisation in Britain' at the annual conference of the Economic History Society, University of Nottingham, 8–10 April 1994

Hudson, Pat, *The Industrial Revolution* (London, Edward Arnold, 1992)

Hudson, Pat (ed.), *Regions and Industries: a Perspective on the Industrial Revolution in Britain* (Cambridge, CUP, 1989)

Hufton, Olwen, *The Prospect before Her: a History of Women in Western Europe*, Vol. 1, *1500–1800* (London, HarperCollins, 1995)

Hufton, Olwen, 'Women in History. Early Modern Europe', *Past and Present*, 101 (1983), pp. 125–41

Humphries, Jane, 'Class Struggle and the Persistence of the Working Class Family', *Cambridge Journal of Economics*, 1 (1977), pp. 241–58

Humphries, Jane, 'Enclosures, Common Rights and Women: the Proletarianisation of Families in the Late Eighteenth and Early Nineteenth Centuries', *Journal of Economic History*, 50 (1990), pp. 17–42

Humphries, Jane, 'Mainstreaming Women's History', unpublished contribution to 'Towards a New History of Industrialisation in Britain' at the annual conference of the Economic History Society, University of Nottingham, 8–10 April 1994

Humphries, Jane, '". . . The Most Free from Objection . . ." The Sexual Division of Labour and Women's Work in Nineteenth Century England', *Journal of Economic History*, 47 (1987), pp. 929–49

Humphries, Jane, 'Protective Legislation, the Capitalist State, and Working Class Men: the Case of the 1842 Mines Regulation Act', *Feminist Review*, 7 (1981), pp. 1–32

Hunt, Margaret, 'Wife Beating, Domesticity and Women's Independence in Eighteenth-century London', *Gender and History*, 4 (1992), pp. 10–33

Hutchins, B. L. and Harrison, A., *A History of Factory Legislation* (Westminster, P. S. King, 1903)

Ittman, Karl, *Work, Gender and Family in Victorian England* (Basingstoke, Macmillan, 1995)

John, Angela V., *By the Sweat of their Brow. Women Workers at Victorian Coal Mines* (London, Routledge and Kegan Paul, 1984)

John, Angela V., *Coalmining Women. Victorian Lives and Campaigns* (Cambridge, CUP, 1984)

John, Angela V. (ed.), *Unequal Opportunities. Women's Employment in England 1800–1918* (Oxford, Basil Blackwell, 1986)

Johnson, Paul and Nicholas, Stephen, 'Male and Female Living Standards in England and Wales, 1812–1857: Evidence from Criminal Height Records', *Economic History Review*, 48 (1995), pp. 470–81

Jordan, Ellen, 'Female Unemployment in England and Wales 1851–1911: an Examination of the Census Figures for 15–19 Year Olds', *Social History*, 13 (1988), pp. 175–90

Jordan, Ellen, 'The Lady Clerks at the Prudential: the Beginning of Vertical Segregation by Sex in Clerical Work in Nineteenth-century Britain', *Gender and History*, 8 (1996), pp. 65–81

Joyce, Patrick (ed.), *The Historical Meanings of Work* (Cambridge, CUP, 1987)

Kent, D. A., 'Ubiquitous but Invisible. Female Domestic Servants in Mid-eighteenth Century London', *History Workshop Journal*, 28 (1989), pp. 111–28

King, Peter, 'Customary Rights and Women's Earnings. The Importance of Gleaning to the Labouring Poor 1750–1850', *Economic History Review*, 44 (1991), pp. 461–76

Kingsley Kent, Susan, 'Mistrials and Diatribulations: a Reply to Joan Hoff', *Women's History Review*, 5 (1996), pp. 9–18

Koditschek, Theodore, 'The Gendering of the British Working Class', *Gender and History*, 9 (1997), pp. 333–63

Kriedte, Peter, Medick, Hans and Schlumbohm, Jurgen, *Industrialisation before Industrialisation* (Cambridge, CUP, 1981)

Lambertz, Jan, 'Sexual Harassment in the Nineteenth Century English Cotton Industry', *History Workshop Journal*, 19 (1985), pp. 29–61

Land, Hilary, 'The Family Wage', *Feminist Review*, 6 (1980), pp. 55–77

Lazonick, William, 'Industrial Relations and Technical Change: the Case of the Self-acting Mule', *Cambridge Journal of Economics*, 3 (1979), pp. 231–62

Lemire, Beverly, 'Consumerism in Pre-industrial and Early Industrial England: the Trade in Secondhand Clothes', *Journal of British Studies*, 27 (1988), pp. 1–24

Lemire, Beverly, 'Developing Consumerism and the Ready-made Clothing Trade in Britain, 1750–1800', *Textile History*, 15 (1984), pp. 21–44

Lemire, Beverly, *Dress, Culture and Commerce. The English Clothing Trade before the Factory 1660–1800* (London, Macmillan, 1997)

Lewenhak, Sheila, *Women and Trade Unions: an Outline History of Women in the Trade Union Movement* (London, E. Benn, 1977)

Liddington, Jill, 'Beating the Inheritance Bounds: Anne Lister (1791–1840) and her Dynastic Inheritance', *Gender and History*, 17 (1995), pp. 260–74

Lown, Judy, 'Not so much a Factory, more a Form of Patriarchy: Gender and Class during Industrialisation' in Eve Garmarnikow *et al.* (eds), *Gender, Class and Work* (Aldershot, Gower, 1983), pp. 28–45

Lown, Judy, *Women and Industrialisation. Gender at Work in Nineteenth Century England* (Cambridge, Polity, 1990)

Lyons, John S., 'Family Response to Economic Decline: Handloom Weavers in Early Nineteenth Century Lancashire', *Research in Economic History*, 12 (1989), pp. 45–91

McBride, Theresa M., *The Domestic Revolution. The Modernisation of Household Service in England and France 1820–1920* (London, Croom Helm, 1976)

McClelland, Keith, 'Some Thoughts on Masculinity and the "Representative Artisan" in Britain, 1850–1880', *Gender and History*, 1 (1989), pp. 164–77

McKendrick, N. (ed.), *Historical Perspectives: Studies in English Thought and Society* (London, Europa, 1974)

McKendrick, Neil, 'Home Demand and Economic Growth: a New View of the Role of Women and Children in the Industrial Revolution' in *Historical Perspectives*, pp. 152–210

McKendrick, N., Brewer, J. and Plumb, J. H. (eds), *The Birth of a Consumer Society. The Commercialisation of Eighteenth Century England* (London, Europa, 1982)

MacKenzie, Donald and Wajcman, Judy, *The Social Shaping of Technology. How the Refrigerator Got its Hum* (Milton Keynes, Open University Press, 1985)

Mark-Lawson, Jane and Witz, Anne, 'From "Family Labour" to "Family Wage"? The Case of Women's Labour in Nineteenth-century Coalmining', *Social History*, 13 (1988), pp. 151–74

Medick, Hans, 'The Proto-industrial Family Economy' in Kriedte *et al.*, *Industrialisation*, pp. 38–73

Medick, Hans, 'The Proto-industrial Family Economy: the Structural Function of Household and Family during the Transition from Peasant Society to Industrial Capitalism', *Social History*, 3 (1976), pp. 291–315

Middleton, Chris, 'Women's Labour and the Transition to Pre-industrial Capitalism' in Lindsey Charles and Lorna Duffin (eds), *Women and Work in Pre-industrial England* (London, Croom Helm, 1985), pp. 181–206

Morgan, Carol E., 'Women, Work and Consciousness in the Mid-nineteenth-century English Cotton Industry', *Social History*, 17 (1992), pp. 23–41

Morris, Jenny, 'The Characteristics of Sweating: the Late Nineteenth Century London and Leeds Tailoring Trade' in John (ed.), *Unequal Opportunities*, pp. 95–121

Morris, Polly, 'Incest or Survival Strategy? Plebeian Marriage within the

Prohibited Degrees in Somerset, 1730–1835', *Journal of the History of Sexuality*, 2 (1991), pp. 235–65

Nardinelli, Clark, 'Were Children Exploited during the Industrial Revolution?' *Research in Economic History*, 11 (1988), pp. 243–76

O'Brien, Patrick and Quinault, Ronald (eds), *The Industrial Revolution and British Society* (Cambridge, CUP, 1993)

Phillips, Anne and Taylor, Barbara, 'Sex and Skill: Notes towards a Feminist Economics', *Feminist Review*, 6 (1980), pp. 79–88

Pinchbeck, Ivy, *Women Workers and the Industrial Revolution 1750–1850* (London, Routledge, 1930)

Prior, Mary (ed.), *Women in English Society 1500–1800* (London, Methuen, 1985)

Purvis, June, 'Editorial' in *Women's History Review*, 1 (1992), pp. 5–7

Purvis, June, 'Using Primary Sources when Researching Women's History from a Feminist Perspective', *Women's History Review*, 1 (1992), pp. 273–306

Purvis, June, 'Women's History and Poststructuralism', *Women's History Review*, 5 (1996), pp. 5–7

Randall, A. J., 'Industrial Conflict and Economic Change: the Regional Context of the Industrial Revolution', *Southern History*, 14 (1994), pp. 74–92

Ramazanoglu, Caroline, 'Unravelling Postmodern Paralysis: a Response to Joan Hoff', *Women's History Review*, 5 (1996), pp. 19–23

Rendall, Jane, *The Origins of Modern Feminism: Women in Britain, France and the United States, 1780–1860* (Basingstoke, Macmillan, 1984)

Rendall, Jane, *Women in an Industrialising Society; England 1750–1880* (Oxford, Blackwell, 1990)

Richards, Eric, 'Women in the British Economy since about 1700; an Interpretation', *History*, 59 (1974), pp. 337–57

Roberts, Elizabeth, *A Woman's Place. An Oral History of Working Class Women 1890–1940* (Oxford, Blackwell, 1984)

Roberts, Elizabeth A. M., '"Women's Strategies", 1890–1940' in Jane Lewis (ed.), *Labour and Love. Women's Experience of Home and Family 1850–1940* (Oxford, Basil Blackwell, 1986), pp. 223–47

Roberts, Elizabeth, *Women's Work, 1840–1940* (Basingstoke, Macmillan, 1988)

Rose, Mary B., *The Gregs of Quarry Bank Mill. The Rise and Decline of a Family Firm, 1750–1914* (Cambridge, CUP, 1986)

Rose, Sonya O., 'Gender Antagonism and Class Conflict: Exclusionary Strategies of Male Trade Unionists in Nineteenth Century Britain', *Social History*, 13 (1988), pp. 191–208

Rose, Sonya O., '"Gender at Work": Sex, Class and Industrial Capitalism', *History Workshop Journal*, 21 (1986), pp. 113–31

Rose, Sonya O., 'Gender Segregation in the Transition to the Factory: the English Hosiery Industry, 1850–1910', *Feminist Studies*, 13 (1987), pp. 163–84

Rose, Sonya O., *Limited Livelihoods: Gender and Class in Nineteenth Century England* (London, Routledge, 1992)

Rose, Sonya O., 'Protective Labor Legislation in Nineteenth-century Britain: Gender, Class and the Liberal State' in Laura L. Frader and Sonya O. Rose (eds), *Gender and Class in Modern Europe* (Ithaca, Cornell UP, 1996), pp. 193–210

Rose, Sonya O., 'Protoindustry, Women's Work and the Household Economy in the Transition to Industrial Capitalism', *Journal of Family History*, 13 (1988), pp. 181–93

Rose, Sonya O., 'Respectable Men, Disorderly Others: the Language of Gender and the Lancashire Weavers' Strike of 1878 in Britain', *Gender and History*, 5 (1993), pp. 382–97

Ross, Ellen, ' "Fierce Questions and Taunts": Married Life in Working-class London, 1870–1914', *Feminist Studies*, 8 (1982), pp. 575–602

Ross, Ellen, *Love and Toil: Motherhood in Outcast London 1870–1918* (New York, OUP, 1993)

Ross, Ellen, 'Survival Networks: Women's Neighbourhood Sharing in London before World War I', *History Workshop Journal*, 23 (1983), pp. 4–27

Rowbotham, Sheila, 'The Trouble with Patriarchy' in Raphael Samuel (ed.), *People's History and Socialist Theory* (London, Routledge and Kegan Paul, 1981), pp. 364–9

Rushton, Peter, 'The Matter in Variance: Adolescents and Domestic Conflict in the Pre-industrial Economy of Northeast England, 1600–1800', *Journal of Social History*, 25 (1991–2), pp. 89–107

Sabel, C. and Zeitlin, J., 'Historical Alternatives to Mass Production', *Past and Present*, 108 (1985), pp. 133–76

Saito, O., 'Labour Supply Behaviour of the Poor in the English Industrial Revolution', *Journal of European Economic History*, 10 (1981), pp. 633–52

Samuel, Raphael (ed.), *People's History and Socialist Theory* (London, Routledge and Kegan Paul, 1981)

Samuel, Raphael, 'The Workshop of the World', *History Workshop Journal*, 3 (1977), pp. 6–72

Sanderson, Elizabeth C., *Women and Work in Eighteenth Century Edinburgh* (Basingstoke, Macmillan, 1996)

Savage, Mike, 'Capitalist and Patriarchal Relations at Work: Preston Cotton Weaving, 1890–1940', Lancaster Regionalism Group, *Localities, Class and Gender* (London, Pion, 1985)

Sayer, Karen, 'Field-faring Women: the Resistance of Women who Worked in the Fields of Nineteenth-century England', *Women's History Review*, 2 (1993), pp. 185–98

Sayer, Karen, *Women of the Fields. Representations of Rural Women in the Nineteenth Century* (Manchester, Manchester UP, 1993)

Schmiechen, James A., *Sweated Industries and Sweated Labour. The London Clothing Trades* (Urbana, University of Illinois, 1984)

Scott, Joan, *Gender and the Politics of History* (New York, Columbia UP, 1988)

Scott, Joan W., 'Gender: a Useful Category of Analysis', *American Historical Review*, 91 (1986), reprinted in Robert Shoemaker and Mary Vincent (eds), *Gender and History in Western Europe* (London, Arnold, 1998)

Scott, Joan Wallach, 'On Language, Gender and Working Class History' in

Lenard R. Berlanstein (ed.), *The Industrial Revolution and Work in Nineteenth-century Europe* (London, Routledge, 1992), pp. 163–75

Scott, Joan W., 'Women in History: the Modern Period', *Past and Present*, 101 (1983), pp. 141–57

Scott, Joan W. and Tilly, Louise A., 'Women's Work and the Family in Nineteenth Century Europe', *Comparative Studies in Society and History*, 17 (1975), pp. 36–64, reprinted in Alice H. Amsden (ed.), *The Economics of Women and Work* (New York, St Martin's Press, 1980), pp. 91–124

Seccombe, Wally, 'Patriarchy Stabilised: the Construction of the Male Breadwinner Wage Norm in Nineteenth Century Britain', *Social History*, 11 (1986), pp. 53–76

Seccombe, Wally, *Weathering the Storm. Working Class Families from the Industrial Revolution to the Fertility Decline* (London, Verso, 1993)

Sharpe, Pamela, *Adapting to Capitalism. Working Women in the English Economy 1700–1850* (Basingstoke, Macmillan, 1996)

Sharpe, Pamela, 'Bigamy among the Labouring Poor in Essex, 1754–1857', *The Local Historian*, 24 (1994), pp. 139–44

Sharpe, Pamela, 'Continuity and Change: Women's History and Economic History in Britain', *Economic History Review*, 48 (1995), pp. 353–69

Sharpe, Pamela (ed.), *Women's Work. The English Experience 1650–1914* (London, Arnold, 1998)

Sharpe, Pamela and Chapman, Stanley D., 'Women's Employment and Industrial Organisation: Commercial Lace Embroidery in Early Nineteenth-century Ireland and England', *Women's History Review*, 5 (1996), pp. 325–50

Shoemaker, Robert B., *Gender in English Society, 1650–1850. The Emergence of Separate Spheres?* (London, Longman, 1998)

Shoemaker, Robert and Vincent, Mary (eds), *Gender and History in Western Europe* (London, Arnold, 1998)

Shorter, Edward, 'Women's Work: What Difference did Capitalism Make?' *Theory and Society*, 3 (1976), pp. 513–28

Simonton, Deborah, 'Apprenticeship; Training and Gender in Eighteenth Century England' in Berg (ed.), *Markets and Manufacture*, pp. 227–58

Simonton, Deborah, *A History of European Women's Work, 1700 to the Present* (New York, Routledge, 1998)

Smail, John, 'Manufacturer or Artisan? The Relationship between Economic and Cultural Change in the Early Stages of the Eighteenth Century Industrialisation', *Journal of Social History*, 25 (1991–2), pp. 791–814

Smith, Ruth L. and Valenze, Deborah M., 'Mutuality and Marginality: Liberal Moral Theory and Working Class Women in Nineteenth-century England', *Signs*, 13 (1988), pp. 277–98

Snell, K. D. M., 'Agricultural Seasonal Unemployment, the Standard of Living, and Women's Work in the South and East, 1690–1860', *Economic History Review*, 36 (1983), pp. 407–37

Stedman Jones, Gareth, 'Rethinking Chartism' in Gareth Stedman Jones, *Languages of Class: Studies in English Working Class History, 1832–1982* (Cambridge, CUP, 1983), pp. 90–178

Steedman, Carolyn, 'Bimbos from Hell', *Social History*, 19 (1994), pp. 57–67

Styles, John, 'Embezzlement, Industry and the Law in England 1500–1800' in Maxine Berg *et al.* (eds), *Manufacture in Town and Country before the Factory* (Cambridge, CUP, 1983), pp. 179–211

Taylor, Barbara, *Eve and the New Jerusalem. Socialism and Feminism in the Nineteenth Century* (London, Virago, 1983)

Taylor, Barbara, 'Socialist Feminism: Utopian or Scientific? in Raphael Samuel (ed.), *People's History and Socialist Theory* (London, Routledge and Kegan Paul, 1981), pp. 158–63

Thomas, Janet, 'Women and Capitalism: Oppression or Emancipation? A Review Article', *Comparative Studies in Society and History*, 30 (1988), pp. 534–49

Thomis, Malcolm I. and Grimmett, Jennifer, *Women in Protest 1800–1850* (London, Croom Helm, 1982)

Thompson, Dorothy, *Outsiders. Class, Gender and Nation* (London, Verso, 1993)

Thompson, Dorothy, 'Women, Work and Politics in Nineteenth Century England: the Problem of Authority' in Jane Rendall (ed.), *Equal or Different. Women's Politics 1800–1914* (Oxford, Basil Blackwell, 1987), pp. 57–81

Tilly, Louise A. and Scott, Joan W., *Women, Work and Family* (New York, Holt, Rinehart and Winston, 1978)

Tomaselli, Sylvana (ed.), *A Vindication of the Rights of Men* and *A Vindication of the Rights of Woman* (Cambridge, CUP, 1995)

Tomes, Nancy, 'A "Torrent of Abuse": Crimes of Violence between Working Class Men and Women in London 1840–75', *Journal of Social History*, 11 (1978), pp. 328–45

Tosh, John, 'Authority and Nurture in Middle Class Fatherhood: the Case of Early and Mid-Victorian England', *Gender and History*, 8 (1996), pp. 48–64

Tosh, John, 'What should Historians do with Masculinity? Reflections on Nineteenth Century Britain', *History Workshop Journal*, 38 (1994), pp. 179–202

Valenze, Deborah, *The First Industrial Woman* (Oxford, OUP, 1995)

Valverde, Mariana, '"Giving the Female a Domestic Turn": the Social, Legal and Moral Regulation of Women's Work in British Cotton Mills, 1820–1850', *Journal of Social History*, 21 (1988), pp. 619–34

Vickery, Amanda, 'Historiographical Review. Golden Age to Separate Spheres? A Review of the Categories and Chronology of English Women's History', *Historical Journal*, 36 (1993), pp. 383–414

Vickery, Amanda, 'The Neglected Century: Writing the History of Eighteenth-century Women', *Gender and History*, 3 (1991), pp. 211–19

Wajcman, Judy, *Feminism Confronts Technology* (Cambridge, Polity, 1991)

Wajcman, Judy, 'Patriarchy, Technology and Conceptions of Skill', *Work and Occupations*, 18 (1991), pp. 29–45

Walby, Sylvia, 'Patriarchal Structures: the Case of Unemployment' in Eva Garmarnikow *et al.* (eds), *Gender, Class and Work* (Aldershot, Gower, 1983)

Walby, Sylvia, *Patriarchy at Work. Patriarchal and Capitalist Relations in Employment* (Cambridge, Polity, 1986)

Weisner, Merry E., *Women and Gender in Early Modern Europe* (Cambridge, CUP, 1993)

Winstanley, Michael (ed.), *Working Children in Nineteenth-century Lancashire* (Preston, Lancashire County Books, 1995)

Wrigley, E. A., *Continuity, Chance and Change: the Character of the Industrial Revolution in England* (Cambridge, CUP, 1988)

Index